Philosophical History and the Problem of Consciousness

The problem of explaining consciousness today remains a problem about the meaning of language: the ordinary language of consciousness in which we define and express our sensations, thoughts, dreams, and memories. This book argues that the contemporary problem arises from a quest that has taken shape over the twentieth century, and that the analysis of history provides new resources for understanding and resolving it.

Paul Livingston traces the development of the characteristic practices of analytic philosophy to problems about the relationship between experience and linguistic meaning, focusing on the theories of such philosophers as Carnap, Schlick, Neurath, Husserl, Ryle, Putnam, Fodor, and Wittgenstein.

Clearly written and avoiding technicalities, this book will be eagerly sought out by professionals and graduate students in philosophy and cognitive science.

Paul M. Livingston is Assistant Professor of Philosophy at Villanova University.

Philosophical History and the Problem of Consciousness

PAUL M. LIVINGSTON

Villanova University

CAMBRIDGE
UNIVERSITY PRESS

PUBLISHED BY THE PRESS SYNDICATE OF THE UNIVERSITY OF CAMBRIDGE
The Pitt Building, Trumpington Street, Cambridge, United Kingdom

CAMBRIDGE UNIVERSITY PRESS
The Edinburgh Building, Cambridge CB2 2RU, UK
40 West 20th Street, New York, NY 10011-4211, USA
477 Williamstown Road, Port Melbourne, VIC 3207, Australia
Ruiz de Alarcón 13, 28014 Madrid, Spain
Dock House, The Waterfront, Cape Town 8001, South Africa

http://www.cambridge.org

First published 2004

Printed in the United States of America

Typeface ITC New Baskerville 10/13.5 pt.   *System* LATEX 2$_\varepsilon$ [TB]

A catalog record for this book is available from the British Library.

Library of Congress Cataloging in Publication data
Livingston, Paul M., 1976–
Philosophical history and the problem of consciousness / Paul M. Livingston.
p.   cm.
Includes bibliographical references and index.
ISBN 0-521-83820-7
1. Consciousness – History.   2. Philosophy – History.   I. Title.
B105.C477 L58 2004
126'.09'04 – dc22   2003069570

ISBN 0 521 83820 7 hardback

Contents

Preface

The following is an interpretive investigation in the history of analytic philosophy. With it, I hope to begin to show what sort of significance the twentieth-century analytic inquiry into the nature of mind, experience, and consciousness has had for the continuing philosophical consideration of the human self-image. I argue that the contemporary debate about the explanation of consciousness, in particular, embodies an important and unresolved set of concerns about this self-image, and that historical investigation allows us to understand the hitherto obscure ways in which the analytic tradition has been defined by its responses to the distinctive philosophical problems of our understanding of ourselves.

Throughout this inquiry, I have adhered to the methodological assumption that the power of philosophy to yield means and methods of understanding that elucidate and edify – its way of making meaning out of the unthought foundations of our ordinary lives – depends, at each specific historical moment, on its way of imaging or imagining the human, of articulating the specific kind of being that human existence involves. In the broader history of philosophy, however, the greatest enduring significance of this articulation has probably not been its theoretical specification, once and for all, of some fixed truth of human nature, but rather its furtherance of the dialectic of our self-understanding, the interminable historical movement in which each successive image of the human defines the means and practices of thought that will ensure its own partial overcoming.

Descartes' consideration of the thinking subject as *res cogitans* articulates one such image, inaugurating the modern inquiry into conscious experience and making room for the conception of experimental science that continues to structure our understanding of nature to the present. Kant's philosophy of transcendental subjectivity, another image of the human, inaugurated the forms and methods of self-critique and social criticism that would be extended and radicalized, with precipitous consequences, by Hegel, Marx, and Nietzsche. In the twentieth century, Freud's discovery of the unconscious made possible a whole new set of interpretive methods and techniques for bringing us, through the speaking of our memory, to the truth of ourselves. The outcomes of these practices of self-conception are so many ways of envisioning the specific character of our complicated way of life, so many ways of understanding what it is to think, to act, to relate to one another in human community.

The analytic tradition of philosophy founded by Frege, Russell, Moore, and Wittgenstein and still definitive of much of the practice of philosophy in the Anglo-American world has sometimes seemed to disclaim any specific consideration of subjectivity in its determinative focus on language. And it is true that the decisive turn of twentieth-century philosophy toward intersubjective language – a turn as deeply definitive of what is called the twentieth-century "continental" tradition as it is of the analytic one – separates its heirs categorically and irreversibly from any philosophy that founds itself on the egoistic selfhood of a wordless and mute subject of experience. But as I argue in this work, historical interpretation can actually reveal the turn toward language, capturing in each of its methods of philosophical illumination the unique insight that our ways of understanding and defining ourselves are ineleminably and decisively linguistic, as defining the most sophisticated and sustained inquiry into our own nature that is today available to us.

The historical analysis conducted here has direct consequences for the discussion of the problem of explaining consciousness that has emerged and developed over the last two decades. Interpreted against the backdrop of the history of linguistic methods of philosophical understanding, this debate, in itself one of the most interesting areas of contemporary analytic philosophy, bears witness to the endurance and relevance of our onging inquiry into the human self-image. Historical reflection on the deep roots of the current debate in the specifically linguistic practices of analysis and investigation characteristic of the analytic tradition points the way for the questions and issues of self-understanding that have in fact organized the contemporary discussion to be recovered for it explicitly. This recovery of the forgotten origins of the contemporary discussion reveals the real philosophical issues that have determined it, pointing the way to a more self-conscious form of the discussion that does not, indeed, offer any final or definitive "explanation" of consciousness but nevertheless, by showing what is really at issue, can bring the debate to substantial resolution.

Analytic philosophy characteristically and definitively develops and practices methods of philosophical insight that operate by furthering our understanding of the meaning of language – of (among other things) what *we* mean when we make the claims and issue the expressions that define us to ourselves and others, and of the significance for our human form of life of the fact that language definitively mediates this self-understanding. The history of its methods, from the earliest conceptions of "logical analysis" to today's more flexible and multiple explanatory practices, reveals the decisive significance of specifically linguistic inquiry for the kinds of understanding of ourselves that we seek from philosophy. Accordingly, the four studies that comprise the body of this work focus on important moments of theoretical development and change in the history of analytic philosophy, moments at which issues about experience and consciousness have caused trouble for existing analytic programs and methods and led to the invention of new ones.

Though the case studies collectively aim to give a revealing and characteristic portrait of the struggles and tensions underlying some of the most significant projects of analytic philosophy, they make no attempt to provide a comprehensive or exhaustive history of the tradition. Instead, they look for insight into the contours of analytic philosophy generally by focusing on the moments most decisive in creating its characteristic methods and practices. For this reason, I have given a great deal of attention to some figures whose views are today rarely explicitly examined, but I have sometimes devoted little space even to the philosophers whose work has most visibly contributed to the contemporary debate.

The great and decisive contribution of Wittgenstein, moreover, I have mostly discussed only at one remove, by discussing the generally more systematic positions of two of the philosophers who were most deeply influenced by him, Schlick and Ryle. The decision to treat Wittgenstein's work here primarily in this insulated way reflects the continuing complexity of the question of his reception within the tradition of analytic philosophy – a question that, I believe, calls on the deepest insights of historical and methodological reflection to define, over the next several decades, successor methods of linguistic insight and interpretation that integrate his conception of philosophy with the further critical inheritance of the analytic tradition. But the determinative role of Wittgenstein's ideas in bringing about the history related here should nonetheless be apparent to anyone who understands his work. I have also devoted substantial attention, in Chapter 2, to a philosophical program that is not generally considered part of the analytic tradition, Edmund Husserl's phenomenology. My aim in that chapter is to shed light on the development of analytic philosophy by considering its historically decisive divergence from one of its closest and most important programmatic competitors in the investigation of the self. The investigation undertaken there exemplifies a kind of reflection on the historical and conceptual boundaries of analytic philosophy as a specific tradition that can, I think, illuminate its deepest conceptual determinants.

The investigations to follow do not confine themselves to what is today defined as "philosophy of mind" (and still less to one side of the currently fashionable distinction, within philosophy of mind, of the "philosophy of consciousness" from the analysis of intentionality), but they necessarily involve, just as centrally, issues in the philosophy of science, epistemology, logic, and metaphysics. Indeed, one of the chief results of the investigation as a whole is that the characteristic means and methods of analytic philosophy in its consideration of consciousness and experience remain, to this day, determinatively grounded in philosophy of *language* – that is, in determinate conceptions of the nature of language and the practice of the illumination of linguistic meaning – even when they superficially seem to have departed from it.

Beyond its revelation of the deep and often obscured unity of the practice of analytic inquiry into experience in its underlying dependence on, and determination by, specifically linguistic means of investigation, the yield of the historical investigation is the methodological self-awareness that could allow the analytic tradition to understand and articulate its own most significant contribution to philosophical history. In particular, the methods and practices of analytic philosophy, typically and definitively linguistic in their orientation and practice, have, I argue in what follows, repeatedly encountered significant and revealing difficulties in their attempts to understand the *language of experience*, the ordinary language with which we articulate and define our own memory, our consciousness of ourselves, and our particular understanding of the world. The historical investigation shows that, over the course of the twentieth century, the philosophical struggle for the intelligibility of this language has taken the form of a struggle of the means and methods of linguistic analysis and interpretation against theories of language and meaning that threaten to make this intelligibility impossible, to reduce or deny the kind of truth that the language of consciousness brings to expression.

In the history I examine here, analytic philosophers have repeatedly supposed that their method demands what I call a *structuralist* picture of language, a picture according to which the essence of language is its total, comprehensive logical or conceptual structure and according to which the analysis of language is the location of terms and propositions within this structure. Though philosophers throughout the history of the tradition have voiced dissatisfaction with the structuralist picture, it remains deeply characteristic of the projects and methods of analytic philosophers even today. But the assumption of the structuralist picture has also repeatedly and determinatively, I argue here, threatened to render the language of consciousness unintelligible, obscuring the kind of contribution that the methods of linguistic analysis and interpretation otherwise definitive of the analytic tradition can in fact make to our understanding of ourselves.

This struggle between theory and method has determined, I argue, a consistent theoretical oscillation between totalizing structuralist theories of language and the world and the repeated complaint that consciousness escapes or resists them, a dialectic struggle that has not only frustrated analytic philosophy's hopes for a comprehensive theory of consciousness but also driven some of its most significant methodological innovations. The dialectic continues, and perhaps culminates, in the contemporary debate about the explainability of consciousness, where the comprehensiveness of physicalist and functionalist forms of explanation, themselves direct descendents of the conceptions of language and meaning that oriented some of the first projects of the analytic tradition, encounters significant but inarticulate resistance from the thought that consciousness cannot be explained in these terms. Historical interpretation provides the basis on which this debate and its predecessors alike can be understood in their real underlying methodological character, paving the way for the means and methods of specifically linguistic analysis and inquiry to produce the kind of understanding of ourselves that the contemporary debate unself-consciously and obscurely seeks.

Acknowledgments

This book grew out of my doctoral dissertation at the University of California, Irvine, and my first debt is to friends and colleagues there who read and critiqued parts of the manuscript at various stages of its development. I would especially like to thank Timothy Schoettle and Strefan Fauble, both of whom read and commented on virtually every page of the manuscript at one time or another. I would also like to thank the members of my original dissertation committee, Alan Nelson, Jeffrey Barrett, and David Woodruff Smith, for their guidance and advice. Bill Bristow and Jeffrey Yoshimi also helped with discussions of some of the material contained herein. Among those at other schools and institutions, I would like to thank Thomas Uebel, Amie Thomasson, David Chalmers, and three anonymous referees for Cambridge University Press for their helpful comments and responses.

An earlier version of Chapter 1 appeared in the *Journal of Consciousness Studies*, volume 9, no. 3 (March 2002), under the title "Experience and Structure: Philosophical History and the Problem of Consciousness" (pp. 15–33). A version of Chapter 3 appeared in *Synthese*, volume 132, no. 3 (September 2002), pp. 239–72, under its current title. I would like to thank the editors of these publications for their permission to reuse this material.

Finally, I would like to thank my wife, Elizabeth, for her constant support over the three and a half years it took to complete this project.

1

Introduction

Philosophical History and the Problem of Consciousness

The history of analytic philosophy, if viewed as more than a repository for superseded theory, could provide the basis for a transformation in the problem of consciousness with which philosophers of mind are currently grappling. Philosophers of mind seldom discuss or investigate, more than cursorily, the history of the interrelated concepts of mind, consciousness, experience, and the physical world that they rely upon in their theorizing. But these concepts in fact emerge from some of the most interesting and decisive philosophical struggles of the analytic tradition in the twentieth century. Historically, these struggles and their results set up the philosophical space in which contemporary discussion of consciousness moves, defining and delimiting the range of theoretical alternatives accessible to participants in the discussion of the explainability of consciousness and its relation to our understanding of the physical world.

Most contemporary philosophical discussions of consciousness address the question of its explainability in terms of objective, scientific description or the question of its ontological reducibility to objective, scientifically describable phenomena. Philosophers often raise these questions, moreover, against the backdrop of the thought that consciousness has certain properties or features that may make it especially resistant to scientific explanation and description. Paramount among the features of consciousness usually cited as problems for its explanation or reduction are its *privacy, subjectivity, ineffability, phenomenality, immediacy,* and *irreducibly qualitative character.*[1] These features or properties are typically taken as problematic for one or both of two "naturalistic" programs of explanation: either *physicalism,* which holds that a successful explanation of consciousness accounts for it as wholly physical, or *functionalism,* which holds that a successful explanation accounts for conscious states as functional states of the brain or person. The debate about the reality and reducibility of these special features of consciousness, having developed over the 1980s and 1990s, shows no sign of being resolved, and indeed, it is unclear what sort of consideration, empirical or philosophical, might decisively settle it.[2] But historical analysis offers to reinvigorate the debate, bringing it to a greater richness and philosophical depth. It does so by showing that each of the determinate notions used in these various types of arguments to characterize (or to contest the characterization of) the specific properties of consciousness, and the forms of explanation appropriate to understanding them, in fact originate in the historical context of bygone philosophical theories and concerns, often seemingly quite distant from those of philosophers who apply those notions today.

Broadly speaking, several of the main aspects of the contemporary discussion of consciousness – in particular, the discussion of its alleged privacy, ineffability, and subjectivity – first arise historically from tensions present in analytic philosophy's longstanding attempt to describe the relationship between linguistic meaning and experience.[3] Historical analysis elucidates this attempt, revealing its underlying form and clarifying its significance for today's debate. Characteristically, analytic philosophy is a *linguistic* inquiry. For the purposes of historical reconstruction, it can be defined as a specific tradition in terms of its determinative and unique attention to language and its logic, and this attention determines the historical and contemporary form of its inquiry into the nature of experience. In particular, analytic philosophy typically investigates the *conceptual and logical structure of language* in order to understand experience and to explain its relationship to objective knowledge about the physical world. From around the turn of the twentieth century, the explanatory projects that would define analytic philosophy of mind sought to elucidate the epistemology and ontology of our knowledge of the objective world on the basis of reasoning about the *structure* of experience or consciousness, the total pattern of the logical or conceptual interrelationships of its basic elements.

One of the inaugural innovations of analytic philosophy was to tie this explanatory project to a program of *linguistic analysis*, whereby the structure of experience is specified by means of a clarification of the logical relationships between *propositions*, both those immediately describing experience and other, more highly conceptual and interpretive ones. Within this program, the analysis of experience, consistently identified with the analysis of the *language* of experience, is the analysis of the logical and conceptual structure of this language, of the network of the syntactic and semantic interrelationships of the terms and sentences that describe, explain, and express experience. The goal of analysis is then the identification and description of this structure of relations. But from the beginning of the analytic tradition, the basic elements of experience figure as the indefinable *relata* of this network of relations, the elements that can be described and explained only by reference to their semantically and conceptually relevant interrelations, and never in themselves. This configuration – in which consciousness is constantly understood as immediate content, and objective language and explanation as relational – has, despite changes in detail and emphasis, continued to characterize the discussion of the problem of consciousness to the present, through the various shifts in doctrine and method that the analytic inquiry into experience has undergone over the twentieth century.

A *structural* or *structuralist* explanation (in the sense in which I use these terms in this study) is one that accounts for particular items by *locating* them in a broader structure of *relations* of one kind or another.[4] Structuralist explanation typically operates by *first* characterizing the nature of the system of interrelations in which a type of events or objects stand, and *then* explaining particular items by locating them within this system. Thus defined, structuralist explanation is an exceedingly general explanatory practice. As we shall see, for instance, it subsumes many forms of *semantic* explanation whereby words, concepts, or meanings are explained in terms of their logical or semantic roles in a language, as well as most forms of *causal* explanation that explain particular objects or events in terms of their position in a structure of causes and effects. The explanatory projects most prominent in the contemporary debate about consciousness are themselves versions of structuralism.[5] *Physicalism* or materialism, for instance, is the doctrine that every real phenomenon can be described and explained in

terms of basic physics. It operates explanatorily by locating each puzzling phenomenon within the total pattern of relations that physics
can capture, typically a pattern of *causal* relations that is conceived
of as exhaustive of reality. *Functionalism* is the doctrine that mental
states, including states of consciousness, are completely explainable
in terms of their functional interrelationships with other mental states
and physical states. Understanding mental states as definable in terms
of these interrelationships, it always explains them by locating them
within a total pattern of relations.[6] These explanatory projects, as we
shall see in the chapters to follow, themselves have a rich and hidden
conceptual history in the analytic tradition, one that entwines them
inseparably with the problems of experience and consciousness that
they were developed to solve. Historical analysis, by exposing this conceptual history, shows the extent and depth of the entwinement of
structuralism with the problems of explaining consciousness, suggesting new possibilities for the understanding and resolution of these
underlying problems.

Not *all* forms of explanation, however, are structuralist in this sense.
Consider, for instance, *genetic* explanations (that explain things in
terms of their origins and histories of descent) and *narrative* explanations (that explain by situating particular things or events within a
larger narrative story). Though these other forms of explanation might
refer to or make use of larger contexts or unities – a specific history,
for instance, or a broader narrative – they do not function primarily,
as structuralist explanations do, by locating items within a larger pattern of interrelations of a particular kind. If the point of explanation
generally is to produce intelligibility of one kind or another, we can
recognize these alternative forms of explanation as producing different kinds of intelligibility and understanding in each of the domains
in which they are felt to be most appropriate.

In this introductory chapter, I argue that the history of philosophy provides a genuine *explanation* for the much-discussed resistance
of consciousness to contemporary structuralist (primarily, physicalist
and functionalist) accounts, and that this explanation, if properly understood, could help to bring the contemporary debate to a greater
level of methodological richness and sophistication. Historical analysis
of concepts is a species of conceptual analysis, and conceptual analysis explains by revealing the underlying conceptual determinants of

patterns of use and description. By unearthing and evaluating the original arguments made for positions that have played a determinative role in structuring our contemporary concepts, historical investigation can remind contemporary philosophers of the original reasons for using concepts of mind and explanation in the ways that we do today. This points the way to a richer and more fruitful discussion, by recommending an explicit reconsideration of these often-forgotten or obscured reasons. Thus conceived, the historical explanation for the intractability of consciousness to physicalist description does not stand in any deep tension with other, more usual explanations for the problem – for instance, that consciousness fails to supervene on the physical or that there is an explanatory gap between our concepts of the physical and our concepts of consciousness.[7] Instead, it contributes to the clarification of these and other descriptions of the problem by clarifying the concepts of consciousness and explanation that they involve.

I

In order to begin to cast the light of historical interpretation on the contemporary discussion of consciousness, it is reasonable to investigate the origin and descent of the interrelated network of concepts that we use to characterize consciousness and the philosophical issues surrounding it. We can make an illuminating beginning by considering the concept of *qualia*. It is in the form of the question of qualia that many investigators today address the question of the explainability of consciousness. In the contemporary literature, qualia are variously thought to be incapable of physicalist or functionalist explanation, resistant to (but capable of) physicalist or functionalist explanation, or, owing to the unclarity or theoretical uselessness of the concept, nonexistent.[8] Argument about the explainability of consciousness, indeed, in many cases amounts simply to argument about the meaning of this concept. Significantly, though, the concept itself has a lengthy and seldom-explored lineage in the discourse of analytic philosophy. Investigation of this lineage provides insight into the philosophical sources of the main features and uses of its contemporary version. The full story of the descent of the concept of "qualia" in the twentieth century would require a detailed study of its own. But the outlines of an explanation for some of the most significant contemporary uses of the term can already be drawn from an examination of some of the earliest uses of the term in the philosophical discourse.

The philosophical uses of the term "qualia" (and the singular "quale") in English trace back at least as far as the writings of C. S. Peirce, who used the term as early as 1867 to describe the immediate or given elements of experience. For Peirce, qualia (often used as cognate to "qualities") were already the most basic constituents of the totality of sensory experience, the ground of what he called Firstness or immediacy.[9] Drawing on Peirce, William James used the term beginning in the 1870s to denote the "irreducible data" of perception, for instance, the whiteness that is one and the same when I perceive it in today's snow and yesterday's white cloud.[10] These items, James argues, are the same no matter where in experience they occur; and they comprise an irreducible set of posits that must, perhaps along with the atoms of physics, be ultimate philosophical data. James's qualia, accordingly, set an utmost limit to the philosopher's project of analysis or rational inquiry, a limit beyond which only speculation can pass.

The most direct early influence on the contemporary debate, though, runs from the epistemology of the phenomenalist pragmatist C. I. Lewis. In the context of his attempt to distinguish the "given element in experience" from the interpretive element placed upon it by conceptual reasoning, Lewis was among the first to use the term "qualia" in substantially the same way it is used by theorists today:

> Qualia are subjective; they have no names in ordinary discourse but are indicated by some circumlocution such as 'looks like'; they are ineffable, since they might be different in two minds with no possibility of discovering that fact and no necessary inconvenience to our knowledge of objects or their properties. All that can be done to designate a quale is, so to speak, to locate it in experience, that is, to designate the conditions of its recurrence or other relations of it. Such location does not touch the quale itself; if one such could be lifted out of the network of its relations, in the total experience of the individual, and replaced by another, no social interest or interest of action would be affected by such substitution. What is essential for understanding and communication is not the quale as such but that pattern of its stable relations in experience which is what is implicitly predicated when it is taken as the sign of an objective property.[11]

Writing in 1929, Lewis already grants qualia the essential properties of immediacy, subjectivity, and ineffability that often characterize them today. In the context of his reasoning about the properties of qualia, contemporary arguments for their existence and properties would be quite at home. As they were for James and Peirce, qualia are, for Lewis, the raw material or underlying substance of our rich and conceptually articulated experience of the world. But for Lewis, qualia are also explicitly *private* items. The ineffability of a particular quale outside its behavioral and relational context means that it is, outside this context, in a certain sense particular to its owner. No one else can possess or even understand my quale itself, for there is no way that I can communicate its intrinsic character to another. All that I can communicate is its place in the global pattern of relations that stands as its only objective sign.

There is also, though, an important contextual difference between the way in which Lewis uses the term "qualia" and its use in most of today's discussions. For instead of basing his conception of qualia on general intuitions or demonstrative thought experiments, Lewis articulates his conception of qualia from within the constraints of his global project of reconstructive analytic epistemology. For Lewis, qualia are the end points of epistemologically illuminating analysis. With their exhibition, we complete our analysis of any complex experience by distinguishing clearly between its interpretive, conceptual elements and that part of the experience that is genuinely "given," immediate, non-interpretive, and unconstrained by conceptual categorization. Aside from their role in this epistemological project, qualia have little significance. Indeed, Lewis says, they are abstractions, for our given experiences always come to us structured and formed, and their elements can be determined only by a process of analysis.

The setting of Lewis's concept of qualia within the larger theoretical project of reconstructive epistemology has historically important consequences for his use, and subsequent uses, of the concept. One consequence is that Lewis's notion of qualia has explicit *semantic* implications that contemporary uses of the concept usually lack. For Lewis ties conceptual interpretation to meaningful expression; it is only by conceptually interpreting a "given" element of experience that we gain the ability to communicate *about* that experience.[12] Consequently, Lewis's qualia are strictly indescribable. Strictly speaking, there is no possibility of describing an isolated quale, and there is no language for expressing the properties of individual qualia out of the context of their relationships with other qualia and conceptual interpretation. It is these patterns of relationship that we do in fact communicate about when we discuss qualia. About the qualia *themselves* we can say nothing, even though we may continually exhibit them to ourselves.[13]

Nor can we, according to Lewis, even *conceive* of an isolated quale. It is ultimately to a *relational* description – a description of their place in relation to a total network of other qualia, external causes, and behavioral effects – that all thought about qualia must relate.[14] For Lewis, then, qualia are real but indescribable, except insofar as we can locate them within a relational structure. It is only in virtue of the quale's having a particular place in a total pattern of relations that it can be referred to at all. Thus, Lewis makes qualia linguistically identifiable only by reference to their positions within a complex relational structure, whose relata we are in no position to characterize independently of that structure.

II

Lewis's conception of qualia as describable only in virtue of the network of their relations, and indescribable in themselves, may at first seem quite uncongenial to contemporary uses of the notion. But even if this implication of indescribability is not always present in contemporary uses of the concept of qualia, the notion of qualia as primary contents set off against a total network of relations nevertheless bears direct relevance to the contemporary discussion of the problem of consciousness. The image of Lewis's original distinction between content and structure appears in David Chalmers's 1996 description of the root of the problem of explaining consciousness physically:

Physical explanation is well suited to the explanation of structure and of function. Structural properties and functional properties can be straightforwardly entailed by a low-level physical story, and so are clearly apt for reductive explanation. And almost all the high-level phenomena that we need to explain ultimately come down to structure or function: think of the explanation of waterfalls, planets, digestion, reproduction, language. But the explanation of consciousness is not just a matter of explaining structure and function. Once we have explained all the physical structure in the vicinity of the brain, and we have explained how all the various brain functions are performed, there is a further sort of explanandum: consciousness itself. Why should all this structure and function give rise to experiences? The story about the physical processes does not say.[15]

Chalmers's complaint articulates a picture of the underlying difficulty with the explanation of qualia that will be recognizable even to those who disagree with it. Accordingly, it is reasonable to begin with this consensus in seeking a historically minded account of the problem. Most importantly for the historical analysis, Chalmers's description of the problem turns on a central distinction between physical description, conceived as exclusively structural and functional, and basic experiences or qualia, conceived as resistant to this sort of description.[16] There is, Chalmers suggests, something direct and immediate about consciousness, something that makes it resist description in terms of structural relationships of concepts and functional relations of properties. It is in these terms, and according to these intuitions, that Chalmers goes on to describe the problem of consciousness as the "hard problem" of explaining the arising of *experience*, distinguishing this problem from the various "easy problems" of psychological explanation, all of which amount to problems of structural or functional explanation.[17] Consciousness is resistant to these kinds of explanation precisely because it is something different, something whose immediacy and directness will not be explained even when *all* the functions and structures in the world are accounted for.

Chalmers's intuition of the simplicity, directness, and immediacy of qualia characterizes both contemporary and older uses of the term. But along with this conception of qualia, Chalmers also gestures toward a conception of scientific explanation that is, in broad terms, shared by physicalists and antiphysicalists in the philosophy of mind. In particular, Chalmers conceives of the realm of physicalist (and, in general, scientific) explanation as a realm of *structural* and *functional* explanation, and he protests that such explanation does not suffice to explain the arising of consciousness. In so doing, he exploits a general conception of the metaphysical structure of the world that is congenial to physicalism and held in common by a variety of contemporary theories and theorists. According to this picture – what Jaegwon Kim has called the "layered model" of the world – reality consists ultimately of elementary particles, or of whatever basic units of matter our best physics tells us everything else is composed of, in *causal* relationships to one another.[18] Accordingly, higher-level entities such as molecules and cells are arrangements of the underlying units, and their properties can be deduced (at least in an idealized sense) from the relations of the underlying units. This makes for a unified *logical* structure of explanation in which all of the causally relevant properties of entities described by the specialized sciences, including psychology, can, in principle, be explained in terms of, or reduced to, relational properties of the underlying units. This logical structure of explanation makes physicalist description essentially relational, for the explanation of a phenomenon adverts either to its compositional relationship to its constituents or to its causal or functional relationships with other phenomena.[19] Given this picture, a characterization of the structural and functional position of a phenomenon is all that the physicalist description has to offer. Reference to nonstructural or nonfunctional intrinsic properties plays no role.

In the underlying motivations of this picture of the world can be sought the underlying motivations of the contemporary discussion of consciousness as a problem for scientific description. The broadly physicalist picture, though, itself has a detailed and important philosophical history; and significantly, this history is not completely distinct from the history of the concept of consciousness to which Chalmers appeals. Historical analysis and reflection reveals the extent to which the conception of consciousness as inexplicable by structural or functional means, and the conception of those means themselves as presupposed in the current discussions, are joined in their origin and philosophical foundations. The philosophical history of the underlying distinction between basic elements of experience and structural or functional description can, in fact, be traced to one of the founding texts of analytic philosophy, Carnap's *Der Logische Aufbau der Welt*:

Now, the fundamental thesis of construction theory (cf. s 4), which we will attempt to demonstrate in the following investigation, asserts that fundamentally there is only one object domain and that each scientific statement is about the objects in this domain. Thus, it becomes unnecessary to indicate for each statement the object domain, and the result is that *each scientific statement can in principle be so transformed that it is nothing but a structure statement*. But the transformation is not only possible, it is imperative. For science wants to speak about what is objective, and whatever does not belong to the structure but to the material (i.e., anything that can be pointed out in a concrete ostensive definition) is, in the final analysis, subjective.[20]

According to Carnap in 1929, the objectivity of any proposition whatsoever – its possibility of referring to the objective domain of scientific explanation – depends on its being a *structural* proposition. Such propositions make no direct use of names. Instead, they comprise only definite descriptions and logical relationships among them. In this way, the total web of science can be described as a logical network of explanation, wherein all evidentiary and theoretical claims are deductively interrelated. Unity of science, Carnap claims, depends on this structuralization, for it is only in virtue of the structural nature of scientific propositions that they avoid referring to private, idiosyncratic experiences. Physics already comprises almost exclusively structural propositions, and other regions of science, as they advance conceptually and empirically, become more fully structural and thus more fully assimilated to a unified explanatory order.

Carnap's claim for the structuralization of scientific propositions already defines the outlines of today's conception of scientific explanation as physicalist or functionalist. Scientific explanation, for Carnap, results in a unified totality of propositions that refer only to the structure of relations comprised by the entities they describe. Structuralization, moreover, makes the explanatory unity of science a *logical* unity. As on Chalmers's picture, the explanatory relationships between structural descriptions are deductive and definitional ones. And, as for Chalmers, physics has a privileged role as the science in which the relational definitions of all sciences have their root. Carnap would soon make "physicalism" – defined as the thesis that all meaningful scientific propositions are expressible in a single language, the language of physics – the basis of his conception of the unity of scientific explanation. By 1932, Carnap even conceived of reports of basic experience as physicalist sentences, reports on the physical state of the observer.[21] This semantic physicalism formed the basis for Carnap's claim for the unity of scientific explanation; the unity of science across all its specialized domains – biology, psychology, and even sociology – could be ensured by the uniform possibility of rewriting the propositions of any of these special sciences in the purely structural language of physics.

In this way, Carnap's picture inaugurates contemporary physicalism's comprehensive claim of explanatory unity. But significantly, the ultimate *relata* of Carnap's system of logical relations in the *Aufbau*'s epistemological project are not physical entities or events, but instead basic or elementary experiences. Like Lewis, then, Carnap makes the description of immediate experiences dependent on their location in a total pattern of relations. And like Lewis, he describes this pattern of relations as a condition for the possibility of meaningful expression; immediate experiences can be described *only* in virtue of their position within it. But Carnap also goes beyond Lewis's picture by treating the "total pattern of relations" as a pattern of *logical* relationships that mirror the logical relationships of linguistic terms. This innovation, in fact, represents a decisive moment in the inauguration of the analytic project of conceptual analysis. For it allows the articulation of a program according to which the analysis of definitional and logical relationships among concepts yields epistemological insight. Because scientific propositions amount to structural descriptions of relationships among elementary experiences, analysis of a proposition allows the analyst to differentiate between the contribution of logical structure and the contribution of empirical content to its meaning. The concepts of science are exhibited as logical constructions from elementary experiences, revealing the epistemological order of inference from elementary experiences to the attribution of these concepts.

Conceiving of elementary experiences as primary, ineffable contents, and setting them off against structural explanation, Carnap's view already provides the outlines of the theoretical configuration within which subsequent stages of the philosophical discussion of consciousness have most often moved. This theoretical configuration, indeed, determines plausible explanatory suggestions even today. This can be seen particularly clearly in one recent reaction to the problem of qualia, a proposal that offers as a new solution Lewis's original view of qualia as identifiable or explainable only in virtue of their structural interrelationships. Recently, several philosophers have suggested that the problem of the relationship of qualia to physical facts can be solved *relationally*: the solution of the problem will depend on the discovery of specific correlations between the overall structure of experience and the structure of neurophysiological, computational, or functional states.[22] Our sense of the mysteriousness of qualia, these philosophers suggest, will dissipate once we describe them in terms of their logical and formal interrelations. Chalmers himself suggests a "principle of structural coherence" whereby "the structure of consciousness is mirrored by the structure of awareness, and the structure of awareness is mirrored by the structure of consciousness" (1996, p. 225).

Even more suggestively, in view of the philosophical history here detailed, several recent writers have sketched arguments for a return to the Russellian view that is sometimes called "intrinsic monism," a view that bears important similarities of motivation and content to Carnap's picture.[23] According to intrinsic monism, physical descriptions of the world are themselves purely relational: they characterize only relations among otherwise undefined entities and properties. Considered intrinsically, however, these entities and properties are themselves phenomenal or proto-experiential. Thus, as on Carnap's view, the relationality of objective, physical description sits alongside the nonrelationality of the phenomenal properties of immediate experience, apparently offering a solution to the problem of the integration of the intrinsic properties of subjective entities with the relational properties of objective ones.

These recent suggestions may seem to bring a new level of attention to phenomenological detail and a new complexity to the contemporary discussion, but in the light of philosophical history they are simply repetitions of positions already investigated and discussed at an earlier moment, albeit in a somewhat different philosophical climate. The second suggestion, in particular, essentially rewrites Carnap's solution to the problem of the relationship of subjectivity and objectivity outside the scope of the primarily epistemological concerns of Carnap's project. The recognition of the deep similarities between this suggestion and older views recommends an explicit discussion of the original reasons for those views and their continuing ability to motivate philosophical argument. In particular, the recognition of the historical parallel recommends an explicit discussion of the underlying reasons for Carnap's and Lewis's distinction between the ineffable, private contents of subjectivity and the objective description of the world, where objectivity is understood as the field of public, linguistic expressibility or communicability and hence as logical structure.

III

The preliminary historical investigation of the concept "qualia" already suffices to reveal the existence of a consistent configuration of theory that unites the claims of Lewis, Carnap, and Chalmers across eight decades of philosophical history. It has two recognizable parts. First, all three philosophers take it that the relevant form of explanation, in terms of which the issue of consciousness can be posed, is *structural* in the sense that I've explained. Second, all three accounts identify qualia, or the elements of consciousness, as *resistant* to such explanation. However successful our explanations of items and objects in terms of relational structures might be in other domains, the intrinsic properties of consciousness appear in each case to have special features that block the possibility of explaining them in this way.

As we shall see in this study, the theoretical configuration that opposes structure to consciousness has remained a consistent determinant of the discussion of consciousness in the analytic tradition. This continuity owes largely to underlying continuities of philosophical *method* within this tradition. In the sweep of the methodological history of analytic philosophy, structuralist methods of analysis and explanation are in fact preeminent and decisive. This preeminence stems, in the first instance, from their use in projects of *linguistic* analysis and from their suitability for producing a kind of philosophical insight into meanings that is distinctively linguistic in nature. A characteristic concern with language and a conception of philosophical elucidation as linguistic analysis are, of course, early marks of the distinctiveness of the analytic tradition. And the methodological contours and demands of the specific inquiry into linguistic meaning have continued to define, as we shall see in detail, the analytic tradition's consideration of consciousness, from its earliest articulations to its most contemporary versions.

For the inaugural projects of analytic philosophy, the *analysis* of a meaningful unit of language – most often a sentence or proposition – consists in the identification of its interrelated, semantically relevant parts.[24] These parts may be the words that obviously constitute the sentence on the level of its surface grammar, but the identification of the meaning of a sentence in terms of its logical role in patterns of inference and definition allows it, in many cases, to be revealed as having a *deep structure* as well. That is, through logical analysis a sentence can be shown to have an underlying pattern of meaningful constituence, or logical structure, different from that of its immediately evident surface grammar. The logical analysis of a sentence, then, shows its genuinely meaningful parts in their logically and semantically significant interrelationships. Given this, it is natural to conceive of meaning *itself* as consisting in logical structure or form. For a sentence to have the meaning that it does, on this picture, is for it to have a particular logical structure, to be composed in a particular way out of simpler significant parts whose interrelations and possibilities of meaningful combination are governed by the general logical or semantic rules that define a language. The analysis of any particular sentence then takes shape within a guiding conception of the overall logical structure of terms in the language.

Insofar as linguistic analysis is explanatory, then, its mode of explanation seems to be a distinctively *structuralist* one. And the structuralist picture of linguistic meaning gained additional early support, as we will see in more detail in the next chapter, from considerations of the *publicity* and *objectivity* of meaning. Since genuine linguistic meaning is not a matter for private or individual decision or determination, it is reasonable to assume that the logical structure of meaning shown by the linguistic analysis of a sentence will be an *objective* structure, one binding on any speaker who uses that sentence meaningfully. Intersubjective communication, after all, depends on *shared* meanings, so the rules followed by a particular speaker in the use of a meaningful language must also characterize her interlocutor's patterns of use, as well as the usage of all speakers of the language. On the structuralist view, then, explanation of meaning in terms of logical structure locates meanings as positions within the stable set of rules and norms that collectively comprise a language and are binding on all of its speakers. Beginning with Frege, this consideration and related ones led analytic philosophers to conclude that a general structuralist account of meaning could also account for the *objectivity* of linguistic meaning. For a sentence to have an objective meaning at all, they supposed, was for it to have a determinate and fixed logical structure, comprehensible in terms of the semantic structure of terms and concepts that characterizes the language as a whole.

Though it varies in details in each of its specific instances, the general structuralist picture of meaning thereby defined provides theoretical support for many of the linguistically oriented projects of analysis and theories of meaning that have characterized the analytic tradition. It supports not only projects, such as Frege's, that conceive of analysis in the context of an artificial, ideal, and logically perfect language meant to eliminate any possibility of logical error, but also subsequent projects that look to ordinary use rather than idealized formal languages and that characteristically understand the logical structure of language as a structure of linguistic rules of use implicit in ordinary practice. For these subsequent projects, the elucidation of the logical form of a sentence is the elucidation of the conventional rules of use followed in using it meaningfully in ordinary practice rather than the ideal rules of a logically perfect language, but elucidation of meaning remains grounded in elucidation of the general logical structure of the language. A structuralist picture of meaning, then, underlies and provides theoretical support to virtually all of the projects of logical or linguistic analysis, conceptual analysis, conceptual-role semantics, and pragmatist analysis of meaning as use that comprise the methodological history of the first fifty years or so of analytic philosophy.

What is perhaps less immediately evident is that both a structuralist picture of explanation and a structuralist account of objectivity continue to provide support for explanatory projects within the analytic tradition even when the tradition ceases to portray itself as exclusively or predominantly focused on *language* at all. For some of the most prominent explanatory projects and positions of the last few decades of the analytic tradition in fact inherit much of their specific method from their linguistically shaped procedural ancestors, even if they do not present themselves officially as chapters of the philosophy of language. This is shown, in part, in the lines of descent that connect the newer projects to older ones with a specifically linguistic provenance. We shall see, for instance, that contemporary *physicalism*, the ontological or metaphysical view that every object and phenomenon in the universe is ultimately physical in nature, began its philosophical life as the *semantic* doctrine of the reducibility of all meaningful statements to a particular language, the language of physics. But in this and other instances, more than just lines of historical descent connect today's popular metaphysical positions to yesterday's methods of semantic analysis. For, as I argue in the four historical investigations to follow, both the general ontological view of physicalism and the specific analytic project, within the philosophy of mind, of functionalism inherit not only their claim to characterize objectivity but also their determinate *methods* of elucidation from an application of structuralism that is formally identical to that of their analytic ancestors.

Like the earlier projects from which they descend, physicalism and functionalism explain phenomena by locating them within a comprehensive, relationally described network. As on the earlier accounts, as well, for a state of affairs to be objectively existent is for it to be locatable within this network. The relations that now define the network can be described as causal rather than logical, but this makes little difference either to the formal structure of the theory or to the character of its explanatory method. The chief and most decisive resource of physicalist or functionalist explanation remains, as the following investigations show in historical detail, reasoning about the structure of language and the semantic interconnections of its descriptive terms. Even if the contemporary projects officially disclaim their own linguistic character, they retain a determinative concern with the logical structure of language in the very form of their explanations. The retention of a basically structuralist picture of explanation within physicalism and functionalism leads, as we have already seen in outline, to the complaint, evident in Chalmers's formulation of the "hard problem," that consciousness is left out of any physicalist or functionalist account. If the complaint is right, no physicalist or functionalist explanation of consciousness can succeed, because no structuralist form of theory is appropriate to explaining consciousness itself. Determining the general reason for this failure – and explaining the recalcitrance of consciousness to physicalist and functionalist description – therefore requires that we reflect methodologically and historically on the underlying nature of structuralist explanation, the continuing reasons for its predominance in analytic philosophy, and the possibility of gaining alternative forms of insight into the nature and structure of consciousness that improve upon it.

Simply recognizing the continuity of structuralist modes of explanation within the analytic tradition already produces an improved understanding of the contemporary problem of explaining consciousness. For the recognition allows the conception of *explanation* operative in the problem to be brought out and discussed explicitly. Standard histories and presentations of the contemporary problem of explaining consciousness often present it as simply an updated version of the traditional "mind–body problem," the problem (as it is envisioned) of accounting for how "the mind" can be "physical," or "material," or a part, aspect, state, or condition of the human body or brain. But foregrounding the role of structuralism in determining the contemporary problem allows us to see that it is not accurately representable in this crude and general way. For the contemporary problem gains its character as much from a historically specific conception of explanation as from the nature of what is to be explained. Roughly speaking, there are as many "mind–body" problems as there are conceptions of what it is to explain something physically or materially. These conceptions take shape in particular historical contexts and for specific philosophical reasons. The particular structuralist conception of explanation that determines the contemporary problem is hardly recognizable (either in its specific linguistic character or in its determinative connection with an overall conception of objectivity) in older, pre–twentieth century versions of "materialism" or "mechanism" about the mind. In order to understand the problem, it is therefore necessary to reflect not only on the properties of consciousness itself, but also on the specific philosophical reasons for holding a structuralist picture. This reflection contributes decisively to the kind of improved insight into the nature of the problem that can help to provide new and improved grounds for its resolution or dissolution.

In the recent history of the discussion of the problem of consciousness, then, the omission of a level of historical and methodological reflection has contributed not only to obscuring the underlying nature of the problem but also to depriving theorists of the means by which it might be resolved. For standard descriptions of the problem hide both the conceptual structure and the history of the structuralist conception of explanation that comprise it. This obscuring of the context of the problem in historically specific conceptions of explanation has also contributed to encouraging theorists, in recent decades, to present their inquiry as a metaphysical, ontological, or empirical one into the nature of one particularly puzzling phenomenon, rather than as a linguistic or semantic inquiry about meaning and the language of consciousness. In so doing, they miss the linguistic provenance and the enduring, basically linguistic orientation of their own methods and programs of investigation, as well as the original partial determination of these very methods by the problem of explaining consciousness in its more general form. This omission leads, in turn, to the frustrating dialectical situation in which the debate can come to seem to concern the bare existence or nonexistence of the phenomena of consciousness themselves, conceived as having the sorts of special and puzzling properties discussed in section I. The issue then seems to be a conflict between those who, in service of a general explanatory project, deny the existence of consciousness, reasoning that nothing in the objective world could have such unusual and distinctive properties as those claimed for consciousness by its defenders, and those who respond by affirming its existence on the ground of the plainest and most immediate evidence of self-consciousness or introspection. At this point, the debate becomes a bare battle of intuitions, with little more to say in favor of one side or the other.[25] Understanding the real source of these intuitions, as I argue in this work, requires identifying their source in originally linguistic issues of the explanation of meaning. Recognizing the debate as a basically semantic one rather than a metaphysical or ontological one allows its methodological specificity to emerge from obscurity by showing the real historical and conceptual determinants of the picture of explanation it presupposes.

Philosophers of mind are not, I hasten to admit, generally completely unaware of the history of concepts here related. Many contemporary philosophers have felt there to be a tension between descriptions of qualia as "intrinsic," on the one hand, and behaviorist, physicalist, functionalist, and other forms of "relational" explanations of them, on the other.[26] And philosophers who appeal to qualia are generally not unaware of the similarities between their view and the views of adherents to "sense-data" and epistemologically foundationalist views, like those of Lewis and Carnap. Indeed, the history here related suggests that the identification of particular tensions between the explanation of qualia as immediate, nonrelational content and the relational explanatory tools of analysis has repeatedly driven methodological and thematic innovation in philosophy of mind, and continues to drive it today. However, the continuing influence of the problem has not generally ensured the explicit recognition of its underlying conceptual determinants. Though the tension between the characterization of the properties of qualia as nonrelational and the formal, relational tools of explanation has repeatedly driven theoretical innovations, and although this tension has indeed sometimes been recognized, little has been said about exactly why it might arise, or about what deeper problem it represents. It is here that historical investigation proves particularly useful.

IV

Throughout the history here examined, characterizing the ordinary *language of consciousness* has posed particular and instructive difficulties for philosophers of mind and language. By "the language of consciousness" I mean the ordinary, generally first-person language in which we express thoughts and beliefs, report perceptions and sensations, complain of pains and discomforts. The investigation of the meaning and reference of this language is, I argue here, the ultimate basis of the analytic inquiry into consciousness in each of its historical versions. The language of consciousness, so described, does not rely on any philosophical or contentious picture of subjectivity or mentality in order to be recognized and employed. But even without rigorously delimiting this language or exhaustively distinguishing it from other regions or versions of linguistic explanation, it is possible to begin to see how the investigation of the language of consciousness can tend to play both a determinative and a problematic role within methods and theories of linguistic reflection generally.

Within the scope of structuralist theories and methods, the ordinary language of consciousness has alternately seemed either *inadequate*, as if its way of describing its subject were in some distinctive way unsuited to that subject, so that what really accounts for it must be some manner of reference or meaning quite unlike that which characterizes other regions of descriptive discourse; or *impossible*, as if there were no question of description, since the objects or events that would be described by it do not – as we can see from one or another structuralist total picture of objectivity – really exist as objective phenomena and so must be relegated to the realm of the unspeakable, if they are real at all. Within the configuration of theoretical opposition that I've described here, positive accounts of the meaning and basis of our language of consciousness repeatedly fail to articulate a phenomenon comprehensible in terms of the very structuralist picture they are meant to support. The result is an ambiguous historical dynamic of oscillation between structuralist explanatory projects and a feeling of the specific inadequacy of these projects for the explanation of consciousness.

The theoretical configuration of opposition so described has, I argue in the detailed case studies to follow, determined and driven debate in the philosophy of mind at several key moments in its history. The ability of this basic configuration both to constrain and to motivate debate through various stages of the history of the analytic tradition can be traced, in large part, to the peculiar explanatory dynamics of the relationship between its two parts. For the conceptual configuration that sets consciousness off against a total pattern of structuralist, ultimately linguistic explanation has been, in a philosophically unique way, both *conceptually stable* and *historically unstable*.

It has been conceptually stable because every general structuralist account requires for its intelligibility some description of the nature of the interrelated *elements* that comprise the relational structure it adduces. As we shall see, within decisive projects in the history of analytic philosophy, the basic elements of consciousness have filled this role. They have been the elements in terms of which everything else is to be explained, while they themselves, owing to this situation, remain unexplainable. Conversely, the thought that consciousness cannot be further decomposed, analyzed, or explained by structural means naturally suggests the thought that we should understand other events and phenomena in terms of the structural configurations of basic elements of consciousness. This mutual support, as we will see, provided important motivation for the introduction of the enduring theoretical configuration that opposes consciousness to structure. But even when, at a subsequent stage of the discussion, structuralist accounts ceased to explicitly envision the explanatory structures they introduced as comprised of elements of consciousness, the sense of a specific resistance of consciousness to structuralist explanation (of whatever type) would remain, reappearing in general complaints such as Chalmers's and continuing to determine the form of discussion of the problem of explaining consciousness today.

The consistent theoretical configuration of opposition has been *historically unstable*, however, in that the linguistic provenance of structuralism as an account of meaning and communication demands that the simple and basic elements of consciousness be *inexplicable* in the structuralist terms that suffice for the analysis of language describing public states of affairs. Since structure is identified with meaningfulness, and since clarification of meaning is clarification of structures of relation, it becomes impossible, by the lights of the theory, to understand language purporting to characterize the simple elements as they are, nonrelationally and in themselves. The intrinsic character of consciousness in itself, then, becomes literally *unspeakable*, incapable of finding expression in any form of language comprehensible as having objective meaning, even though it remains a presupposition for the structuralist analysis as a whole. Within this configuration, therefore, any positive description of the character of consciousness undermines itself. For if the character of consciousness is expressible at all, structuralist methods can analyze the language in which it is expressed. They can reveal any purported positive description of the contents of consciousness, if meaningful, as having the same determinacy of meaning, understandable in terms of its logical interrelations with other meaningful propositions in the language, that other public-language propositions have.[27] But the imposition of the structural method then invites the recurrence of the original complaint: the putative description of the nature of consciousness has tried to capture the unstructured elements of structure, but its failure to do this is shown by its very structuralizability. There must, the now-recurrent complaint continues, accordingly be an alternative description, one that somehow makes intelligible the nonstructural character of consciousness itself, even given that the meaningfulness of language is generally intelligible in terms of its logical structure.

The following four case studies trace the methodological fates and fortunes of twentieth-century philosophy of mind, at some of its most decisive moments, to this ambiguous dynamic. At each of the four moments of theoretical development considered here, a positive structuralist explanatory project is challenged by the particular difficulties of giving a structuralist account of some aspect of the ordinary language of consciousness. But because the general problem has typically not been articulated on its actual level of generality, the complaint of inadequacy, though it has a recurrent form, has most often seemed to figure only against the *particular* structuralist project for which it arises. The most consistent theoretical response has accordingly been, not to

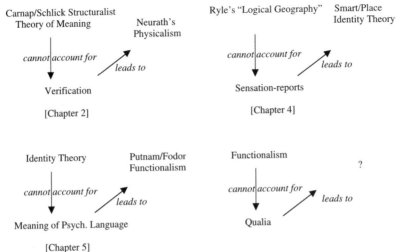

FIGURE 1.1. Some instances of the historical dynamic. The form of the historical dynamic between conscious experience and analytic explanation at four of the historical moments discussed here. In each case, the recalcitrance of some phenomenon of conscious experience to a particular analytical program leads to its replacement by a new one.

recognize the problem with structuralist explanations of consciousness as a general one, but to replace the particular structuralist project for which the problem arises with another such project, characterized by different specific means but sharing a structuralist form. The underlying complaint that consciousness resists structural explanation, then, recurs in the context of the new theory, and this consistent recurrence again leads to methodological innovation that preserves a structuralist form. Figure 1.1 outlines this dynamic, as it is shown to have occurred in the following investigations, at several decisive moments in the history of analytic philosophy of mind. It culminates in the contemporary configuration, where qualia are felt to be a decisive problem for physicalist or functionalist means of explanation, but it remains unclear what successor project might accommodate them.

This kind of methodological reflection provides grounds not only for criticizing specific structuralist projects, but also for raising the question of the limitations of structuralist explanation itself. And because of the special and determinative link, running through the history of analytic philosophy, between structuralist methods and forms of insight that are distinctively linguistic, reflection on the figuring of the language of consciousness in the projects and explanatory schemes of analytic philosophy becomes a historically grounded way of considering the more general questions of the relationship of specifically linguistic forms of intelligibility to the understanding of consciousness, of the privilege or fatefulness of language as structuring the kinds of intelligibility of which we are humanly capable, and of the relationship between this privilege and the kind of understanding shown in our ordinary, untheoretical language of self-description.

In each of the four case studies that follow, the problems of explaining consciousness appear in the particular infelicities of particular attempted accounts of the ordinary language of consciousness, accounts that figure this language as extraordinary or peculiar, as having a special status or needing a special explanation, as demanding new forms of linguistic analysis or explanation. In Chapter 2, we see that Carnap and Schlick's structuralist project of accounting for objectivity leads them to consider basic perceptual reports or protocol sentences to depend, for their meaning, on the performance of special acts of inward-directed ostension or demonstration, or on the bare presence of subjective, private items, exterior to the system of language but nevertheless having a justificatory role with respect to linguistic utterances. The picture thus envisions experience as, paradoxically, both inside and outside the linguistic system it describes, leading not only to its ultimate incoherence but also to its historical demise and replacement by other projects. The same logical positivist theory, as we see in the examination of Chapter 3, pictures the logical structure or form of experience as governed by conventional rules of semantic use for the language, but it comes to grief in the attempt to explain the nature and force of these rules. In the fourth chapter's examination of Gilbert Ryle's widely influential program for the analysis of the concepts of mind, the first-person language of sensation emerges as an area of particular and indicative difficulty for Ryle, seeming to demand the modification or abandonment of his program and leading to Place and Smart's formulation of the psychophysical identity theory as a replacement. Finally, the fifth chapter shows how the demands of capturing the logic of ordinary psychological language, a logic that fits only poorly the more general logic of causal or physicalist description, drove theorists in replacing the identity theory with functionalism as a method of investigation and a theory of mind.

Still, though, it was clear from almost the beginning of functionalism's career that it had a special problem with the characterization of consciousness, and particularly with qualitative states or (using the old term, which soon began to reappear) qualia. Old puzzles, like the puzzle of the inverted spectrum, made a prominent reappearance in the form of a challenge to functionalism to explain qualia, and evocative new thought experiments capitalizing on the generality and abstract character of functional state descriptions further embarrassed the functionalist claim to explain the qualitative.[28] Most of all, qualia seemed obviously different from other, functionally explainable mental states because of their independence from functional descriptions. This independence was soon captured in a compelling allegory: that of the zombie, or the physical and functional duplicate of a conscious being that nevertheless completely lacks qualia or consciousness. As the metaphysical concepts of possible worlds and supervenience developed during the 1980s and 1990s, these concepts offered a compelling picture of scientific explanation and a natural description of the problematic cases that, given their apparent conceivability, makes consciousness and qualia seem stubbornly resistant to physicalist and functionalist accounts.

V

I have argued that structuralist modes and methods of explanation derive their preeminence in the analytic tradition from their suitability to the specifically linguistic forms of analysis or inquiry that define that tradition, and also that structuralist projects, in each of their historical instances, fail to explain consciousness because, while retaining a basically linguistic orientation, they nevertheless fail to adequately handle the ordinary language of self-description and self-awareness. So much the worse, someone might be tempted to conclude, for linguistic modes of explanation; what we ought to do in order to improve the debate is to forget about the *language* of consciousness and try to understand the nature of consciousness directly. Since any attempted explanation of consciousness according to linguistic means or methods of clarification seems to leave it unintelligible (we might conclude), we would do better to abandon linguistic methods of clarification entirely and make a fresh start with means of analysis that are more directly, or more honestly, metaphysical, ontological, or empirical in character.

But to draw this conclusion would be to miss something else that is shown by the four case studies to follow, something that is, in its own way, just as important as showing that consciousness systematically resists structuralist theories. For each of the investigations, in showing how consciousness has failed to adequately figure within particular structuralist theories, at the same time shows how modes of explanation that work by investigating logic and language are, in a sense, *unavoidable* for the project of understanding consciousness. As we shall see, particularly in Chapter 3, forms of inquiry and analysis that do not accord linguistic methods a privileged status miss substantial and decisive insights that linguistic inquiry can capture; and in the course of the history here detailed, projects that do not present themselves as linguistic nevertheless most often actually share or recapitulate the explanatory structure of overtly linguistic ones. Even as they show why consciousness systematically resists structuralist theories that have their home in linguistic analysis, then, the historical investigation suggested here also suggests the unavoidability of linguistic means for any satisfying understanding of it.

One way of putting the insight of this unavoidability would be to say that the attempt to make consciousness intelligible is never in fact wholly separable from the attempt to make the language of consciousness intelligible. For as we shall see in the following investigations, there is no source of evidence about consciousness, and no means of making a description of it more intelligible, that does not in some way rest on, or relate to, judgments about what we can ourselves *say* about our own experience. Even the results of pure introspection, if they are to be useful in an account or description of consciousness, must be propositionally stated, and clarified, in the language that we use to describe consciousness. The analytic tradition's investigation of mind embodies this discovery of the unavoidability of linguistic means, even as it repeatedly submits the language of consciousness to general structuralist theories of language that threaten to make this language unintelligible; and the historical investigation of method conducted here provides the conditions for the language of consciousness to be brought out explicitly and determinately. The structuralist picture figures the linguistic analysis of any particular sentence as an episode in, and as possible only on the precondition of, a general theory of the logical and semantic structure of language as a whole. What remains possible – if we can find historically based grounds for resisting this general structuralist picture *while nevertheless retaining some of the particular methods of linguistic analysis and clarification that it historically subsumes* – is that an application of these linguistic methods to the language of consciousness, but *outside* the guiding picture of structuralism, might be capable of producing the specific intelligibility that we desire from a theory of consciousness and that we repeatedly find lacking within structuralist theories.

The history of theories of consciousness in the analytic tradition could then be reread as a history of linguistic methods and of the specific kinds of intelligibility they produce, and these methods and their results could then be prized apart from the structuralist theories in which they have usually figured. On this rereading, the methods of linguistic analysis, clarification, and explanation that have comprised the analytic tradition could be seen to yield significant insights into the nature of consciousness through the investigation of language, even as the structuralist picture has repeatedly obscured these insights. The specific contribution of analytic philosophy of mind to the ongoing history of our philosophical attempts to understand ourselves might then be viewed as its recognition, in general and in detail, of the *priority* of language for our self-understanding – its recognition (in other words) that the specific kind of self-intelligibility that we want a theory of consciousness to produce is determinatively *shown* in the language with which we describe, and through which we understand, ourselves; and accordingly, that any form of clarificatory inquiry that elucidates consciousness will derive its specificity and force wholly from its employing methods continuous with our ordinary linguistic means of self-description. To read the specific insights of analytic philosophy in this way would be to read them as embodied in methods rather than stated in theories, and in particular, to consider the possibility that the elucidation of consciousness requires means and methods other than those of *any* general theoretical description of language or objectivity. But this might be just what is necessary in order to produce an improved discussion that both *dissolves* the recurrent problem of the recalcitrance of consciousness to structuralist explanation and *captures* the significant insights into its nature that analytic methods have produced.

If meaningful language were a structure or system of signs for the purpose of describing and explaining objects and events in the world, the elements of consciousness would be its mute foundation or center, the simple *relata*, themselves incapable of further explanation, that support it both epistemologically and semantically. When the ordinary language of consciousness, in its descriptive specificity and straightforward meaningfulness, belies this picture, philosophers have for too long drawn the conclusion of the inadequacy or incoherence of this language. What they have missed in drawing this conclusion is the possibility of an alternative linguistic mode of intelligibility for consciousness that does not depend on locating it within a comprehensive structuralist picture. Historical reflection allows us to formulate and understand the suggestion that the possibility of our understanding consciousness may depend on our recognizing such a mode as implicit in the practices and methods of analytic philosophers, even as they have themselves repeatedly failed to recognize it by submitting consciousness to a structuralist picture. It is the burden of the four historical investigations that follow to support this suggestion by showing the philosophical and conceptual roots of the difficulties, at some of the most decisive moments in the history of analytic philosophy of mind, of explaining consciousness.

Structuralism and Content in the Protocol Sentence Debate

Beginning in the 1920s, the philosophers of the Vienna Circle sought to explain the possibility of scientific knowledge with a new theory of meaning that joined the empirical content of experience to the formal structure of logical inference and derivation. Drawing upon the logical and mathematical tools recently developed by Frege, Hilbert, Russell, and Wittgenstein, proponents of what might be called the *structuralist* theory of meaning set the private, ineffable, or incommunicable content of subjective experience off against the linguistic form of intersubjective communication and conceptual articulation. The theory drew its ultimate conceptual warrant from the method of logical analysis that inaugurated the analytic tradition itself, but it took specific shape in response to the need to account semantically for the contribution of experience to empirical meaning within a unified, empiricist epistemology of scientific knowledge. Its conception of meaning as ultimately structural, and its assertion of a link between this conception and the possibility of objectivity, would continue to orient the theories and projects of analytic philosophers long after the breakup of the Circle in 1935. But in this conception lay, as well, the ultimate seeds of the downfall of the Circle's originally unified theoretical project. The project came to grief when the philosophers of the Circle could not agree about the logical form of basic observational or "protocol" sentences, sentences capturing the immediate observations to which, the members of the Circle supposed, all empirical knowledge must ultimately trace.

Although the story of the protocol sentence debate has often been told, its standard retelling in the analytic tradition has obscured its significance by concealing its conceptual origin. That origin, I argue in this chapter, lies in tensions inherent to the positivists' structuralist model of the relationship between experience and meaning. On a standard and received interpretation, the debate revealed the necessity of basing the epistemology of an empiricist description of scientific knowledge on public, intersubjectively verifiable claims rather than on essentially private, subjective, or phenomenalist ones. Otto Neurath's insistence on physicalism, confirmation holism, and the fallibility of observational claims is most often seen as a decisive and original repudiation of the Cartesian, infallibilist, and foundationalist picture initially held by his Circle disputants, Moritz Schlick and Rudolf Carnap. Schlick's foundationalism, by contrast, is seen as embodying a "correspondence" theory of truth demanding, at the basic level of justification, that protocol or observation sentences designate immediately and apodictically evident facts, whereas Neurath's fallibilism about protocol sentences is thought to fit within a general holist "coherence" theory.[1] Schlick's theory failed – so the usual story goes – when he could not make sense of the relationship that he supposed to hold between language and the world in virtue of which it is possible for a proposition to directly confront or be compared with a fact. For this reason, Neurath's coherence theory triumphed, even if residual doubts remained about its tendency to relativism and about its entitlement to the credentials of genuine empiricism. It was then left to Quine to accommodate Neurath's coherentist insights with his own holistic model, while reconstructing "confrontation with the facts" in terms of the causal responses of an observer to her environment.[2]

This received interpretation has recently been challenged by a variety of interpreters seeking a more historically accurate, nuanced, and comprehensive picture of the debate.[3] Neither Schlick nor Neurath, these interpreters object, could have based his position in the protocol sentence debate on a general theory of truth, for neither philosopher held any such theory.[4] Even more significantly, though, the received interpretation fails to situate the debate within the context of the issues of the relationship of experience to meaning that provided its actual conceptual background. This failure obscures the central importance of the structuralist conception of meaning inaugurated by

Schlick, Carnap, and Neurath and conceals its subsequent endurance within the analytic tradition. From its beginnings, the structuralist theory of meaning opposed the structural form of linguistic meaning to the contents of experience, conceived as ineffable and indescribable in themselves. The question of protocols raised, for the structuralist theory, the difficult question of the place of sentences *directly* characterizing experience, sentences expressing contents that were, by the lights of the structuralist theory, in themselves inexpressible. Paradoxically, structuralism *needed* its characterization of the content of experience as incommunicable in order to give its theory of meaning, and the concrete project of structuralization, their determinate significance and shape. But at the same time, the asserted incommunicability of content imperiled its ability to theorize the contact between experience and meaning that the verification of protocol sentences seemed to require. The resulting tensions generated the conflicting positions of Schlick and Neurath on the nature of protocols, and drove Carnap from a project of phenomenalist epistemological reconstruction to a generalized physicalism that accords experience no special role in empirical justification. At the conclusion of the debate, the implications of the underlying structuralist model forced all three philosophers to abandon the hope for a coherent account of the relationship between experience and meaning.

From the structuralist picture of Carnap, Schlick, and Neurath would later arise physicalism, the view that reality can be exhaustively characterized in terms of physical states and events causally related, and it is against the backdrop of a physicalist worldview that the problem of consciousness is today most often discussed. After the debate, structuralism survived, in the discourse of the analytic tradition, as the *ontological* (rather than semantic) doctrine of physicalism. But despite its shift to ontology and its role in generating subsequent projects in the philosophy of mind and epistemology, the physicalist worldview could not avoid the recurrence and repetition of the objection that structuralism fails adequately to characterize the language of consciousness. The underlying problem of how to accommodate experience, first prepared by the basic structuralist model of experience and meaning, would survive, and recur, as a problem for the successor forms of structuralist explanation that continued to characterize the analytic tradition long after the breakup of the Vienna Circle, and that continue to provide the backdrop for the problem of explaining consciousness today.

I

When Carnap wrote his masterpiece, *Der Logische Aufbau der Welt*, in 1928, he sought to provide an epistemological reconstruction of all scientific concepts on the basis of the given elements of immediate experience. Officially, the *Aufbau* undertakes the construction of an epistemological "genealogy" of all concepts on the basis of a simple set of basic ones in accordance with the method of logical analysis developed by Frege, Russell, and Wittgenstein.[5] The ultimate aim of the book is to sketch, at least in outline, the development of a complete "constructional system" of concepts linked by derivability relations, in terms of which all scientific propositions can be stated, and in virtue of which these propositions can be reduced to simpler ones through meaning-preserving constructional rules.[6] In particular, the construction system Carnap develops in outline bases all scientific concepts on immediately given "elementary experiences" and a single relation of recollected similarity between them.[7] The text shows how, given the project, one might actually carry out the logical construction of an individual's spatio-temporal world from the synthesis of elementary experiences, and it gives in rough outline the further construction of the "heteropsychological" or intersubjective domain of physical reality. Finally, Carnap indicates that cultural objects and values can be constructed on the basis of the heteropsychological domain. In this way, the total hierarchical concept system of science is constructed from the given basis of the elementary experiences alone.

Because of its emphasis on the possibility that the intersubjective world can be constructed from a basis of private experiences, Carnap's project can seem to amount to a species of idealism or phenomenalism. But as recent scholarship has revealed, the philosophical surroundings of the apparently phenomenalist project of the *Aufbau* are much more complicated than many of Carnap's readers in the analytic tradition have appreciated.[8] For instance, the constructional system based on elementary experiences is intended to be only an incompletely worked-out example. By Carnap's own claim, other constructional systems, with other kinds of bases, are possible and equally valid. The choice of the autopsychological basis of elementary experiences is particularly advantageous for the purposes of epistemology, but a constructional system with a physical basis would also be possible.[9] It is clear, moreover, that Carnap did not intend the basis of his system to be anything as simple as Russell's sense-data. The "elementary experiences," though basic, are already richly interrelated by relations of partial similarity, and an elaborate procedure of "quasi-analysis" is needed in order to discover the network of these relations from the extensionally given list of them.[10] Quasi-analysis characterizes the interrelationships of basic experiences in such a way that they can be used for the construction of higher-level domains by adumbrating "similarity circles" that relate them according to particular characteristics.[11] Carnap emphasizes, moreover, that the choice of an autopsychological basis is not metaphysically committal and that construction theory in general does not make any ontological or metaphysical claim about the constitution of the world.

Even more important to a full understanding of Carnap's philosophical goals, however, is an appreciation of the guiding role played in his epistemology by the concept of *structural definite descriptions*.[12] At the end of section 2 of the *Aufbau*, Carnap indicates that the task of building constructional systems involves demonstrating the possibility of bridging the gap between subjective, private experience and the objective world described by science:

Even though the subjective origin of all knowledge lies in the contents of experiences and their connections, it is still possible, as the constructional system will show, to advance to an intersubjective, objective world, which can be conceptually comprehended and which is identical for all observers.[13]

All scientific propositions, Carnap goes on to argue, are themselves descriptions of the *structural* properties of objects, those properties that can be defined entirely by means of structural descriptions:

Thus, each scientific statement can in principle be transformed into a statement which contains only structural properties and the indication of one or more object domains. Now, the fundamental thesis of construction theory (cf. s 4), which we will attempt to demonstrate in the following investigation, asserts that fundamentally there is only one object domain and that each scientific statement is about the objects in this domain. Thus, it becomes unnecessary to indicate for each statement the object domain, and the result is that *each scientific statement can in principle be so transformed that it is nothing but a structure statement.* But the transformation is not only possible, it is imperative. For science wants to speak about what is objective, and whatever does not belong to the structure but to the material (i.e., anything that can be pointed out in a concrete ostensive definition) is, in the final analysis, subjective. One can easily see that physics is almost altogether desubjectivized, since almost all physical concepts have been transformed into purely structural concepts.[14]

Designation of an individual, particular object may be accomplished, Carnap thought, by ostension. But the terms of objective, intersubjective science, in virtue of which agreement between individuals about the designation of objects is possible, cannot be essentially tied to ostension but must instead rest on purely structural properties of those objects. Structural descriptions sufficient to uniquely designate their objects are possible on the basis of a purely formal characterization of the relations obtaining among those objects.

In the course of the development of science, as Carnap reconstructs it, the progressive characterization of the structural interrelationships among objects in a particular domain ensures the objectivity of the science that handles them. The statements of physics are, according to Carnap, already almost completely structuralized.[15] For physical statements, even ones that designate particular objects or events uniquely, can be reduced to statements about world lines and four-dimensional tensor and vector fields. Given relations of coincidence and time order, particular events and objects can be described and identified purely in terms of their place in the total relational network of world lines, and this network can itself be reduced to purely relational concepts of mathematics. Other sciences, such as sociology, however, are not yet as completely structuralized, in the sense that we still lack a comprehensive description of the network of the interrelationships of their objects. Constructional theory facilitates the increasing structuralization of science by showing how to construct the objects at higher levels of scientific description, such as persons and cultural objects, from objects at lower levels, such as the phenomenal and the physical, that are already structuralized.

In order to show how structuralization works in the context of the development of scientific knowledge, Carnap considers a simple example of the determination of the identity of objects in a specialized domain by way of their pattern of structural relations.[16] Such a pattern of relations is represented by a railroad map that portrays the railroad stations in a certain area and the rail lines that interconnect them. We can imagine that the map is metrically distorted – as railway maps often, in fact, are – so that it represents not the actual distances between stations but only the pattern of their interrelations by way of the rail lines, and we can also imagine that the names of the stations have been removed. How, then, could we go about determining the names of the stations represented as intersection points? We would begin by looking for the stations in which the largest number of lines meet. For instance, we might find several stations, in each of which eight different rail lines intersect. This does not yet suffice to determine the identity of each, but now we can consider each such station in turn with respect to the eight stations adjacent to it. By considering the number of rail lines that these stations, in turn, collect, we can generally determine the identity of the stations we started with. We can now proceed to stations with only seven lines intersecting, then six, and so on. Proceeding in this way, the determination of the structural interrelations of the railway stations generally suffices to disambiguate them and specify them uniquely in the total network. Of course, it is possible that, even when all the interconnections have been considered, there might remain two stations that are indistinguishable from one another structurally, that stand in the same pattern of interconnections by way of rail lines to the rest of the network. If this happens, it will be necessary to consider additional kinds of relations between the stations, for instance their interconnections by way of telephone lines or highways. Ultimately, given enough objective relations, it ought to be possible to identify each station uniquely.

As in the railway network, progressive scientific investigation elaborates the entire structure of relations in a particular domain. As it does so, the individual objects become specifiable in virtue of their unique position in the structure. Carnap admits the possibility that even when the total description of the relational structure of a domain of objects is complete, it may not distinguish between two distinct but structurally similar elements. But he argues that in such a case, the subjective distinction between the two elements is not accessible to science either:

From the preceding example, we can see the following: on the basis of a structural description, through one or more only structurally described relations within a given object domain, we can frequently provide a definite description of individual objects merely through structure statements and without ostensive definitions, provided only that the object domain is not too narrow and that the relation or relations have a sufficiently variegated structure. Where such a definite description is not unequivocally possible, the object domain must be enlarged or one must have recourse to other relations. If all relations available to science have been used, and no difference between two given objects of an object domain has been discovered, then, as far as science is concerned, these objects are completely alike, even if they appear subjectively different. (If the given assumptions are all fulfilled, then the two objects are not only to be envisaged as alike, but as identical in the strictest sense. This is not the place to give a justification for this apparently paradoxical assertion.) Thus, the result is that a definite description through pure structure statements is generally possible to the extent in which scientific discrimination is possible at all; such a description is unsuccessful for two objects only if these objects are not distinguishable at all by scientific methods.[17]

According to Carnap, a difference that is not a structurally discernable difference cannot *make* any difference for the terms of objective science, for the very terms of scientific description are purely structural terms, or can at least become such when all dependence on ostension is eliminated. This elimination of ostensive reference is itself, moreover, necessary for the objectivity of science. For concepts and names depending on ostension remain essentially subjective and dependent on individual experiences, which vary from subject to subject. The only way for science to assure genuine intersubjectivity in its description of objects is to "desubjectivize" its designations by structuralizing them.

Using this structuralist conception of knowledge, Carnap hoped to exploit the formal resources of the new logic in order to provide epistemological reconstructions of scientific concepts and terms suitable for genuine objectivity without sacrificing the epistemic basis of all empirical knowledge in immediate, subjective experience. Central to this project was his guiding conception of the necessity of structuralized descriptions of experience for the possibility of intersubjective communication and objective knowledge. If scientific terms and propositions could be structuralized, their deductive connection with the subjective, experiential basis of knowledge could be clarified without threatening their objectivity. In this way, the epistemological reconstruction of actual scientific claims could yield a justificatory explanation of the possibility of scientific knowledge itself.

Versions of the claim that all knowledge is structural were relatively common among turn-of-the-century epistemological projects. At times, this doctrine had also issued in ontological claims about the structural nature of entities in the universe.[18] The view that all physical description is relational, for instance, had been defended influentially by Russell, who used it as the basis for his *neutral monism*, which combined structuralism about physical entities with phenomenalism about the mental.[19] And the idea of logical form as essential to both the meaning of propositions and the structure of the world had been the centerpiece of Wittgenstein's "picture" theory of meaning in the *Tractatus.* The most significant innovation of Carnap's view was, then, neither its structuralist picture of knowledge nor his application of *logical* structure to the world, but rather the application of structuralism to yield a *semantically* based picture of the relationship of experience to knowledge. This picture begins with an underlying commitment to the identification of meaning with logical structure:

Structuralist theory of meaning: A description of the derivational and definitional *logical structure* of a proposition displays the proposition's meaning.

The structuralist theory of meaning already suggests the outlines of the program of constructional analysis: the constructional analysis of a proposition exhibits the derivational relationships between it and other propositions, as well as the definitional relationships between its constituent concepts and others. The analysis elucidates the meaning of the proposition by showing its logical structure. To this basic view of meaning as logical structure, though, Carnap also added further claims about the expressibility or inexpressibility of various states of affairs. Because all propositions are dependent for their meaning on their logical structure, expressible or communicable distinctions between states of affairs must be formalizable (that is, capable of expression in purely structural terms) as well. Carnap developed this thought, for instance, with the example of the railroad map. As the relational structure of the network is elaborated, the structural description uniquely designates more and more of the particular stations. At the limit, when not only the spatial relations but also all other scientifically describable relations have been captured in the relational description, any differences that remain are literally inexpressible:

> If there should still be two locations for which we have found no difference even after exhausting all available scientific relations, then they are indistinguishable, not only for geography, but for science in general. They may be subjectively different: I could be in one of these locations, but not in the other. But this would not amount to an objective difference, since there would be in the other place a man just like myself who says, as I do: I am here and not there.[20]

For Carnap, then, the *objectivity* of a state of affairs or a difference between two states of affairs implies its *expressibility*, which in turn implies its formalizability. An unformalizable difference between two states of affairs is possible, but because of the purely formal character of linguistic meaning, such a difference would be literally inexpressible. It follows that all expressible states of affairs are capable of being expressed by formalized propositions, ultimately by structural, definite descriptions. And insofar as scientific knowledge is possible at all, it treats of objective states of affairs; so all scientific knowledge must be capable of formalization.

The structuralist theory of meaning bears an essential, but also a somewhat equivocal, relation to the main epistemological project of the *Aufbau*. As we have seen, the project of the *Aufbau* involved not only a description of objectivity, but also an epistemologically enlightening "construction" of objectivity based on the reduction of the structure of science to the relational structure of immediate, given experiences. But the claims that all expressible states of affairs are formalizable and that all formalizable states of affairs are objective do not by themselves suggest anything in particular about the relationship of scientific propositions to their empirical basis. From Carnap's identification of objectivity with expressibility, it follows that unformalizable states of affairs are *subjective*, but an additional step is needed in order to motivate the claim that such states of affairs are identical with, or composed by, the elements of experience. The additional step is, moreover, necessary in order to forge a link between the structural conception of knowledge and the claim that such a conception yields an epistemologically plausible reconstruction of scientific propositions. Without it, a completed structuralization of scientific claims might indeed yield completely formalized descriptions, but it would not be evident that these descriptions have any special relationship to experience at all. In order to make the required link, then, Carnap must be construed as being committed to an additional proposition about experiences:

The Incommunicability of Content: (At least some) unformalizable, and hence inexpressible, items are private, individual experiences. These private, individual experiences are only describable in virtue of the logical structure of their interrelations.

Carnap comes closest to arguing for this when he appeals to the irreducible difference in content between the experiences of two epistemic subjects:

The series of experiences is different for each subject. If we want to achieve, in spite of this, agreement in the names for the entities which are constructed on the basis of these experiences, then this cannot be done by reference to the completely divergent content, but only through the formal description of the structure of these entities.[21]

If individual experiences are irreducibly divergent and intersubjectively incomparable, then their specific contents are presumably inexpressible in an intersubjective language, making them good candidates for an elucidatory structuralized redescription. But such a description will not be *epistemologically* relevant unless, in addition to their inexpressibility, private, subjective experiences also *justify* the scientific claims based on them. Assuming that they do, a structuralized redescription of immediate, subjective experiences can plausibly claim to shed light on the epistemological order of justification: the reduction of a complex scientific claim to a relational structure description concerning only immediate experiences can then claim to reveal the actual or idealized order of justificatory inference from immediate, subjective experience to public, intersubjective proposition.

Carnap is clearly aware of the need to forge this specific connection between the structuralist picture of meaning and the reductive, epistemological project. He admits, for instance, that the phenomenalist basis of the system given in the *Aufbau* is not the only possible basis for a constructional system; a physicalist basis is also possible and legitimate.[22] But the primary reason for choosing a phenomenalist basis of immediate experiences is epistemological: it rests on the "intention to have the constructional system reflect not only the logical-constructional order of the objects, but also their epistemic order."[23] Fidelity to the epistemological order, in turn, means accuracy with respect to the order of recognition of entities. That one entity is epistemically primary with respect to a second means that the second can be recognized by recognizing the first.[24] There can be little doubt, therefore, that Carnap thought of the order of epistemic justification as flowing from immediately recognizable subjective experiences to the intersubjective propositions of science. Only in this way could a structuralist redescription of scientific propositions plausibly illuminate the actual justificatory basis of those propositions in subjective experience. Even more significantly in the context of Carnap's goals, only in this way could the possibility of objective knowledge itself be explained within the same framework.

II

With its linguistic focus on the inexpressibility of subjective content and its assumption of the possibility of an epistemologically illuminating formalization of scientific concepts, Carnap's structuralism set up the conditions under which the protocol sentence debate would be argued. But the structuralist conception of knowledge already had a long history when Carnap made it the setting of the *Aufbau*'s project in 1928. Carnap himself drew the idea of structuralism from Poincare, Russell, and Schlick;[25] of these, the most significant antecedent for the subsequent development of the protocol sentence debate is Schlick's structuralist model of knowledge, developed in the *General Theory of Knowledge* of 1918. Aiming to produce an epistemological account of the process of cognition and the possibility of scientific objectivity, Schlick here takes as his central problem the bridging of the gap between intuitive experience and conceptual knowledge. Whereas intuitive images and perceptions are fleeting, particular, and, above all, vague, conceptual knowledge can be permanent, universal, and precise.[26] If science can indeed make use of absolutely precise concepts, their definition cannot ultimately rest on any particular intuitions but must be specified in some other way. Schlick found the answer to the problem in the procedure of *implicit definition*, originally discovered by Hilbert in his influential axiomatization of geometry.[27] Rather than defining the

basic terms of geometry (such as "point," "line," and "plane") by reference to actual examples of drawn figures, Hilbert's system begins with
a set of axioms asserting various relations to hold among the bearers
of these basic terms. The basic terms are implicitly defined simply as
the *bearers* of all the relations asserted by the axioms. The resulting
system yields all the theorems of geometry by structural means alone,
without ever having to refer to an actual figure or perception. Similarly, Schlick thought, the total system of scientific concepts can be
implicitly defined in terms of the laws governing their objects. In actual practice, the meanings of basic terms may initially be established
ostensively or by reference to experience. But as the set of scientific
propositions is elaborated, it becomes possible to replace all of these
definitions by a single conceptual system that implicitly defines all scientific concepts relationally, with no essential reference to experience;
and it is this system that allows for the possibility of predicting future
events.[28]

By exploiting the method of implicit definition, Schlick proposes
to explain the connection between intuition and conceptual knowledge while preserving an extreme nominalism with respect to concepts
themselves. For Schlick, concepts are nothing more than symbols or
signs capable of performing certain functions owing to the conventional stipulation of the rules governing their use.[29] Because conceptual knowledge itself ultimately amounts simply to the recognition of
objects or states of affairs, clarity sufficient for the purposes of science
is attained as soon as the implicitly defined network of concepts can
uniquely designate each possible individual state of affairs. This establishes the possibility of an exact conceptual system of science that
responds to empirical data. But the relationship between intuition and
concept can still seem strained, at best, as Schlick himself admits:

> It is therefore all the more important that in implicit definition we have found
> an instrument that enables us to determine concepts completely and thus to
> attain strict precision in thinking. To achieve this end, however, we have had to
> effect a radical separation between concept and intuition, thought and reality.
> While we do relate the two spheres to one another, they seem not to be joined
> together at all. The bridges between them are down.[30]

Tying the fate of knowledge to the possibility of successfully designating
states of affairs with conceptual names, Schlick must admit that there

is, strictly speaking, no such thing as intuitive *knowledge* or knowledge by acquaintance.[31] All knowledge – all recognition of present states of affairs – does bear some relation to experience, but no experience alone is sufficient for knowledge.

Schlick's subsequent writings leading up to the protocol sentence debate further specify the relationship between experience and meaning with a more sophisticated and linguistically influenced development of the *Allgemeine Erkenntnislehre* picture. Having become convinced by Carnap himself that the content of immediate experience must be not only insufficient for conceptual knowledge but also actually incommunicable, Schlick now conceived of the difference between experience and knowledge in terms of a generalized content/form distinction that set the structure of language (on the side of form) off against the empirical content in virtue of which an empirical proposition could be understood. According to the 1932 essay "Form and Content," a scientific proposition has meaning in virtue of its ability to designate the place of its object in a system of relations.[32] For example, a specific color can be designated by reference to its position in the spectrum. In the context of a language with definite grammatical rules, a proposition about that color indicates it by *showing* its logical or relational form.[33] Thus knowledge of the relational form of a state of affairs, in the context of a language capable of showing relational form through its conventional rules of use, is sufficient for intersubjective designation and objectivity; even a blind man could understand the truth of propositions about the color green by knowing its relational place in the color spectrum.[34] But beyond communicable, public form, there is incommunicable, private content – in this case, the "ineffable quality of greenness." To understand the meaning of a proposition is to provide private content for communicable form, to "fill in" the structure of the proposition with material provided by the sense organs.[35] A difference in the content available to two persons, however, poses no threat to the possibility of communication. One and the same structure will simply be filled in differently in each case. In fact, owing to the fundamental incommunicability of content, there is actually no sense in speaking of sameness or difference of content intersubjectively at all.[36]

Even more importantly for the protocol sentence debate, Schlick's construal of content as radically private and incommunicable means that an elucidatory explanation of a proposition can only replace one *structure* with another:

> We can ask for a meaning only as long as we have not understood a statement. And as long as we have not understood a sentence it is actually nothing but a series of words; it would be misleading to call it a proposition at all. A series of words (or other signs) should be regarded as a proposition only when it is understood, when its meaning is comprehended.... Now there is not the slightest mystery about the process by which a sentence is given meaning or turned into a proposition: it consists in defining the use of the symbols which occur in the sentence. And this is always done by indicating the exact circumstances in which the words, according to the rules of the particular language, should be used. These rules must be taught by actually applying them in definite situations, that is to say, the circumstances to which they fit must actually be *shown*. It is of course possible to give a verbal description of any situation, but it is impossible to understand the description unless some kind of connection between the words and the rest of the world has been established beforehand. And this can be done only by certain acts, as for instance gestures, by which our words and expressions are correlated to certain experiences.[37]

The purely formal rules that define an actual language, Schlick now thought, could not float completely free of any connection to experience; to understand the meaning of a sentence is to understand the rules governing *which* states of affairs it expresses. But because of the incommunicability of content, the experiential states of affairs themselves cannot be described, but only *shown* by means of ostensive acts. The specification of the meaning of a sentence does not, therefore, consist in the public display of some state of affairs. All that can be given publicly is propositions, and in order to be comprehended these must be accompanied by certain private experiences.

III

By early 1931, discussion in the Vienna Circle's weekly meetings had turned to the topic of the nature of protocol sentences, the sentences recording or describing an investigator's actual observations. The immediate impetus for the debate was the challenge posed by the sociologist Otto Neurath to Schlick's and Carnap's implication that protocols must be drawn from a phenomenalist language essentially linked to private experience. In accordance with the semantic view that he would call *physicalism*, Neurath argued that protocol sentences, like all other meaningful sentences, are corrigible and must be part of a public, intersubjective language from the beginning. For Neurath, the unity of science demanded universality of language as well, and only a physicalist language could succeed in putting *all* propositions into an intersubjectively comparable form with no dependence on individually variable private experience. Already in 1928, Neurath had praised the structuralism of Carnap's *Aufbau* for its elimination of epistemological dependence on the individual content of private experience:

Carnap undertakes to characterize sense impressions on the basis of certain structures, structures in which 'red', 'hard', 'loud' ... do *not* appear, but only facts which can be captured by mathematical-logical means – *and that suffices!* Carnap consciously turns away from taking empathy in any form, or personal attitudes, as his starting point. He only knows that kind of insight which can be grasped by every human being! Order is the most common, the most universal [property] which we experience in things.[38]

With Neurath's repudiation of "empathy" and "personal attitudes" went his physicalist view of language. Language, for Neurath, is always itself a phenomenon of the physical world. And because spoken sounds and written marks are themselves physical, there is no need for a transcendental or metalinguistic account of the meaningfulness of a proposition.[39] It was just such an account that he saw as presupposed by Schlick's reliance on "content." And even though Carnap's picture did not go as far as Schlick's in making the understanding of structural propositions dependent on a private act of "filling in" subjective content, Neurath already considered even Carnap's reliance on a separate stratum of language capable of describing experience untenable.

Most importantly for the protocol sentence debate itself, though, Neurath's physicalist view of language was also generated by a conception of meaning drawing on Carnap's and Schlick's structuralism:

Unified science expresses everything in the unified language that is common to the blind and the sighted, the deaf and those who hear, it is "intersensual" and "intersubjective." It connects the statements of a man talking to himself today with his statements of yesterday; the statements he makes with his ears closed, with those he makes with his ears open. In language nothing but order is essential, and that is already represented by a sequence of signs of Morse code. "Intersubjective" and "intersensual" language in general depends on order ("next to," "between," etc.), that is, on what can be expressed by sign sequences in logic and mathematics. All predictions are formulated in this language.[40]

With this, Neurath shows his commitment to the underlying structuralist theory of meaning, according to which the exhibition of structure clarifies the meaning of a proposition, as well as to the more specialized connections between structure and expressibility and between expressibility and objectivity. However, Neurath's understanding of the reasons for these commitments was from the start somewhat different from Carnap's and Schlick's. For Neurath's argument for a physicalist language for unified science depends both on his antimetaphysical insistence on the essentially physical character of spoken or written signs and on the further claim that whatever intersubjectivity language achieves is ultimately dependent on the physical and relational properties of these signs alone. It is only in virtue of these physical and relational properties, Neurath argued, that a sentence has the meaning that it does. Ultimately, semantics depends on syntactic properties expressible in terms of the physical shape of written signs or the acoustic shape of spoken signs and their combination into sequences. And because purely formal or syntactic public properties of physical signs suffice to determine the meaning of any proposition, no reference to subjective or first-personal items is ever needed, even in the case of protocol sentences.[41]

Despite sharing a structuralist motivation, therefore, Neurath's picture of meaning, with its emphasis on the essentially public character of meaning determination, diverges from Schlick's requirement of private acts of "filling in" for the understanding of a proposition. Both the determination of a sentence's meaning and its verification, Neurath thought, could mean only the comparison of that sentence with other sentences; no "comparison" to the extralinguistic facts and no private act of meaning bestowal was necessary or even possible. Neurath's first exchanges with Schlick over protocol sentences focused on this point, with Neurath insisting on the impossibility of any "confrontation" between language and experience whatsoever.[42] Soon Neurath would back up his general claim of the impossibility of comparison to the given with specific arguments against the possibility that a protocol language could describe essentially private objects or events. The ascertainment of any state of affairs relevant to the verification of scientific propositions, Neurath argued, traces ultimately to physical changes in the sensory system of the verifier.[43] The utterance of a proposition asserting that an event occurs at a certain time, for instance, depends on the observer's access to an intersubjectively observable clock. Even a sentence apparently referring only to the observer's perception – a sentence, for instance, predicting the appearance of a red spot together with a blue spot in the visual field – can ultimately be referred to facts about the central nervous system of the observer.[44]

Both sides of the subsequent exchange between Neurath and Schlick, representing the extreme positions of the debate proper, often have the appearance more of attacking an ill-understood straw man from widely divergent positions than of seriously investigating an issue of common concern. Schlick's first official treatment of protocols – the *Erkenntnis* article "On the Foundation of Knowledge," written in 1934 – reaffirms what may seem to be a foundationalist model of empirical knowledge, emphasizing the need for a secure and unshakeable foundation of absolute certainty for epistemological theory. Important to this defense is Schlick's criticism of what he took to be Neurath's "coherence theory" of truth. Coherence in the sense of noncontradiction among a set of beliefs cannot be sufficient for truth, Schlick argues, except in the case of tautologies. For empirical or material propositions, truth generally demands the additional constraint that they not contradict a special and nonarbitrary set of propositions, those deriving immediately from experience.[45] Agreement with *these* propositions, Schlick says, deserves the name of "agreement with reality," and it is to these propositions that all empirical certainty must be traced.[46] Still, Schlick admits that a protocol sentence asserting the observation of a particular state of affairs by a particular observer cannot be considered certain. Such a sentence may have been produced by the observer in error, or as the result of a hallucination.[47] It follows that, as Neurath maintained, protocol sentences themselves have no special status of unrevisability; they are public, intersubjective sentences of science like any other. But unrevisability and incorrigibility *does* characterize another set of statements concerning what is immediately perceived. These Schlick calls "observation statements" or "affirmations":

> In this way the actual procedure of science is described schematically. It is evident what role is played in it by the statements concerning what is "immediately perceived." They are not identical with those written down or memorized, with what can correctly be called "protocol statements," but they are the occasions of their formation. . . . What I call an observation statement cannot be identical with a genuine protocol statement, if only because in a certain sense it cannot be written down at all. . . . [48]

Since the actual writing down or speaking of a sentence always allows some possibility of uncertainty as to whether it has been written correctly, the absolutely certain basis of empirical knowledge must be traced to observation statements that are strictly inexpressible.

As commentators have noted, the inexpressibility of Schlick's "affirmations" poses problems for their foundational status. How, after all, are propositions that cannot be written or spoken supposed to serve as the certain inferential basis for anything? But Schlick intended the "affirmations" to serve as the certain basis of science only in the special sense that they provided for the *verification* of empirical propositions. Schlick had the idea that, rather than requiring the inferential derivation of scientific hypotheses from propositions about experience or the given, one could ensure sufficient contact with reality simply by maintaining the requirement that hypotheses, once stated, actually be tested by experience and observation. The outcome of the act of verification ultimately depends on the result given by experience on the occasion of a particular observational test; and only in this case is it necessary to resort to an "affirmation."[49] For this reason, neither the actual nor the idealized order of empirical cognition requires that affirmations come *before* the formulation of hypotheses. All that is required is that they allow for experience to pass judgment, in particular instances, on the truth of particular empirical propositions, once these propositions have been formulated. Moreover, the alleged certainty of affirmations does not trace, on Schlick's theory, to the Cartesian assumption of the incorrigibility of immediate experience, but rather to considerations about the source of their *meaning*. As the expression of a concrete act of verification, each affirmation, Schlick argues, will contain an irreducibly *demonstrative* element capturing the direction of attention on the observed circumstance. For instance, an affirmation might have the form "Here two black points coincide" or "Here now pain"; in each case, an ineliminable demonstrative element captures the dependence of the affirmation on reference to a currently experienced state of affairs. Because the meaning of such a demonstrative element is dependent, in each case, on the presence of the actual state of affairs indicated, the conditions for the truth of an affirmation are not distinct from the conditions under which it has meaning at all. Like tautologies, affirmations can be misunderstood, but they cannot be false if correctly understood.[50] It was thus the essentially demonstrative feature of affirmations that, Schlick thought, accounted for their incorrigibility. In this way, the essential tie of affirmations to a basis in actual experience could be preserved formally without endangering their connection to other empirical propositions.

In his 1934 response to Schlick's article, Neurath emphasized again the corrigibility and revisability of protocol sentences.[51] Neurath's own theory, elaborated two years earlier, called for protocol sentences to be public, physicalistic statements embedding other statements to be taken as records of the subject's experience, themselves couched as descriptions of physical events. For instance, Neurath gives as a typical protocol sentence the following: "Charles' protocol at 9:14: 'Charles' formulation at 9:13 was: "there was a table in the room at 9:12:59."' "[52] The three-level form of the protocol sentence is meant to allow for the possibility of error, both in the immediate experience itself (as in the case of hallucination) and in the recording of the proposition based on it.[53] The resulting proposition, though necessarily embedding other propositions, can be understood in physicalist terms; never refers to private experience; and bears straightforward inferential relations to other propositions of public, intersubjective science.

In the article, Neurath reacted especially sharply to Schlick's description of affirmations as unstateable, demanding a behavioristic description of the act of verification. Without such a description, Neurath averred, Schlick's claims for affirmations themselves remained unverifiable and metaphysical. But because affirmations were by hypothesis unstateable, no behavioristic description of them could be given.[54] Similarly, Neurath resisted for behaviorist reasons Schlick's claim for the certainty of affirmations: because any description of a particular set of sentences as certain depends ultimately on the behavioristic criteria of widespread acceptance and reluctance to abandon the sentences in question, Schlick could claim certainty only if he could manifest a set of sentences that are in fact never altered or abandoned. But even a priori and analytic statements, Neurath argued, are sometimes abandoned, for instance when they are found to have been misunderstood. Because Schlick could not point to any actual set of sentences, relevant to the practice of language, that are never revised, he could not make good on his promise to build an unshakable foundation of knowledge from the protocol sentences.

Given Neurath's steadfast maintenance of a behaviorist picture of meaning, Schlick's affirmations doubtless appeared not only irrelevant to the practice of science but also meaningless. Essentially private or subjective items need never appear, Neurath reasoned, in the unified intersubjective language of science, and the admitted inexpressibility of affirmations simply proved the point of their uselessness for epistemology. Such contact with experience as was necessary for the purposes of scientific or epistemological practice could be assured, in any case, by Neurath's version of protocols, carefully formulated to allow for the possible inaccuracy of an individual's perception.

It is instructive to note, however, that behind this disagreement on the need for a connection to private, subjective experience in science lay a somewhat more subtle disagreement about the source of a proposition's meaning, one ultimately tracing to Neurath and Schlick's slightly different inflections of the structuralist model that they had shared. One of Schlick's reasons for declaring the affirmations unstateable in the first place was the Neurathian observation that an actually written (or, presumably, spoken) sentence could always be in error. Any actually written sentence, after all, might have been produced by a slip of the pen or an error in transcription rather than as an accurate report of primitive experience. The only way to ensure the accuracy of the primary sentences was to make them epistemically prior to the written reports of them, as Schlick did with the theory of affirmations. For Neurath, by contrast, the standing possibility of error in the actually written primary sentences simply meant that all such sentences must be revisable and that science could in fact do no better. As a consequence of this claim of revisability, Neurath misunderstood Schlick's claim for the self-validation of affirmations. Rather than taking the point that certain propositions, because of either their

analyticity or their essentially demonstrative character, must be seen to
be true as soon as they are understood, Neurath maintained that even
analytic sentences might be revised under the right sort of conditions.

Correspondending to this disagreement about revisability was a subtle but significant difference between the two philosophers with respect to their conceptions of the identity of propositions. For Neurath,
a proposition was simply a physical sequence of written or spoken signs.
No such sequence could be held immune to revision, since any such
sequence might turn out to have been misunderstood. For Schlick, on
the other hand, a proposition was a physical sequence of signs *together
with the rules of its use*, including such rules as define the conditions under which it can be verified. Even affirmations, then, could be treated
as dependent for their meaning on concrete rules of use; the only difference between the rules of use for affirmations and those for other
propositions was that, in the case of affirmations, these rules of use
comprise rules demanding the immediate display of a private, ineffable content.[55] Given the satisfaction of these rules by the display of
a private content, the affirmation calling for this content is *automatically* true. There could be ambiguity, correspondending to confusion
about rules of use, about *which* proposition a physical sign sequence
stood for; but given consistent rules, the misunderstanding of a physical sign sequence would never require the *abandonment* or *revision* of
any proposition.

It is true that Schlick's picture, even so characterized, must make
affirmations unstateable if they are to remain certain. But the characterization of affirmations in terms of rules of use calling for the display
of a private contents gave Schlick considerable resources for defending his conception.[56] Most importantly, it gave Schlick the ability to
characterize subjective contents as the *occasion* for the formation of
protocol sentences rather than, or in addition to, characterizing them
as the *subject matter* of protocol sentences. If affirmations essentially
involve demonstratives, then the rules of use defining their meaning
include rules dictating the performance of essentially ostensive acts of
demonstration. Schlick doubtless considered the connection of these
acts to knowledge to be the point of affirmations, since he thought
that all verification occurred through such subjective acts. It remains
true that the description of such an act cannot be given in generally
applicable intersubjective terms – in other words, the affirmations are

essentially private and inexpressible – but given its essentially demonstrative character, it does not seem obvious that there is any reason it should be.[57] In "Form and Content," Schlick had understood the subjective "filling in" of content as the nexus of the contact between experience and meaning. Now he thought that such contact between knowledge and experience as occurs in the course of verification must also depend on essentially subjective acts.[58] In this way, Schlick developed a picture of verification that ties the meaning of protocols to essentially subjective conditions, without denying the Neurathian moral that protocols are revisable and that they must yield inferences to intersubjective states of affairs.[59]

The positions of Schlick and Neurath can therefore be traced to minor inflectional differences between two conceptions of the same picture of meaning. But these relatively minor differences did make a substantial difference for the possibilities of reconstructive epistemology. For Schlick, verification always involved contact with experience. Only in this way could experience authorize an empirical proposition for use in the system of science. Neurath's physicalist protocols, by contrast, bore no particular relationship to experience or subjectivity; they could be used as justifications only in the same way, and subject to the same defeasibility, that any physicalist proposition could. This left room for a difference of *degree* in epistemological status between protocol sentences and theoretical propositions, but Neurath drew no fundamental distinction of *kind* between the two types of sentence. For this reason, no epistemological project connecting subjectivity to objectivity or offering a general explanation for the possibility of objectivity is even *conceivable* on Neurath's picture. The act of formulating a (physicalist) protocol sentence might still be thought to represent the forging of a kind of link between experience and knowledge, but there is now no reason to think of this act as epistemically special; it remains a physical event like any other. It follows that protocol sentences have no more claim to provide justification, or to solve philosophical problems, than any other empirical propositions do. The *Aufbau*'s plan for a reconstructive epistemology becomes unrealizable, because the problem that it set out to solve becomes unformulable.

Schlick's brief and final rejoinder, written in 1935, reveals the extent to which mutual understanding between the two philosophers had by this time broken down. Responding directly not to Neurath but to Hempel, who had put Neurath's objections into a form more acceptable to Schlick in his article "On the Logical Positivists' Theory of Truth,"[60] Schlick reaffirms his belief in the possibility of comparing linguistic propositions to empirical states of affairs and repeats his objections to a coherence theory of truth, chiefly that the coherence theory makes the truth of propositions depend on the judgment of "the scientists of the culture circle" rather than on experience and observation.[61] For Schlick, a proposition remains a physical sign sequence together with the rules of its use, including such rules as define the conditions under which it can be verified.[62] Within the context of the theory of affirmations, these rules pose no special problem and indeed provide for the only possibility of maintaining empiricism by accounting for the relation of scientific propositions to experience.

IV

By the time of Schlick's final rejoinder to Neurath in 1935, the Circle was in disarray. The protocol sentence debate had ended inconclusively, with neither Neurath nor Schlick convincing the other to depart from his basic position. It would be years yet before Neurath's naturalism, updated and transmitted by Quine, would begin to convince the philosophical community at large of the possibility of replacing phenomenalist justifications with physicalist ones in epistemology generally. But it is doubtful whether the debate between the extreme positions of Schlick and Neurath could have been undertaken and sustained at all without the constant mediating influence of Carnap, who consistently sought to accommodate the apparently conflicting intuitions driving Neurath and Schlick apart within a common theoretical and programmatic framework deriving from his turn to syntax of 1931.

Inspired by Wittgenstein, Tarski, and Gödel's method of arithmetizing logic, Carnap in 1931 conceived of a new program for metalogic based on the possibility of representing the logical structure of a language in that language itself. Carnap's idea of logical syntax would not be fully developed until 1934, but he already envisioned far-ranging philosophical implications. Given the claim of the complete representability of the logical structure in virtue of which a language is capable of expressing meaning, Carnap no longer sought to describe the structure of the *one* language of science. Instead, he allowed a multiplicity of possible languages, subject only to the constraint that the logical form of each be syntactically specifiable. The choice of a language could then be conventional, based only on the free stipulation of particular syntactic rules. Carnap also saw in his syntactic conception of language a new tool for the elimination of metaphysics and a new purpose for philosophical explanation. The only way for philosophy to speak unmetaphysically, Carnap thought, was for it to speak of nothing more than the syntactic form of various possible languages. This way of speaking Carnap called the "formal mode" of speech, contrasting it with the "material mode" in which objects and states of affairs are themselves described. Only strict adherence to the formal mode, Carnap reasoned, could prevent the arising of metaphysical psuedoproblems about the nature of the objects spoken of in a particular language.

Carnap's 1932 article "The Physicalist Language as the Universal Language of Science" turned to the syntactic conception and the formal/material distinction in order to solve the problem of the semantic form of protocol sentences. Ostensibly devoted to confirming Neurath's claim that a physicalist language could serve as the universal language for the description of all states of affairs (formally speaking, the equivalent claim is that every meaningful sentence can be translated into the physicalist language), the extended essay treated the language of protocols, used for recording direct experience, as a sublanguage of the unified physicalist language.[63] Like Schlick, Carnap thought that the verification of a scientific claim consisted in the derivation from it of one or more protocol sentences, which were then compared to the scientist's actual protocol (his set of protocol sentences) in order to check their accuracy.[64] This necessitated that transformation rules of the physicalist language permit the deduction of protocol sentences from physicalist sentences.[65] Accordingly, Carnap devoted the rest of the essay to explaining the possibility of translating the protocols of a specific investigator into the intersubjective language of physics. As in the *Aufbau*, such translations are in general possible owing to the contingent existence of certain structural ordinal properties of the contents of experience (formally: of the protocol sentences themselves). The translation rules correlate quantitative physical states with sets of protocol sentences by means of these regularities. In general, the physicalist translation of a protocol sentence specifies the physical conditions under which the quality named by the protocol sentence is experienced.[66] This allows an individual to connect his protocols to intermodal and quantitative propositions usable in the language of science, but the true intersubjectivity of the physicalist language depends on the additional possibility that one investigator can determine the physical conditions corresponding to a particular qualitative determination in *another* investigator's protocol language. In this way, physical determinations gain intersubjective validity from the existence of structural correlations among the protocols of various investigators.[67]

By translating protocol sentences into the language of physics, Carnap thought it possible to maintain simultaneously the distinctness of the protocol languages of various observers, the foundation of all scientific knowledge in the immediate experience of individuals, and the intersubjectivity and universality of the physical language. He could do this, he thought, by treating the individual protocol languages as disjoint sublanguages of the universal physicalist language, each one describing the condition of an individual's body.[68] As long as strict adherence to the formal mode was preserved, Carnap thought, the familiar objection that such descriptions of bodily states do not genuinely describe experience could not be maintained:

Let us assume that S_2 makes a report, based on physical observations, of the events in S_1's body yesterday. Then (in the material mode), S_1 will not accept this report as a complete account of yesterday's section of his life. . . . Now, we will assume that S_2 introduces by definitions, terms such as 'seeing red' . . . into the physical language. He can then formulate a part of his report with the help of such expressions in such a way that it runs identically with S_1's protocol. In spite of this S_1 will not accept this new report. He will object that although it is true that S_2 now uses expressions such as 'joy', 'red', 'memory', etc. he means something else than S_1 does by the same words in his protocol; the referends of the expressions are different. For S_2, he says, they denote physical properties of a human body, for himself, personal experiences. . . .

S_1 connects different associations with the statements P and p respectively for, on account of their linguistic formulation, P is thought of in connection with physical statements whereas p is associated with the protocol. The difference in associations is however no argument against the thesis that the two propositions have the same content (i.e. express the same), for the content of a proposition is constituted by the possibility of inferring other propositions from it. If the same statements can be inferred from two given statements they must both have the same content, independently of the images and conceptions that we are accustomed to associate with them.[69]

Formally speaking, identity of meaning amounts to identity of inferential consequences, so a protocol sentence will have the same content as a physicalist one if the same statements can be inferred from it. That this identity of content is possible is, in turn, established by the consideration that the condition described by each protocol sentence occurs just when certain physicalistically describable states of affairs obtain. The possibility of hallucinations and perceptual error blocks, it is true, the immediate derivation of an external state of affairs from a protocol sentence so conceived. For this reason, Carnap thought, each protocol sentence must be translated into a physicalist sentence concerning the state of a particular observer's body and nervous system.[70] Only by means of further assumptions concerning causality could the inference to a reported state of affairs in the external world be made.[71] Nevertheless, knowledge of the content of the protocol adequate for use in scientific description did not depend on detailed knowledge of brain physiology. Pending such knowledge, the physical internal state of the observer identified with the protocol sentence could simply be treated as a complex dispositional state characterized by the observer's responses to various stimuli and questions (e.g., "Do you see red now?")[72]

With the formal-level identification of protocols with physicalist descriptions of bodily states, Carnap believed he had done justice to Neurath's claim for the universality of physicalist language while preserving the epistemological basis of science in immediate experience by redescribing, rather than eliminating, the role of phenomenalist protocol sentences. As in the *Aufbau*, both the physicalist and the phenomenalist language have their place in scientific practice; but it is instructive to note just how different a picture is suggested by "Physical Language" with respect to the possibility and aims of reconstructive epistemology. In the *Aufbau*, the derivability of intermodal and then intersubjective propositions from structural propositions describing only the similarity relationships among elementary experiences matched, at least in an idealized way, the order of epistemic justification. In the "Physical Language" picture, by contrast, the epistemological use of a protocol sentence in actual science is from the start tied to the possibility of its being reconstructed as a physicalist sentence. The definitional rules leading from a particular protocol sentence to its physicalist reconstruction *could*, it is true, follow the complex definitional route of the *Aufbau*'s epistemologically accurate constructions. But given the possibility of simply redefining a protocol sentence in terms of the physical states of affairs that elicit its affirmation, "Physical Language" suggests no reason that they should.

In this way, Carnap's picture of protocols in "Physical Language" suggests the abandonment of the *Aufbau*'s assumption of the epistemic priority of experience. Later in 1932, Carnap took this abandonment further in the article "Protocol Sentences." Carnap wrote the article as a response to Neurath's refusal to accept the idea that he had done justice to the physicalist position. Neurath had opposed Carnap's claim of the incorrigibility and unalterability of even physically reconstructed protocol sentences. Now Carnap thought that the difference between his proposal and Neurath's was simply the difference between two possible forms of language that one could use for science. In the first language form, corresponding to Carnap's own proposal, the protocol sentences in virtue of which the system of science is justified stand outside the system language itself, and so are not revisable in that language. In the second, corresponding to Neurath's proposal, the protocol sentences are already within the system language. Carnap thought that both language forms were possible; they had differing advantages, and either might be used, depending on one's specific investigative purposes. In order to establish the possibility of the first language form, Carnap considers that a protocol sentence is nothing more than an observable process (a set of spoken or written symbols) for which a translation rule to the system language has been constructed.[73] In constructing such rules, we attempt to maintain the accuracy of as many protocol sentences as possible. We may translate them into statements concerning external states of affairs or – more reliably – into statements concerning the behavioral dispositions of the speaker.[74] Finally, as in "Physical Language," we can take as protocols our own reports of experience, translating them into the system language by determining the physical conditions under which they are elicited. In general, Carnap suggests, our freedom in determining translational rules for the protocols means that we can, if we wish, make all of our protocols come out true under translation. In case of inconsistencies, we simply alter the translational rules to make all of the translations mutually consistent. In no case are we constrained to assume the falsity of any of the protocol sentences themselves in the uninterpreted protocol language.

In practical terms, then, the incorrigibility and unrevisability of protocol sentences, on Carnap's proposal, is established by the conventionality of the translational rules linking them to physicalist sentences. Carnap now drops the requirement, however, of any special connection of the protocol sentences to experience itself. The translation of an individual's protocol sentences into the physical language does not depend on the protocol sentences' having any specific content at all. All that is required is that they be translatable, in virtue of *some* rules, to propositions describing the states of affairs eliciting them. Nor does it matter whether the protocol languages are private or intersubjective. Even a protocol language spoken by only a single subject can be translated into the physicalist language in virtue of Carnap's proposal.

By refusing to describe the content of protocol sentences, Carnap just leaves room for the possibility that they still do describe experience after all; but he leaves himself no possibility of describing *how* they do so. Given the "Protocol Sentences" picture of the meaning of protocols, any direct description of the bearing of experience on their formation is illicit, and any idiosyncratic contribution of experience to their meaning is incomprehensible unless already expressible in physicalist terms. In the second part of the essay, Carnap discusses Neurath's proposal for using system-language sentences of a certain form as protocols, and endorses a modification of that proposal suggested by Popper.[75] In Popper's proposal, protocols are relativized to specific explanatory purposes. Any system-language sentence whatsoever may be taken as a protocol in the context of the arising of a specific explanatory question. Even an observation sentence may in a particular case not serve as a protocol sentence, if there is some doubt, for instance, as to the reliability of the observer uttering it; in this case, additional protocols attesting to reliability will be needed.[76] In this way, the choice of protocols is completely relativized to the explanatory purpose at hand, and Carnap characterizes this choice as a free decision. The supposed epistemological primacy of individual experience remains only in the form of physicalistic facts about the possibilities of testing:

> If S_1 (speaking, writing, or thinking) advances and tests a specific sentence, then that happens immediately only on the basis of his own experience. Even if S_1 evaluates statements of S_2 this always happens through the mediation of S_1's own perceptions, perhaps his hearing of S_2's statements. (By the expressions 'thoughts', 'perceptions', 'hearing' obviously the physical processes in the nervous system of S_1 are meant.) More precisely: the causal chain from the perception of S_2 to the testing thought or discourse of S_1 occurs by way of the speech act of S_2, the process on the sense organs of S_1, and the perception process on the brain of S_1. This fact, that testing rests on the perceptions of the tester, forms the legitimate kernel of truth in "methodological solipsism." . . . [77]

To the obvious objection that, however one tests an empirical proposition, one does not do so by discovering the character of one's own brain processes, Carnap would by now have had little to say. Formally, that the process of testing occurs by means of certain physical and brain processes is enough – for the purposes of the kind of epistemology that Carnap now contemplated – to ensure the possibility of retracing the actual epistemic order, including such doubts as one might have about the accuracy of a perception.

V

The question of protocol sentences generated the debate that drove the Vienna Circle apart. But historical reflection shows that the tensions that led to it in fact originated with the structuralist model of language that the philosophers of the Circle shared. In identifying meaning with publicly communicable meaning, the structuralist model from the beginning set the language of science off against something else to be eliminated from scientific description, something variously conceived of as private, subjective, ineffable, and indescribable. It was the hope of Schlick and the early Carnap that the identification of this "something else" with subjective experience could make good on the promise of empiricism to fund the synthetic propositions of science with the validity of experiential content. In this way, structuralism became both a theory of meaning and a theory of verification. Experience provided both the subjective verification of structural propositions and the content whose intersubjectively invariant relational structures they represented. But trouble arose for the compatibility of these two sides of the structuralist picture as soon as the question of protocols put pressure on it. For whereas the structuralist theory of *meaning* required experiential content to be private, subjective, and ineffable, the structuralist account of *verification* required a description of the contact between this experiential content and actual propositions.[78] For the purposes of epistemology, experiential content had to be sufficiently close to propositions to be capable of actually verifying or refuting them. In some way, then, the subjective content of experience had to be described after all, if only to clarify how it is that experience verifies anything.

The historical outcome of the protocol sentence debate, then, left the structuralist theorist of meaning with two options, neither of which was completely satisfactory from the perspective of the original epistemological project with which Carnap and Schlick had begun. The first was to uphold, with Neurath and the late Carnap, a generalized physicalism that accords immediate experience no special role among the objects or contents of structuralized, objectively meaningful sentences. This amounts to denying the incommunicability-of-content doctrine that organized the structuralist model in its original forms. Because protocol sentences and other propositions describing or reporting immediate experience now have no special role, either semantically or logically, the claim that they are authorized or verified by contents that are themselves extralinguistic or inexpressible drops out of the picture. The approach of a generalized semantic physicalism, as we have seen, had the advantage of allowing a unified and coherent account of verification, but taking it meant abandoning all hope of a reconstructive epistemology that begins with experience as the ultimate empirical basis for objectively meaningful claims. Within the purview of physicalism, the language of experience, including the protocol sentences that might naturally be taken to express direct reports of experience, has no special role, logically or semantically. It follows that there is no hope, once such a position has been adopted, of clarifying the objective status of scientific propositions by referring to their relation to subjective experience.

The second theoretical alternative consistent with the underlying structuralist model is to maintain the incommunicability-of-content doctrine, holding in one way or another that the content of experience, though incommunicable, provides a semantic basis for meaningful and communicable public claims. This second alternative, as we have seen, receives its original inspiration from considerations about the way in which the logical analysis of an empirically meaningful sentence might reasonably clarify not only its meaning but also its epistemological form. Standardly, the logical analysis of an ordinary proposition reduces it to another proposition, perhaps a longer one, that shows more clearly the conditions under which the original proposition has meaning. The new sentence may clarify the definition of a vague term, show more clearly how the original sentence achieved reference to its object, or reveal more clearly the significant content of the original sentence, freeing it from linguistic ambiguities. Given a basically empiricist outlook, it was natural, therefore, to imagine that the tools of logical analysis could produce from an empirical proposition a clear description of its empirical content, leaving conventional, definitional, and conceptual features of language, as far as possible, to one side. Still, in order to be linguistic at all, the outcome of such a reduction had to have *some* conceptual and definitional structure. For the early Schlick and the *Aufbau* Carnap, the maximal closeness of such bottom-level propositions to empirical content could be assured by reducing their conceptual structure to a purely relational structure of experiences, and by making the definitions of their terms definitions of the simplest possible sort – namely, acts of ostension or simple recognition.

But as we have already seen in the historical dynamics of the protocol sentence debate itself, the appeal to simple ostension proved incapable of providing the basis in experience that the Vienna Circle philosophers had sought. Maintaining the incommunicability-of-content doctrine consistently left the philosophers who held it without any account of how the content of experience could in fact contribute to the verification of propositions. This theoretical cost might legitimately be borne, were it required by the nature of objective meaning itself or demanded by the character of our insight into conscious experience. And the incommunicability-of-content doctrine did provide, as we have seen, substantial support for the original formulation of the structuralist theory of meaning by defining the incommunicable elements against which structural objectivity was to be set off. Nevertheless, historical reflection on the structuralist model itself demands that we consider what sort of basis there might be, in the nature of meaning or the phenomenology of experience, for concluding that the subjective elements of experience are incommunicable in themselves.

One possible answer cites ineliminable differences between the experiences of distinct individuals. Carnap, remember, made this the basis of the only argument he gives for the incommunicability of the subjective, holding that "the series of experiences is different for each subject" and that these differences make for "completely divergent content" in the experiences of individuals. Because of the ineliminable difference between individual streams of experience, Carnap appears to have thought, immediate, ostensively defined names for the elements of individual experience would never converge enough to support agreement on the names of objective entities, even if these entities must ultimately be derived from subjective ones. Objectivity required a basis in what was *invariant* between individual streams of experience – their relational structure rather than their qualitative content. In this way, the idiosyncratic divergences in individual streams of experience could be overcome without threatening the epistemic basing of objectivity on subjective experiences. The qualitative contents of individual experiences, while perhaps nameable, would remain inexpressible in the sense that, because of their divergence, no public agreement could be reached on their character or on the identity of objects constructed from them.[79]

Carnap's argument from the difference in subjective streams of experience to the incommunicability of content doubtless provided important motivation for his project, justifying its claim to establish an objective basis for scientific propositions that bracketed the differences between the limited epistemic perspectives of distinct observers.[80] But aside from its rhetorical suggestion of the eliminability of differences in perspective, the argument fails by undercutting its own premises. For as Schlick had already noted, the intersubjective *incommunicability* of content implies the *unintelligibility* of claims of intersubjective similarity or difference in content.[81] If Carnap had really established that private content cannot be described, what basis could there be for holding that content is "completely divergent" between individuals? Given the possibility of intersubjective communication about experiences, it would seem just as legitimate to conclude that the intrinsic character of two subjects' experiences must be, by and large, similar. More generally, though, if any description of two people's experiences as different or similar is itself a structural description, then there is no warrant for concluding, as Carnap does, that the indescribable *contents* that comprise the structure are in themselves similar or divergent from one subject to the next. Where description is impossible, neither sameness nor difference makes sense. Any intelligible difference between streams of experience that could serve as a basis for Carnap's argument, moreover, would by the lights of his own theory be a *structural* difference, fully describable in terms of relational structure, and not the kind of *intrinsic* difference that alone could show the general need for structuralization of claims about experience. Carnap's conclusion, therefore, seems to deprive him of the possibility of making sense of the premise he needs, that individual streams of experience differ in their qualitative content. Of course, there may be differences between the character of my experience, in a particular situation, and yours. But according to the structuralist model itself, these differences, where it makes sense to speak of them at all, are structural, and hence communicable. Any basis or ground we can meaningfully adduce or cite for holding that my experiences differ from another person's is, according to the structuralist model itself, a matter of structure rather than of content. We may, just barely, continue to speak of an essential difference that is ineliminable, indescribable, and incommunicable; but the structuralist model itself deprives us of any meaningful basis for doing so.

Alternatively, Carnap *might*, admittedly, have meant only that individuals differ in their epistemic perspectives and that objective science must abstract from this difference. But from this difference it would not at all follow that anything about experience is incommunicable. For differences in epistemic perspective trace to differences between individuals' locations in space and time or to contingent facts about their perceptual devices, not to the fundamental incapability of their experience to support intersubjectively agreeable propositions. (If you and I are standing in different places, or if I am color-blind, we may disagree about the facts. But in neither case does this tend to show that we cannot describe our different experiences or that these different experiences could not be the basis of eventual agreement on the facts, once we allow for the differences.) Even if individual differences of epistemic judgment may be in a sense insurmountable, because of their reliance on normative claims or their relativity to particular circumstances, still there is no evident reason why such differences should not be straightforwardly describable. Only if Carnap intends the difference between two individual streams of experience to be the insurmountable difference of incommunicable qualitative content does he establish his structuralist conclusion. But in so doing, he deprives himself of the ability to speak of a difference in content at all.

Carnap's appeal to the difference between two subjects' streams of experience formulates the only basis that he provides, independent of considerations following from the structuralist picture of meaning, for thinking that the content of experience must be incommunicable. The incommunicability-of-content doctrine itself provides, as we have seen, substantial support for his initial formulation of the structuralist picture and for the project of epistemological reconstruction that he undertakes in the *Aufbau*. Ironically, though, the argument from the difference between two subjects' streams of experience becomes unintelligible when submitted to the structuralist model it aims to support. For on the model, talk of a divergence between streams of experience is, where meaningful, *structural* talk, licensed by the comparison of different structures and incapable of establishing the general claim of intrinsic difference that Carnap relies upon. The failure of Carnap's argument in this respect is instructive, and bears historical consequences beyond Carnap's project itself. For as the subsequent history of the protocol sentence debate itself shows, the structuralist theory of meaning, conjoined with the incommunicability-of-content doctrine that originally provided substantial support for it, eventually undercuts itself by failing to provide any coherent positive account of experience. *Given* the incommunicability-of-content doctrine, it is true, this theoretical failure is not surprising to its adherents, and might even be considered a necessary cost of a comprehensive theory of meaning. But it threatens to leave the structuralist model without any external support, in considerations about the nature either of experience or of meaning, that is intelligible on its own terms. Faced with the consequences of the incommunicability-of-content doctrine, moreover, the structuralist theorist must admit that his theory fails (even if, according to the model itself, this failure is necessary) to provide what he had wanted: a coherent positive account of the relationship between experience and meaning.

Another possible reason for holding content to be incommunicable, suggested by both Carnap's and Schlick's versions of structuralism, can be found in the thought that the epistemic basis of scientific claims depends ultimately on acts of *ostension*. When Carnap develops the example of the structural description of a railway network, he allows that a subjective difference may remain in the position of two structurally indistinguishable positions, but holds that such a difference would be incommunicable because it could be expressed only in essentially indexical terms.[82] Both occupants of two structurally indistinguishable positions could designate their position as "here," but neither could express the difference between the two positions in nonindexical terms. This situation, Carnap suggests, mirrors the situation of subjectivity in science: the first designation of a particular state of affairs depends on its concrete ostension, and hence on the irreducibly demonstrative act of ostensive indication. The job of construction theory is then to generate structuralized propositions suitable for intersubjective communication that do not depend on any such essentially subjective gesture. The essential indexicality of the ostensive gesture, then, makes its meaning incommunicable, suggesting the need for the structuralization of any state of affairs originally involving such a gesture.

Schlick, taking the same point differently, maintained that an essentially demonstrative component remained in the meaning of *all* propositions (not only those that have not yet been structuralized) and that the incommunicable meaning of an ostensive gesture, to be carried out in each case of understanding, contributed essentially to the establishment of any proposition whatsoever. The thought that scientific claims originate in essentially indexical propositions tied to ostensive acts evidently figured, though, in both philosophers' conceptions of the epistemological task and provided some intuitive motivation, in both cases, for declaring the empirical basis of science to be essentially demonstrative in form. But upon further examination, there is little reason to suppose that this thought helps at all to establish the incommunicability of experience. First, there is no evident reason why even essentially indexical propositions might not be rewritten as intersubjective ones without losing any of their empirical content. On the structuralist account, after all, the meaning of any meaningful proposition whatsoever depends upon its objective, logical form; so even essentially indexical propositions, if they have any meaning whatsoever, can be rewritten without loss of content in an objective, structuralized form. Carnap himself came to think, during the *Syntax* period, that an ostensive description of an object is always replaceable by a perfectly objective description of the state of affairs at a particular spatio-temporal location.[83] If this is so, then the indexicality of an indicative proposition formulated on the basis of an ostensive act has no implication whatsoever for the communicability of its content. The very same content can be described, without any need to involve the character of an individual's experience, in straightforwardly objective terms.

Second, even essentially demonstrative claims are generally *expressible*, even if they are not immediately suitable for inclusion in a general scientific description of the world. Construed as involving a demonstrative *act* of gesturing or pointing, ostension makes an indexical connection to a particular state of affairs. But it does so in a way that is publicly accessible – at least to the other observers positioned in such a way as to witness the ostensive act – and has no obvious dependence on any particular subjective experience. Only if the ostension involved in providing a basis for scientific claims is thought to be the *private* ostension of an experience to *oneself* is the necessary connection made. But it is notoriously difficult to make sense of the nature or result of any such purely private act of ostension, completely independently of the public conditions of meaningfulness and truth that are typically taken to account for the meaning of ordinary demonstrative and indexical claims.[84] Again, it remains *possible*, even while clearly distinguishing between public and private ostension, to continue to maintain that essentially private acts of attending or focusing provide the ultimate basis for the verification and establishment of scientific claims. But accepting the structuralist model of objective meaning itself demands that the meaningful propositional contents *established* by any such acts be structural, and thus essentially objective and public. The relationship between the private ostensive act – in itself strictly meaningless, according to the structuralist model – and the public, objective proposition that it will be called upon to support becomes essentially unclear and unclarifiable. It remains possible to assert that, despite the impossibility of describing it, there nevertheless *is* such a relationship. But this admission again renders inaccessible any description of the relationship between private ostension and objective contents as one of verification or evidence, depriving the structuralist of any positive picture of the relationship between experience and meaning that he had sought to capture.

A somewhat different kind of connection between ostension and experiential content is suggested by Schlick's claim for the *self-verification* of incommunicable affirmations. Recall that Schlick construed affirmations as essentially ostensive and reliant for their meaning on the presence of the experiential state of affairs indicated. It follows that any public expression of an affirmation differs in meaning from the affirmation itself, for no nonanalytic public expression is self-verifying. This will be the case even if the affirmation is replaced by an essentially ostensive proposition indicating some public state of affairs by way of an indexical term, for it is always possible that, because of perceptual distortion or error, the experiential state of affairs indicated by the affirmation does not match the public state of affairs indicated by a public ostensive description. This possibility suggests that what was for Schlick really decisive for the meaning of an affirmation was not actually the reliance of affirmations on ostensive acts, but rather their reliance on the *presence* of particular subjective experiences. On this account, for a particular affirmation to be possible and true is just for a particular subjective experience to exist. But the affirmation is not now the *proposition* or *claim* that that experience exists; for even in a purely demonstrative form, this proposition could be false. Instead, the affirmation consists, in whole or in part, simply in the presence of the experience it affirms.

This view – that affirmations not only depend semantically on but also *consist in* the presence of particular experiences – seems to capture the only coherent way of making sense of Schlick's commitment to the self-verifying character of affirmations.[85] But if this was Schlick's view, his holding of it marks the ultimate failure of his version of structuralism to accommodate experience as semantically relevant at all, in the way he had hoped to do with his earlier form/content distinction. For to characterize affirmations as essentially consisting in the presence of experiences is to admit that, in all semantically relevant contexts of verification and justification, the experience itself would do as well as the affirmation. With the claim of existential dependence on the presence of a particular experience, the affirmation has lost any distinctively linguistic form or content whatsoever. This saves the incommunicability of content, but leaves it deeply mysterious how affirmations can interact rationally with linguistic propositions at all.

As much as the incommunicability of content might have been necessary to motivate the epistemological project of structuralism, then, none of Schlick's or Carnap's arguments for it, independent of structuralism, are sufficient. Why, then, *did* Schlick and the early Carnap hold the incommunicability-of-content doctrine? Reflection on the history of the debate, and on the unsatisfactoriness of those of their arguments for the doctrine that were independent of the structuralist theory of meaning, motivates the suggestion that the structuralist theory was itself their only real basis for affirming the incommunicability of content. Within the ambit of the structuralist configuration, which theorizes meaning and expressibility as public, logical structure, the elements of experience (insofar as they are elements, and not structures) had to appear as inexpressible and ineffable, even if they were theorized as being capable of animating or informing empirical propositions with their empirical meaning. The incommunicability-of-content doctrine could be dropped, as it was on Neurath's physicalist theory, but only at the cost of portraying experiential propositions as being no different in their semantic status from any other structurally meaningful, objective propositions. The desire to retain a special role for experience in the verification and meaning of empirical propositions required, given the structuralist theory of meaning, that experience appear as both incommunicable in itself and capable of directly authorizing basic empirical propositions such as protocol sentences. This produced, in turn, the temptation to theorize experience as capable of justifying basic empirical propositions from a position outside language, and led to the pictures of ostension or bare presence to which Schlick and Carnap appealed. Given the underlying structuralist picture of meaning, experience could appear (if indeed it appeared at all) only as its unspeakable support. The necessary result was the theoretical unsatisfactoriness of the explanations of the empirical meaningfulness of protocol sentences that structuralist theorists provided. But since the only way to avoid these explanations, given structuralism, was to affirm a semantic physicalism that denied experience any special or privileged role, the theoretical unsatisfactoriness of these pictures of the semantic privilege of experience was just the inevitable result of its affirmation.

VI

By the end of the protocol sentence debate, Carnap was convinced of the generalized semantic physicalism that Neurath had consistently defended. As we have seen, this physicalism construed protocol sentences as essentially no different in their semantic status from any other structural sentences of objective science. What we use as protocols for a particular science might in fact be sentences asserted on the basis of the functioning of our perceptual apparatuses, but this makes no important difference, according to the physicalist, to their semantic content or status. Within the consistent physicalist picture, "experience" can now refer only to the status or configuration of perceptual devices and cognitive or behavioral structures expressible in, or translatable without loss of meaning into, the objective language of physics. It follows from this that the project of epistemological reconstruction that Carnap had originally envisioned, and that he had made the basis of the *Aufbau*, loses its point. Since the meaning even of protocol sentences is already *fully* structural, there is nothing to be gained by epistemology's demonstration of how to "structuralize" them. With the affirmation of physicalism, the very contrast between subjective contents and objective structure that had given the project of structuralization its point drops out of the picture, along with the intelligibility of subjectivity itself. We might still, of course, be interested in knowing better, in particular cases, how it is that we know what we know. Epistemology now gets its point, in particular cases, from its ability to show the capacities and limitations of human beings, themselves conceived biologically and physically, as knowers. But the thought that experience itself has, in general, any distinctive role in the ultimate support of empirical propositions – the thought that had linked Carnap's constructional project with the empiricism of Locke and Hume – now drops out of the epistemological picture of physicalism entirely, along with the prospect of any general epistemological reconstruction of objectivity itself.

The elimination of experience as a distinctive contributor to epistemology might not seem to represent a problem for the tenability of physicalism, despite the implausibility of this elimination from the perspective of ordinary reasoning and language about knowledge and experience. Indeed, the defeat of the "foundationalist" claim that knowledge has an intelligible basis in experience has sometimes been celebrated as among the most significant insights of midcentury analytic philosophy. But the idea that individual, subjective experience retains a determinative significance for empirically meaningful claims survives in the logic and grammar of ordinary language and in the practice of scientific inquiry, beyond the repudiation of the foundationalist epistemological projects that figured experience as the ultimate basis for the edifice of knowledge. Insofar as physicalism denies this idea, it falsifies rather than captures the grammar of the ordinary language we use to describe our experience, and the practices by means of which we establish and evaluate empirical claims. The thought, usually inarticulate, that physicalism falsifies the ordinary language of experience in this and other ways resonates through the subsequent history of the analytic inquiry into consciousness, recurring at each stage of the development of physicalism but typically unclear about the general form of the complaint that it embodies. The historical elucidation of the origin of physicalism in Neurath's structuralist picture allows the real ground for this recurrent complaint to be seen and allows the comprehensiveness of physicalism to be challenged in a new way on its basis.

Neurath's semantic physicalism consistently affirmed the structuralist identification of structure with meaning, to the point of denying the possibility of giving *any* account whatsoever of the character of the elements that make up the relational structure of meaning. For Neurath, the only possible candidates for the elements comprising the relational structure of language were the physical signs and sign sequences themselves. But the relational description of signs in their physical configurations and interconnections stops short of showing why structure should be identified with meaning at all, or why analysis of structure should be capable of clarifying meaning. In a sense, Neurath's identifying meaning with structure while providing no account of the *elements* of the structure of meaning was simply the consistent outcome of the structuralist picture that he shared with Carnap and Schlick. We have seen how Schlick was himself forced to recognize the impossibility of providing any such account, even as he attempted to maintain that empirical propositions are ultimately justified by experience. But it is not obviously coherent to describe language as a structure of meaning without being able to say anything whatsoever about the nature of the elements so structured. And even beyond this suggestion of incoherence, Neurath's inability to characterize the elements comprising what he thought of as the structure of meaning poses substantial problems for the concrete meaningfulness of the physicalist program he upheld. Without a distinctive sense of basic experiences as the subjective elements of the objective structure of language, Neurath could not construe the analysis or elaboration of structure as *contributing* to the objectivity of science, for he lacked any distinctive sense of what this contribution could consist in. On the consistent physicalist picture, meaningful propositions, insofar as they are meaningful, are *already* fully structuralized. Since there is nothing opposed to structure, there is no point in elaborating structure further in order to benefit science or to contribute to the intelligibility of its claims. But even the claim that all meaningful scientific propositions are, or ought to be, reducible to propositions in the language of physics had gained its original plausibility from its role in the structuralizing project that sought to increase the objectivity of scientific claims by rewriting them in the objective language of physics. Without the subjective/objective distinction that made this project intelligible, Neurath's doctrine of physicalism threatens to fall into a pragmatic emptiness obscured by the apparent boldness of its claim of reducibility.

A doctrine that is pragmatically empty in this sense may nevertheless be true, and the subsequent history of the analytic discussion of the mind certainly bears witness to the enduring popularity of the physicalism that Neurath inaugurated. But reflection on its origin in the semantic picture that opposed experience to meaning as content to structure allows us to question the truth of its comprehensive claim in a new way, by inquiring into the basis for, and intelligibility of, the picture of meaning on which it ultimately rests. For decades, the doctrine of physicalist explicability has seemed comprehensive because it has seemed that the only way effectively to challenge it would be to manifest a process or phenomenon that is *not* physical or eventually describable in physical language. The very structuralist basis of physicalism itself makes this manifestation effectively impossible, however, since structuralism comprehends *every* objective description of a manifested phenomenon as a structural one and hence one potentially reducible to the language of physics. What emerges from the historical elaboration of the actual origin of physicalism in the semantic picture of structuralism is the possibility of a reconsideration of physicalism on grounds other than those provided by the introduction of nonphysical phenomena, processes, or facts. In particular, set against a historically sensitive reconsideration of the semantic origin of physicalism, the antecedent meaningfulness of the language of consciousness, outside and before any structuralist theory, provides grounds for an inquiry that reconsiders the original claim of structuralism to produce a theory of meaning, and an account of explanation, that is comprehensive for all domains. Remedying the distortions in our understanding of experience that structuralism seems to demand, this inquiry might allow the language of consciousness itself to produce, in the context of a nonstructuralist reflection on its distinctive kind of meaning, the intelligibility proper to our understanding of ourselves.

VII

Only the briefest of glances at the contemporary debate about the explanation of consciousness is necessary to show the continuing significance for it of the physicalist picture of explanation that historically originated with Neurath's version of structuralism. It is in terms of physicalism that the issue of the explanation of consciousness is today standardly raised, and one consistent complaint of those, such as Chalmers, who hold consciousness to be unexplainable by existing theories of mind is that it resists physicalist explanation. We have seen that Neurath's semantic physicalism originated in his structuralist conception of the semantic unity of science: physicalism held that science could be unified in the sense that all objective propositions could be reduced to a single, structuralized language, in particular the language of physics. This explicitly linguistic picture of the unity of science drew much of its support from the conception, shared by all parties to the protocol sentence debate, of logical analysis as capable of specifying the meaning of an objective sentence by displaying its logical structure. But it also yielded Neurath's interpretation, at variance with that of the other logical empiricists, of protocol sentences as semantically, logically, and epistemologically akin to other meaningful propositions in the language and, as such, having no unique or distinguished role in the justification of empirical claims. Consistent adherence to the physicalist position, as Neurath defined it, then, drove theorists such as Carnap to repudiate the earlier project of reconstructive epistemology and to replace it with epistemological and theoretical projects that accorded subjective experience no foundational or primary role. Subsequently, prominent projects such as Quine's suggestion of a naturalized epistemology reconstructed experiential reports and protocol sentences, as Neurath already had, as reports of objective, physical happenings such as stimulations of sensory devices.[86] At the same time, the methodological program of naturalism, taking shape largely under Quine's influence, most often presupposed the physicalist doctrines of the unity of science and the translatability or reducibility of all objectively meaningful claims to the language of physics. Throughout these developments, the various projects that conceived of themselves as "physicalist" shared a basically structuralist picture of explanation, one that holds that the objectivity of meaningful propositions is explicable in terms of their logical or semantic position within a structurally defined unitary language of science.

This structuralist picture of explanation and objectivity would remain the background and basis of physicalism, moreover, even when its adherents began to express its claim primarily as an *ontological* doctrine about the underlying nature of matter and forces rather than as a *semantic* doctrine about the reducibility of claims to a particular language. Through the 1930s and 1940s, the philosophical discussion of the "unity of science" largely took shape, still under the determinative influence of Neurath's semantic position, as a discussion of the possibility of reducing the claims of science to a unified language. The physicalist position, thus understood, gained significant support from logical empiricist pictures of the nature of scientific laws and explanation, including Hempel's "deductive-nomological model" and Ernest Nagel's conception of biconditional definitions mediating between distinct ontological levels in a unified science.[87] By the late 1950s, however, analytic philosophers became increasingly willing to assert physicalism as the *ontological* doctrine that all objects and events in the world are ultimately physical, rather than as the original *semantic* doctrine of reducibility to physical language. A turning point in the development from semantic to ontological physicalism was the publication in 1958 of Paul Oppenheim and Hilary Putnam's influential article "Unity of Science as a Working Hypothesis." In the article, Oppenheim and Putnam sketch the unity of science as involving not only the definitional or analytic reducibility of all scientific *terms* to the terms of physics or some other basic discipline (what they call "Unity of Language") but also (what is a stronger condition) the reducibility of all scientific *laws* to the laws of one basic discipline ("Unity of Laws"). They go on to argue that both kinds of unity can be realized through the development of "micro-reductions" that explain the entities of one field of science in terms of their constituent parts, as describable in a more basic field. Thus, for instance, the biological science of multicellular organisms can be wholly reduced to a more basic field of science that characterizes cells. In this way, Oppenheim and Putnam argue, the possibility of micro-reduction defines a series of reductive levels, with the physics of elementary particles at the bottom level. The scientific description of social groups reduces to the description of individual humans; and it is not implausible, they suggest, that the psychological laws characterizing human behavior can be reduced to laws of the collective behavior of individual neurons. The cellular biology of neurons then reduces to the chemistry of their molecules, and the chemistry of these molecules to the physics of atoms. The claim of the unity of science, then, just amounts to the claim that such micro-reductions are always possible, even if they have not yet in fact been attained. And because each micro-reduction reduces its object to its own constituent parts, the "bottom level" of the whole reductive picture must be the basic particles and laws described by physics.

Oppenheim and Putnam's picture of science presupposes the semantic doctrine of physicalism as Neurath had formulated it but also moves beyond that picture, both in requiring the reduction of laws and by figuring translatability relations among levels of science as grounded in the relation of micro-reduction that explains an entity in terms of its constituent parts. Though Oppenheim and Putnam avoid any clearly nonlinguistic statement of their view, preferring to present it as a program for the unification of science rather than as a general ontological claim, they marshal both pragmatic and empirical evidence for the likelihood of eventual unification. The recent discovery of the molecular structure of DNA is strong support for the program, as is the recent innovation of artificial "nerve nets" that mirror the structure of neuron assemblies in the brain.

Soon thereafter, philosophers would begin to discuss physicalism as the ontological view that all objects and events are ultimately physical in nature and that the laws governing their behavior can always be reduced to the causal laws of physics. Physicalism, thus understood, became a popular position, in particular, in the philosophy of mind, where adopting it was seen as a way of opposing any dualist or epiphenomenalist picture of mental causation. That all events are determined, without remainder, by physical causal laws requires that mental events, including states of consciousness, not be isolated from the unified causal order; as Herbert Feigl put it, in an early statement of the view, there could be no "nomological danglers," mental states outside the unified realm of causes and effects linked by physical causal laws.[88] The commitment to physicalism came to be understood as a basic and straightforward consequence of any thoroughgoing commitment to scientific explanation, shaping and determining the form of the special problem of explaining consciousness.

Despite the shift away from a primarily semantic idiom, the physicalism suggested by Oppenheim and Putnam's article and the physicalistic ontological pictures that succeeded it retain the basically structuralist model of explanation that had characterized Neurath's original picture of the unity of science. For the new picture as for the old one, to explain an event or phenomenon is to locate it in a comprehensive, unified order of events linked by causal laws. Moreover, on both pictures, events and phenomena initially characterized by nonphysical sciences such as psychology are to be explained by reducing the structures and laws treated in these special sciences to their ultimate bases in physical matter and forces and in the causal laws that govern them. Whereas the Neurathian picture envisioned these reductions as "conceptual" or semantic, the newer physicalism figured them as partially empirical micro-reductions depending on the identification of a higher-level structure's constituent parts. But this makes little difference to the form of explanation itself, or to the particular reductions that are possible. Significantly, there is little reason to suppose that a phenomenon unexplainable by the structuralist means of Neurath's semantic picture will be explainable by the structuralist means of the new ontological picture, or vice versa. Since the form of explanation in each case is the reduction of the *explanandum* to simpler physical phenomena characterized by causal laws, the newer picture, despite its change of focus, provides the physicalist no substantially new explanatory or descriptive resources.

VIII

Recognizing the historical continuity of Neurath's structuralism with today's physicalism puts us in a position, therefore, to provide at least a partial historically based *explanation* for the widely held opinion that consciousness is *resistant* to physicalist explanation. For the historical record shows that today's physicalism descends from, and remains formally similar to, a structuralist program of explanation and analysis that itself arose from the breakdown of the program of epistemological reconstruction that accorded conscious experience a privileged role in the justification and meaning of empirical claims. Neurath's physicalism arose, as we have seen, precisely from the exclusion of consciousness (at least, consciousness thought of as having any special logical or explanatory role) from the total explanatory picture of structuralism. Of course, as we've seen in the history of the protocol sentence debate, Neurath had good reasons for this exclusion. Given the structuralism that he shared with Carnap and Schlick, the claim of a special semantic role for consciousness had to emerge as incoherent once the question of the meaning of protocols arose. But given this origin, it is hardly surprising that the special properties of conscious states should today seem to pose a deep problem for their integration into the physicalist order of explanation, or that this problem should be felt as arising particularly from the structuralist form of physicalist explanation. The historical analysis conducted here suggests that one basic reason for this feeling is the continuity of today's structuralist physicalism with its earlier, more explicitly semantic but formally similar version, itself designed in the first instance to provide a unified explanatory order without according consciousness any special role.

If this is right, it follows that in order to attain an adequate understanding of the contemporary problem, we must reexamine the original methodological and conceptual grounds both for the semantic structuralism that Neurath shared with Schlick and Carnap and for the exclusion of consciousness from this picture that characterized

Neurath's physicalism. The historical analysis of this chapter already suffices to yield, in fact, a preliminary suggestion of one way in which the current debate could be brought to a better understanding of itself on the basis of philosophical history. If the suggestion of the present analysis is correct, Neurath's physicalism originated, in large part, as a response to the explicitly *semantic* question of the relationship of experience to public, linguistic meaning; and since contemporary physicalism inherits the basic explanatory form of Neurath's physicalism, it also inherits its primarily semantic character and method, even if it does not make this explicit.[89] It follows that the contemporary problem of explaining consciousness in physicalist terms is essentially the same problem that troubled Carnap, Schlick, and Neurath: the problem of locating the language of conscious experience, including protocol sentences, in a total structural system of logical interrelations. From the exposure of language as the historically determinative field for the current configuration of physicalism and consciousness, the problem can gain philosophical perspicuity and determinacy. To insist that consciousness resists physicalist explanation is, then, to insist that the language with which we report and describe our conscious states does not present itself as logically, semantically, or epistemologically on a level with the objective language of physicalist description. By situating, on the basis of the historical analysis, the problem of explaining consciousness as the problem of the relationship between experience and linguistic meaning, we gain not only historical accuracy, but also the dialectical position from which we might understand how to figure the priority of consciousness or speak it to ourselves *through* the reflective methods and means of linguistic analysis, but *outside* the ambit of a total, structuralist picture in which it can appear only as empty, mute, or unintelligible.

3

Husserl and Schlick on the Logical Form
of Experience

In the last chapter, we saw how the structuralist picture of meaning that the philosophers of the Vienna Circle formulated led to deep and decisive problems with the explanation of experience. The structuralist conception of meaning arose in the attempt to accommodate experience within a general theory of meaning derived from the practice of logical analysis in the special context of epistemological reconstruction. Even when this epistemological project was abandoned, I argued, the underlying opposition of structuralist explanation to the content of experience has remained characteristic of analytic philosophy of mind, and has culminated in the contemporary problem of explaining consciousness. But because this theoretical configuration has remained in place largely owing to *methodological* continuities in the elucidatory and explanatory practices characteristic of the analytic tradition, understanding its role in generating the contemporary problem requires an understanding of the philosophical warrant and extent of the methods that have led to it.

Since the 1930s, the legacy of the philosophical investigation into experience has been one of stylistic discord and disunity between the analytic tradition and the phenomenological tradition founded by Edmund Husserl. Particularly with respect to the elucidation of the nature of experience, though, the phenomenological tradition has long purported to offer a genuine alternative to both the linguistic methods of analytic philosophy and the observational methods of empirical science. Indeed, phenomenology's rigorous and determinative attention to subjectivity, its introspective approach, and its reliance on the primacy of a first-person mode of investigation and description have long seemed to recommend it above all other approaches for the elucidation and characterization of experience. In 1929, for instance, Husserl argued in the *Cartesian Meditations* that, as Descartes had earlier shown, philosophical certainty about any subject must ultimately trace to the evidence of first-person reflection on the subjectivity of the ego – to the foundation of knowledge in actually lived experience.[1] The phenomenological method, therefore, would begin with exploration of the realm of experience available to self-reflection, *prior* to the positing of objective, natural reality that the natural sciences presuppose. In order to maintain steadfastly its basis in actual experience, phenomenological inquiry subjects the natural world to a radical "bracketing" or *epoche*, withholding judgment on its actual existence so as to inquire into subjective conscious experience itself.[2] At the same time, Husserl went beyond Descartes in holding that the phenomenological examination of experience reveals a realm of *transcendental subjectivity* that is not another being or object in the world but rather forms the basis for the existence and reality of the natural world itself.[3] Thus, according to Husserl, first-personal, essentially subjective reflection can reveal the universal and objective laws and principles governing the logical and conceptual interrelations of objects and events in the world. Immanent subjective reflection reveals, running through the data of self-experience, "a universal apodictically experienceable structure" of experience that governs the reality of all phenomena that can appear to the subject.[4]

Recently, the first-person and subjectivist orientation of phenomenology has again seemed to recommend it over other approaches for the investigation of consciousness. The literature on consciousness has witnessed sporadic calls for a return to phenomenological methods of inquiry in order to end the hegemony of "third-person" approaches to consciousness and to clarify its metaphysical position.[5] But because these appeals, like the literature to which they respond, fail to consider deeply enough the underlying methodological character of the project they defend, they mischaracterize the merits of phenomenology and miss the underlying conceptual reasons for its historical failure.

The discord that continues to exist between the analytic tradition and the philosophical descendents of Husserl's project is unfortunate not only because of the legacy of mutual incomprehension it has engendered, but also because this discord has obscured the possibility of a level of methodological reflection that could bring both traditions to a better understanding of themselves. Happily, history offers an opportunity for such reflection in the very polemic argument that led analytic philosophers, beginning in the 1930s, increasingly to distance themselves from phenomenology: the argument between Husserl and Schlick over the nature of propositions describing the overall form or structure of experience. Like the protocol sentence debate that unfolded at roughly the same time, the Husserl–Schlick dispute arose, I argue here, from the difficulties of accommodating experience within a total structural form of explanation. Reflection on the source of these difficulties and the different resources of the two traditions for handling them allows us to comprehend not only the specific failures but also the specific merits of the analytic style of investigation in contrast with phenomenology. This reflection clarifies how attention to the specifically linguistic methods of analytic philosophy – methods that the phenomenological tradition, for all its attention to conceptual analysis, never explored – might provide the basis for a reception or reconception of the problem of explaining consciousness as a specifically semantic and linguistic problem, but as one *outside* the structuralist forms of theory to which analytic reflection on experience has so often been led.

Though it first came to philosophical prominence only around the turn of the century, the idea of the logical form of experience is a straightforward one. It is natural to suppose that the relations of similarity and difference, inclusion and exclusion, among the sensory qualities that comprise the manifold of experience can be represented in a single structural account. Such an account will be *logical*, moreover, in that it helps to establish or reveal the structure of such categories as we bring to any description of, or based on, our experience of the world. In one sense, of course, the structure of our experience is contingent, dependent on the physiological constitution of our particular sensory apparatus and neurological equipment; but there is another sense of the "structure of experience" in which such structure plausibly figures as a precondition of any proposition we will understand as describing a possible experience, or any item of knowledge supposed to be based on experience. Construed in this second way, the structure of experience has the necessity of logic, and the propositions describing it are correspondingly a priori.

The project of elucidating the logical structure of experience bore, for Schlick and the logical empiricists, particular relevance to the prospects for scientific epistemology. For given the empiricist assumption that all scientific knowledge begins with experience, a schematization of the logical grammar of the base-level terms of description of experience is a necessary condition for epistemology's account of the relations of inference between propositions capturing basic experiences or observations and the higher-level inferences to which they give rise. The hope for such a schematization, in particular, invited the logical positivists' most original suggestion for the nature of the a priori: that all a priori propositions might be analytic consequences of conventional stipulations and definitions together with the logical rules governing their linguistic use. If the rules defining the structure of experience could be treated as logical, then the a priori character of propositions about it could be explained without metaphysical commitment; and the purely structural nature of such a description would make good the positivists' claim to deal only in formal terms, without having to make any reference to the purely qualitative, private, or subjective *content* of experience itself.

The idea of the logical structure of experience thus became an essential backdrop for the Vienna Circle's most innovative hopes for scientific epistemology. Based on these hopes, Schlick launched a series of attacks on Husserl's competing phenomenological picture of experience and logic from 1910 to the early 1930s. The immediate focus of Schlick's attacks was Husserl's reliance on the method of *Wesenschau,* or "intuition of essences." Throughout his career, Husserl made the doctrine of the intuition of essences central to his claims for phenomenological insight. In the context of his attacks on Husserl's theory of the structure of experience, Schlick objected, in particular, to Husserl's claim that the intuition of essences could deliver *synthetic* (rather than analytic) a priori propositions describing the nature and structure of experience. Despite Schlick's significant misunderstandings of Husserl's position, his attack isolated a genuine point of difference between the two philosophers on a set of issues with precipitous consequences for the subsequent development of the analytic tradition and for its self-imposed alienation from phenomenology and its descendents.

I

Schlick's reasons for attacking Husserl's method over a period of almost two decades can best be understood against the background of the development of Schlick's own epistemology from an empiricist nominalism to the mature, semantically influenced logical positivism that he would develop under the influence of Wittgenstein and Carnap. As early as 1910, Schlick had criticized Husserl's theory of truth for its appearing to countenance logical truths independently of concrete acts of judgment. For Schlick, although Husserl's distinction of the *object* of an act of judgment from the act itself was quite correct, any attempt to conceive of the logical structure of mental acts, in virtue of which they possessed truth or falsity, in independence of those acts themselves could end only in incoherence.[6] In particular, Schlick criticized Husserl's description of the direct intuition or "grasping" of ideal logical objects or abstractions as nonsensical.[7] The initial criticism drew much of its motivation from Schlick's own developing picture of intuition and logic, and in 1913 this picture became the basis of a sharper and more focused attack on Husserl's doctrine of *Wesenschau*. Schlick now thought purely intuitive knowledge of any sort impossible.[8] Because knowledge, Schlick reasoned, is always recognition or grasping of something *as* something, the immediate, nonrelational faculty of intuition never gives us anything more than the raw material of knowledge. Further conceptual acts of comparison and combination are needed in order to make even the simplest of judgments. Knowledge always has the form of judgments, and it always requires, in addition to intuition, some mediation by general concepts.[9] The necessity of concepts for knowledge, however, does not provide any justification for regarding them as substantial realities above and beyond specific acts of judging.

Three years later, in his comprehensive *General Theory of Knowledge*, Schlick further developed this nominalist vision of concepts. Strictly speaking, Schlick argued, concepts do not exist at all; what really exist are simply *conceptual functions* accomplished by mental acts or spoken or written signs. These conceptual functions serve to coordinate and associate mental images in order to produce knowledge, but they have no existence outside of concrete acts of coordination and association.[10] This picture of concepts provided the basis for a renewed attack on Husserl's *Wesenschau*. Schlick interpreted Husserl as holding that ideal concepts could be directly grasped in a mysterious form of intuitive act that was nevertheless not a real psychological occurrence.[11] The attempt to explain such acts, Schlick averred, led Husserl to speak obliquely of a puzzling "self-evidence" that supposedly accompanies the grasping of ideal concepts; but, Schlick objected, no sense could be made of the nature or purpose of this self-evidence.[12]

In Husserl's only official recognition of Schlick's attack, he bitterly and dismissively rebuffed Schlick's remarks in the *General Theory of Knowledge*, accusing Schlick of completely misunderstanding his doctrine. Husserl's response specifically mentioned only Schlick's assertion that *Wesenschau* involves a nonreal intentional act, calling it a "total impossibility that I should have *been able* to utter so insane an assertion as that attributed to me by Schlick" and calling for an end to criticisms of phenomenology based, like this one, on a failure to understand it.[13] But the larger context of Husserl's comments shows that he thought more than just this particular issue was at stake. According to Husserl, phenomenology, like mathematics, requires of those who would criticize it certain "strenuous studies," without which a philosopher should not even be allowed to comment on phenomenological matters. Husserl perceived the motivation of Schlick's attack to be a complete rejection of the phenomenological method and an irresponsible attempt to pass judgment on it without practicing it. It is not surprising, then, that when Schlick corrected his specific misunderstanding in the second edition of the *General Theory of Knowledge*, agreeing that acts of *Wesenschau* are indeed real psychological acts (which, according to Husserl, additionally have an abstract or "ideal" aspect), he nevertheless took no heed of Husserl's call for phenomenological study, instead leaving the rest of his attack on *Wesenschau* in place.[14]

Nor was this Schlick's final word on phenomenology. In 1930, he again attacked Husserl's methodology, this time focusing his attack on the phenomenologist's defense of synthetic a priori propositions.[15] Schlick had in the meantime absorbed Wittgenstein's Tractarian picture of meaning, and he now tied his reasons for opposing phenomenology to the logical positivists' hope that mathematical and other a priori propositions could be identified as analytic or logically true by applying the new logical tools developed by Frege, Russell, and Wittgenstein. The thought that even the synthetic a priori propositions offered by phenomenology as the results of its eidetic investigations – Schlick's examples were "Every tone has an intensity and a pitch" and "One and the same surface cannot be simultaneously red and green" – might ultimately be tautologies gave Schlick the basis for his criticisms of the phenomenologist's defense of the synthetic a priori and the use of *Wesenschau* to ascertain it. Just as axiomatization had shown, *contra* Kant, the ultimately tautologous character of mathematical propositions (or so Schlick thought), further analysis might well reveal the phenomenologist's synthetic a priori propositions to be tautologous or logically true rather than true in virtue of facts.

In the article, Schlick offered several types of evidence for the plausibility of his claim for the tautologous and nonfactual nature of phenomenological propositions. First, Schlick noted that such claims as that a surface cannot be simultaneously red and green are not normally used in ordinary language, except perhaps rhetorically. This suggests their triviality and their distinction from normal claims that communicate facts.[16] Moreover, Schlick argued, unlike factual propositions and like tautologies, phenomenological propositions have the property that their contraries are nonsensical. The assertion of the existence of a surface both red and green all over, for instance, would not even be understood, and no possible evidence could convince us of its truth.[17] Indeed, according to Schlick, it is a peculiarity of phenomenological propositions that to understand a phenomenological proposition is to know its truth, for to deny its truth is to betray one's incomprehension of its terms. For this reason, the claims of phenomenological propositions are undeniable by any competent language user. This made it clear, Schlick thought, that phenomenological propositions are true in virtue of the conceptual structure of their terms rather than in virtue of facts:

If I hear that [a] dress was both green and red, I am unable to give a meaning to this combination of words; I just do not know what it is supposed to mean. If someone speaks of a tone that lacked a determinate pitch, I know beyond question that it was no simple musical tone; and if someone speaks of a green dress, I know beyond question that it wasn't a red dress; in the same way I know that a man who is 1.60 meters tall, isn't at the same time 1.80 meters tall. Everyone will admit that it requires no special kind of experience or insight in order to know that the lengths corresponding to 1.60 and 1.80 meters are incompatible with one another, for this follows from the nature of the concepts. As long as I take them to be compatible, I simply have not understood what is meant by the words '1.60 meters long.'[18]

Following Wittgenstein's treatment of tautologies in the *Tractatus*, Schlick thought that the internal connection between truth and understanding in the case of phenomenological propositions revealed their purely formal, conceptual, or tautological character.[19] It followed that no facts were needed in order to make them true, and indeed that they had no claim to represent the world as being one way rather than another. As purely conceptual truths, they simply expressed the derivational or transformational structure relating empirical propositions to one another, and made no autonomous contribution to the empirical content expressed. This meant, of course, that the understanding needed in order to grasp their truth was no real knowledge at all and, in particular, that Husserl's intuitional "seeing of essences" had nothing to do with establishing them.[20] And since phenomenological propositions embody no real knowledge, they certainly, Schlick concluded, cannot be the basis of a distinctive special science of phenomenology.

The development of Schlick's criticism of phenomenology instructively mirrors the development of logical positivism itself, from its empiricist roots to the linguistically and logically oriented program of conceptual analysis that Schlick and his Vienna Circle colleagues drew from the suggestions of Russell and Wittgenstein. Representing no genuine knowledge, concrete intuitions provided only, according to Schlick, the occasion for the specific acts of comparison and recognition that allowed the expression of knowledge in linguistic or symbolic form. Following Wittgenstein, Schlick now considered the meaning of terms and propositions to be dependent on nothing more abstract than the semantic rules governing their use. It was on this basis that he sought to explain the tautologous character of phenomenological propositions. "The meaning of a word is solely determined by the rules which hold for its use," he wrote in 1930. "Whatever follows from these rules, follows from the mere meaning of the word, and is therefore analytic, tautological, formal."[21] Phenomenological propositions, then, simply characterized some of the particular rules for the use of their terms. They were in no sense either direct descriptions of the structure of experience or descriptions of any metaphysically real structure. Once these rules were clarified, Schlick thought, all such propositions could be revealed as analytic, and all Husserl's confusion about their allegedly material character would dissipate. Thus the conceptual analysis of the logical structure in virtue of which phenomenological propositions held true could reasonably claim to be mere redescription of the correct use of various terms by competent language users; no special insight into either the specific character of experiences or the ideal structure of any conceptual domain was needed.

II

Largely one-sided though it was, the dispute between Schlick and Husserl unfolded with marked bitterness, resentment, and allegations of misunderstanding on both sides. The perceived stakes of the debate went far beyond the apparently local issues cited by Schlick. Both philosophers regarded it as a struggle for the correct methodology of future philosophy, and both saw the practices of the two schools they represented as incompatible. But their dispute cannot really be understood except against the backdrop of the thematic and methodological consensus that they shared. In particular, Husserl and Schlick broadly agreed on a single post-Kantian conception of logic as displaying the formal structure of language and knowledge and on the relevance of a logical analysis of concepts to the clarification of linguistic propositions and the solution of the problems of epistemology. Even Schlick's ability to characterize the issue as a dispute about the existence of a material a priori presupposed the two philosophers' shared understanding of the universality and necessity of a priori propositions, as well as their agreement on the relevance of a basic distinction between matter and form in handling them.[22] Both philosophers, moreover, substantially agreed about the meaning of this distinction. Form (in the sense relevant to the debate) was, for both Schlick and Husserl, conceptual or logical, whereas to say of a proposition that it was "material" meant that it depended on facts, intuitions, or the nature of experience. On the basis of this distinction, the two philosophers agreed that propositions true in virtue of form are true a priori. Their official difference, on Schlick's construal at least, simply concerned whether there are further a priori propositions whose truth depends not on logical or conceptual form, but on the specific characteristics of experiential "matter" or worldly states of affairs.

In a recent essay, M. M. van de Pitte (1984) undertakes to defend Husserl against Schlick's allegations, both early and late. Central to van de Pitte's defense of Husserl is the suggestion that his phenomenological methodology be understood as a program of "conceptual analysis" that actually differs little from Schlick's own. The phenomenological propositions that Schlick cites as examples in the 1930 article, van de Pitte argues, might well be considered analytic rather than synthetic, at least on a sufficiently rich conception of analyticity.[23] Responding in *Ideas Pertaining to a Pure Phenomenology and to a Phenomenological Philosophy, First Book,* to the reproach of those who consider his system a variety of Platonic realism, Husserl indeed claims that the essences seen in eidetic intuition may be called concepts, as long as one does not confuse them with *acts* of conceiving.[24] This identification of essence with concept motivates a plausible interpretation of the point of eidetic intuition as a kind of conceptual analysis. As van de Pitte points out, the sense in which essences are seen in eidetic intuition emphatically does not require that they exist or subsist in some Platonic or ideal realm; the point of calling essences ideal is precisely that they do not exist as real objects, and phenomenology, in any case, studiously avoids making any positive claims for the existence of any objects, real or ideal. Indeed, van de Pitte argues, the phenomenological consideration of a concept or ideal type never results in any factual claims at all. The analysis of the essences governing colors or sounds, for instance, simply establishes the range of possibilities within these domains, establishing what relations of inclusion or exclusion obtain among the classes and sets that define their types. Given this, van de Pitte suggests, there need be nothing particularly troubling about *Wesenschau.* Indeed, it goes no further than the understanding needed, on anyone's theory, simply to comprehend analytic propositions.[25]

But in bringing Husserl's methodology closer to Schlick's, van de Pitte's argument also obscures the genuine ground of the deep animosity and mutual rejection that characterized the dispute between the two. Schlick clearly lacked a full understanding of Husserl's arguments against construing phenomenology as Platonic realism, and much of his criticism of *Wesenschau* can indeed be ascribed to simple misunderstanding. But even had Schlick appreciated Husserl's arguments for a non-Platonic construal of the phenomenological method, it seems likely that he would not have accepted them. As Jim Shelton (1988) argues in response to van de Pitte's article, for Schlick it was impossible for the objects of any kind of intuition to be *general* entities like concepts; the claim that intuition could grasp only particulars was foundational for his nominalist description of concepts as symbolic functions.[26] This objection brings to the fore at least one significant point that remains at issue between Schlick and Husserl even if they are construed as joint participants in a common method of conceptual analysis. From the beginning, Schlick had objected to Husserl's theory not only on the basis of a nonspecific distaste for Platonic realism (or the appearance thereof) but also, more significantly, on the basis of his own empiricist and nominalist picture of the relationship between abstract concepts and particular intuitions. What, then, was the source of judgments about concepts, and what did such judgments represent?

By the time of the 1930 article, Schlick was prepared to answer this question with a sophisticated conception of the nature of language and logic according to which the knowledge of certain a priori "conceptual" propositions could be internally connected to the understanding of competent language users, as embodied in the rules they followed in speaking. And Schlick clearly thought this picture an improvement over all previous descriptions of abstraction and the a priori, including phenomenology's. It is not difficult, indeed, to see why Schlick might have thought his theory superior in the special case of propositions describing the structure of experience. For he thought that his linguistic picture of their origin could explain their necessity and a prioricity without utilizing any metaphysical resources beyond those already presupposed by the conditions of meaningful language in general (which, in turn, were no special problem, given an account of rules of use). For Schlick, the nonsensicality of the contraries of phenomenological propositions showed that insofar as the specific structure of experience operates as a condition on possible knowledge, it does so as a condition on the possibilities of linguistic meaning. Such possible items of knowledge as are excluded by our experience's having the structure that it does are already nonsensicalities. It follows that an adequate theory of the general conditions of meaning yields an explanation of the structure of experience automatically, without involving any additional metaphysical or epistemological commitment. Schlick thought his insight crucial to the nonmetaphysical understanding of the structure of experience; any alternative theory that missed the specific link between the structure of experience and the possibilities of meaning would be forced to posit a material a priori and incur all of its metaphysical problems.

Even if many of Husserl's actual results, therefore, can be recast in the mold of Schlick's linguistic theory, and whatever the status of their analyticity, it is not at all clear that Husserl would have agreed with Schlick about their epistemological ground or their metaphysical origin. But the question of the epistemology and etiology of conceptual judgments clearly has a deep relevance to the investigation of their status, not least to whether and in what sense they might be "material" or synthetic. Especially since a new conception of logical truth was one of the most important early results of the logical positivist project, and since problems with this conception would be responsible for some of the most significant developments in post-positivist analytic philosophy, the similarities and differences between Husserl's account of logical truth and Schlick's bear closer examination in the light of the hope the two philosophers shared for the instructive connection of logic with meaning.

III

What was, then, Husserl's real understanding of the origin and epistemology of phenomenological judgments of the sort that Schlick singled out in his 1930 article? What, in particular, was Husserl's conception of the relationship of such judgments to the meaning of ordinary language propositions? In order to address these questions, it is necessary to examine in somewhat greater detail the specific concepts and distinctions that Husserl himself brought to bear on them. Upon closer analysis, Husserl's treatment of *Wesenschau* is no mysterious or mystical doctrine of the "seeing of essences," but rather a sophisticated and complex theory of abstraction and of the epistemological relation of particularity to generality that was the focus of some of his most devoted efforts throughout his development of phenomenology.

Beginning in 1900 with the first edition of his *Logical Investigations*, Husserl envisioned an overarching mathematical/logical/ontological project that he called (using terminology taken from Leibniz) *mathesis universalis* or the pure "theory of theory." One of its tasks was to describe the formal unity of each of the particular theories of the formal and empirical sciences by defining "pure categories of meaning, the pure categories of objects and their law-governed combinations."[27] Because each empirical or formal theory must have a unified, deductive character and concern a particular domain of possible or actual objects, the semantic metatheory given by logic would comprise, in each case, a theory of the possible logical relations of objects in that domain as well as a theory of the logical relations of propositions about those objects. The pure "theory of theories" would, in addition, comprise a description of the possible logical forms of any objectivity whatsoever, as well as the logical forms and relations in virtue of which semantic meaning is possible at all. Thus, examples of the pure categories of meaning include "Concept, Proposition, [and] Truth." In close connection with the pure categories of meaning, pure logic also establishes the highest-level categories of ontology. These ontological categories, such as "Object, State of Affairs, Unity, Plurality, Number, Relation [and] Connection," are "formal" in the sense that they govern the possible forms of existents in any objective domain whatsoever.[28] Epistemologically, the determination of both the pure categories of meaning that allow for the systematic unity of a theory and the formal categories of ontology requires the use of essential or categorial intuition, the "seeing" of abstract concepts or categories:

In both cases we are dealing with nothing but concepts, whose notion makes clear that they are independent of the particularity of any material of knowledge, and under which all the concepts, propositions and states of affairs that specially appear in thought, must be ordered. . . .

All these concepts must now be pinned down, their "origin" must in each case be investigated. Not that psychological questions as to the origin of the conceptual presentations or presentational dispositions here in question, have the slightest interest for our discipline. This is not what we are enquiring into: we are concerned with a phenomenological origin or – if we prefer to rule out unsuitable talk of origins, only bred in confusion – we are concerned with insight into the essence of the concepts involved, looking methodologically at the fixation of unambiguous, sharply distinct verbal meanings. We can achieve such an end only by intuitive representation of the essence in adequate Ideation, or, in the case of complicated concepts, through knowledge of the essentiality of the elementary concepts present in them, and of the concepts of their forms of combination.[29]

Already in the *Logical Investigations*, then, Husserl connects the intuition of essence to the establishment of both the overriding categories of ontology and the "categories of meaning" governing the unity of all possible theories. The intuition of essences – their representation "in adequate Ideation" – will suffice to fix and disambiguate the meanings of the terms with which we establish the ontological and pure categories into which we divide the world and meaningful language. Essential intuition is therefore at least in part concerned with establishing the conceptual conditions under which purely formal truths, truths depending on meaning alone, are possible, as becomes clear when Husserl explains the second task of pure logic:

Our *second* group of problems lies in the search for the *laws* grounded in the two above classes of categorial concepts, which do not merely concern possible forms of complication and transformation of the theoretical items they involve (see Investigation IV), but rather the *objective validity* of the formal structures which thus arise: on the one hand, the truth or falsity of *meanings* as such, purely on the basis of their categorial formal structure, and on the other hand (in relation to their objective correlates), the being and not being of objects as such, of states of affairs as such, again on the basis of their pure, categorial form.[30]

In addition to establishing the most general categories of meaningful language and objects and events in the world, then, essential intuition clarifies the laws governing the possibility that a proposition is formally or logically true. Within it will, accordingly, be found the basis for the truth of any analytic truth. At the same time, essential intuition also establishes the *existence* of certain kinds of *objects* that owe their existence purely to form, including numbers, sets, and other mathematical objects.

Why, if Husserl agreed with Schlick in considering a priori propositions to be true solely in virtue of the abstract form of conceptual connections, did he nevertheless insist that a special ability of essential intuition or direct grasping of essences was required to establish them? The answer lies in the *Logical Investigations'* development of a sophisticated theory of abstraction, through which Husserl sought to explain our epistemic access to general concepts and truths. In contradistinction to classical empiricist theories of abstraction, which held that the ability to generalize rests on the use of an intuited particular as a general example, Husserl thought that no theory of abstraction would give an adequate account unless it described our ability to access a generality *as such.* For instance, where Locke, Hume, and Berkeley had sought to explain our knowledge of a general geometrical proposition about triangles by hypostatizing a particular, intuitively graspable triangle – a "general idea" – with no determinate size or shape (Locke), or by treating the generalization as a mere annexation of a general name to a set of several representative particulars (Berkeley), Husserl insisted that such a proposition could be known only through direct knowledge of a general essence that is completely distinct from any of its particular instances.[31] Without the intuition of generalities as such, Husserl thought, any number of acts of comparison or distinction of particulars remains insufficient to establish any general, a priori propositions about the characteristics of their types or species.[32]

Later in the *Logical Investigations,* Husserl further develops the description of essential intuition to cover not only the intuition of the conditions of formal meaning and ontology, but also the possible types and forms of various sensuous and intuitive materials, such as colors, shapes, and sounds. By varying a particular intuitive content (for instance, a color or a shape) in imagination, we can establish ideal laws governing its possibilities of transformation into various forms and combinations. These ideal laws of intuitive possibility may – but need not – match the categorial laws in virtue of which propositions have meaning. Accordingly, it becomes possible for a proposition to express a meaning that cannot be fulfilled by any real intuitive content. Husserl calls such propositions, and the nonintuitive presentations that they embody quite generally, *inauthentic.*[33] For instance, a sentence reporting the existence of a "round square" might fulfill all the syntactic rules necessary for a proposition to have meaning, but it will have no possible intuitive fulfillment.[34] The unimaginability of Schlick's "impossible" propositions (for instance, the proposition asserting that a particular surface is both red and green all over) then corresponds to the formal mismatch between the categorial laws governing the formation of possible meanings and the categorial laws governing the particular sensuous or intuitive domain described. The intuitive content called for by such a proposition cannot even be experienced in imagination, owing to its failure to respect the specific categorial laws governing the possibilities for transformation and combination of intuitive contents in its particular sensory domain.

Husserl's *Logical Investigations* picture, then, calls for essential intuition to establish ideal laws governing both the possibilities of formal or analytic truth and the existence of formal objects such as numbers, and additionally to determine the more specific possibilities of transformation and combination of intuitive contents in particular sensory domains. But what are the relationships among these types of categorial laws, and how does essential intuition operate in each case? In *Ideas* I, Husserl develops the theory of categories further, distinguishing on the level of ontology between formal and regional categories. As in the *Logical Investigations*, formal categories include those ontological categories (such as Object, State of Affairs, and Relation) that can apply in any objective domain whatsoever, and also the ideal logical/ grammatical categories of propositional form in virtue of which propositions have meaning. In addition to formal ontology, however, various regional ontologies with their own particular categorial laws underlie specific domains of experience and theory. The "eidetic seeing" of the particular categorial laws governing a region can be accomplished by a process of "free phantasy" or imaginative variation of intuitive contents:

> If we produce in free phantasy spatial formations, melodies, social practices, and the like, or if we phantasy acts of experiencing of liking of disliking, of willing, etc., then on that basis by "ideation" we can see various pure essences originarily and perhaps even adequately: either the essence of any spatial shape whatever, any melody whatever, any social practice whatever, etc., or the essence of a shape, a melody, etc., of the particular type exemplified.[35]

In this way, regional essence determines regional axioms. These axioms are eidetic truths that Husserl describes as synthetic a priori. Husserl is less explicit about the methodology for establishing formal categories, but as in the *Logical Investigations*, he suggests that one can proceed grammatically, by systematically generalizing specific propositions in order to isolate the formal syntactic structure of their terms.[36] Thus, linguistic-level analysis does for formal categories what imaginative free variation does for regional ones. In each case, the establishment of categorial laws rests on the evidence derived from the arbitrary variation of particular instances of a general type in order to establish the character of that type.

The central importance of the epistemology of categorial form to the phenomenological description of judgment can be seen in *Experience and Judgment*'s account of the distinction between pre-predicative and predicative experience. For Husserl, pre-predicative, intuitive experience suffices only to put one in contact with particular objects or parts of objects. Making a judgment about a state of affairs, or having an experience of a state of affairs as such, requires a specific further act of predication that involves full knowledge of general species, types, or concepts and therefore presupposes their categorial intuition.[37] For instance, the cognitive or experiential judgment that predicates a universal of a particular ("The sky is blue") requires not only sensory intuition of the particular but also abstractive, adequate intuition of the universal in its specific character.[38] The abstract relations of essences therefore establish the preconditions for any sensory or intuitive judgment whatsoever, and the specific phenomenological principles that can be established on their basis are only illustrations of the preconditions of intuitively fulfillable meaning generally.

Husserl applies the method of imaginative free variations explicitly to Schlick's own example of the law holding that every tone has both an intensity and a quality:

[A priori necessity] is attained... in an act of judgment which is connected with the obtaining of pure generalities in free variation. We have, for example, obtained the *eidos* sound and have found that a quality, an intensity, and a timbre belong to it and that these qualities, when we run though like sounds, are also like. We can then make a particular judgment: some particular sound or other of this sound-concretum has in itself a particular moment of the concepts of concrete intensity, quality, etc. But continuing on the basis of an arbitrary repetition, we can also say that the concrete concept "sound" (the sound-*concretum*) includes the dependent partial concepts "this intensity," "this quality" and that every possible individual particular of this sound-*concretum* includes a particular moment of this intensity, this quality. And this is in the activity of free variation. We see that it is in general so and that the universal state of affairs subsists in the realm of *a priori* possibility; that is, just as the concrete concept includes its partial concepts, so in general every possible state of affairs that is some particular sound or other includes the state of affairs that this same particular sound has intensity and quality.[39]

For Husserl, then, the phenomenological "law" that each sound has an intensity and a quality expresses a categorial law or an ideal conceptual structure that governs both the imaginative possibilities of intuition and the ontological possibilities of actual states of affairs, both subject additionally to the overriding laws of formal meaning and ontology. Insight into the categorial law can be described as the intuitional seeing of an essence, but it is always bought by the free variation of intuitive, concrete contents in imagination. Such a basis is necessary, in fact, in order to ensure that any essence is intuited adequately and completely. For, Husserl explains, any mere generalization or induction from a finite set of particular observed examples of a type remains tied to the contingency of that particular set. What is needed for genuine perception of an essence is, in addition to the adumbration of a set of examples of an essential type, the a priori knowledge that the set of possibilities envisioned for that type is indeed exhaustive. Generalizing from a finite number of actually perceived examples of dogs, I may arrive at an incomplete concept that bears the contingent marks of the particular set of examples I happened to observe; the only way to gain adequate insight into the *essence* dog is to gain exhaustive knowledge of the extent and boundaries of its *infinite* range, or horizon, of possible instances.[40] Even in imagination, however, the possibility of attaining such insight does not rest on the entertainment of an infinite number of examples, but only on the *arbitrary* character of imaginative variation:

What matters is that the variation as a process of the formation of variants should itself have a *structure of arbitrariness*, that the process should be accomplished in the consciousness of an arbitrary development of variants. This does not mean – even if we break off – that we intend an actual multiplicity of particular, intuitive variations which lead into one another, an actual series of objects, offering themselves in some way or other and utilized arbitrarily, or fictively produced in advance; it means, rather that, just as each object has the character of exemplary arbitrariness, so the multiplicity of variations likewise always has an arbitrary character: it is a matter of indifference what, in addition, I might be given to apprehend in the consciousness that "I could continue in this way."[41]

In the course of explicit phenomenological investigation of an essence or an essential law, awareness of the arbitrariness of possible variation thus leads to the grasping or intuition of the infinitely open horizon of possibilities encompassed by a specific invariant type.[42] Husserl's theory of judgment calls for any predicative judgment of the type of an object to be based somehow on such a grasping. But explicit and deliberate acts of free eidetic variation are undoubtedly rare; the possibility of each of my predicative judgments could hardly depend on my having explicitly gone through the process of imaginative variation for each of the predicates that one employs in an ordinary judgment. For this reason, Husserl does not require that imaginative free variation be explicit and deliberate. Ordinarily, an ongoing process of *passive synthesis* suffices to "constitute" the universal concept needed for judgment.[43] By synthetically associating similar objects in virtue of their common properties, the process of passive synthesis begins to constitute the concepts of those properties even where no explicit course of phenomenological investigation is undertaken.[44]

The details of Husserl's sophisticated theory absolve him, then, of any accusation of simple obscurity; but even with these details in view, Husserl's theory does not provide him with the resources to resist completely Schlick's attack. This becomes clear upon an examination of the differences between the two theories. Most importantly, unlike Schlick, Husserl does not tie the understanding of regional-categorial laws directly to the conditions under which formal truth and meaning in general are possible, except in the derivative sense that regional categories always remain subject to formal categories and all propositions remain subject to the general logical categories that make propositional meaning possible at all. Indeed, for Husserl, Schlick's "incomprehensible" propositions are actually *meaningful*, albeit "inauthentic." The specific establishment of the material-categorial laws that Schlick describes as "phenomenological propositions" rests in each case on the imaginative establishment of the range of forms and combinations possible for a given intuitive content or type. Because they depend on and establish only imaginational *possibilities*, the material-categorial laws are certainly not "factual" in the sense of being made true by particular facts. Indeed, they have a good claim to be "formal" in the sense of resting only on the formal possibilities of variation and combination in particular intuitive domains. Still, particular material-categorial laws

clearly rest on the specific character of the perceptual or intuitive domains to which they apply. Though the formal structure of these laws is
assuredly an ideal/conceptual structure, it nevertheless emerges only
from the particular perceptual or sensory possibilities evident in free
imaginative variation.

Husserl's two-level account, then, does indeed treat the a priori laws
governing the structure of experience as grounded in determinate and
specific ranges of experience subject to specific material ontologies,
and in this sense, whatever the additional complexities and motivations of the theory of *Wesenschau*, Husserl's theory does indeed require
a material a priori of the sort that it was the aim of Schlick's linguistic
theory to expose as unnecessary. Moreover, the two-tiered character of
Husserl's theory leaves him unable to capture as readily as does Schlick
the guiding linguistic intuition of the latter's theory: that the logical
structure of experience constrains the possibilities of knowledge by
constraining the possibilities of linguistic meaning, thereby making
the contraries of phenomenological propositions nonsensical. Failing
to identify "authentic thinking" with meaningful thinking *tout court*,
Husserl's theory invites the criticism that among the propositions it
describes as meaningful there are many (viz., the "inauthentic" ones)
for which we can certainly envision no clear meaning. Nor can these
propositions evidently enter into meaningful inferential relations with
other propositions; any sentences derived from them by the usual rules
of inference will have no more clarity of sense than they themselves do.
From Schlick's perspective, at least, Husserl's failure to treat the structure of experience as a constraint originating from the conditions for
the possibility of linguistic meaning saddles him with the burden of explaining the determinacy and necessity of the structure of experience
in other, more metaphysically involved terms.

This additional metaphysical burden might reasonably be thought
undesirable in any case, given the availability of a simpler theory; but
it provides specific problems for Husserl's view in that the metaphysical description of the structure of experience necessarily engenders
a correlative epistemology of our knowledge of that structure. In the
broad sweep of Husserl's system, we have seen that the possibility of
essential intuition through eidetic free variation emerges as the crucial link between the phenomenological theory of abstraction and the
equally important theory of judgment, providing at once an account

both of our knowledge of abstract universals and of the possibility of our judging their instances – specific properties – to hold of individuals. Its necessary basis in imagination gives eidetic variation the character of generality it needs to establish genuinely substantial a priori phenomenological knowledge of concepts on the basis of concrete psychological acts, while the possibility of passive synthesis accounts for the epistemology of conceptual knowledge as it figures in ordinary acts of judgment. But even so, specific epistemological problems for his account of phenomenological propositions still emerge from Husserl's reliance on imagination as their original source. These problems point to the genuine difficulty of giving an account of phenomenological propositions, and point as well toward the sense in which, though based on substantial misunderstandings, Schlick's criticisms of Husserl identify a real and important inadequacy in his account.

Because Husserl's account does not – as Schlick's account does – identify the conceptual conditions of possible experience directly with the linguistic conditions of possible meaning, it incurs the additional burden of explaining the origin of experiential concepts and the capability of their a priori relations to constrain possible knowledge. Husserl discharges the additional theoretical burden with his theory of *Wesenschau*, imaginative variation, and passive synthesis, but it is not clear that this interconnected theory, for all its sophistication of detail, really clarifies how the origin of experiential concepts determines the a priori propositions describing the structure of possible experience. One set of difficulties surrounds the applicability of the idea of passive synthesis to the experiential concepts in virtue of which Schlick's "phenomenological propositions" hold true. The preexisting possibility of passive synthesis and its associative comparison of like with like might plausibly be thought to provide as much basis as we have for discerning the type of an ordinary object encountered in experience, or for answering the question of how much it could change while remaining the same type of thing. Here it seems plausible that actually imagining – having images of – a number of variants of a given object might play a necessary role in determining the nature and limits of its conceptual type. But Schlick's special phenomenological propositions describe the structure of experience in general, rather than the essences of specific objects or types of object. Accounting for the sense in which the structure of experience is a presupposition of all of our encounters with the world requires an explanation for that structure that does not simply depend on generalization from a set of observations of things *in* the world.

How, then, are experiential concepts – for instance, color concepts – supposed to originate in passive synthesis? One possibility is that the associative mechanism of passive synthesis just has privileged access to the structures in virtue of which the concepts of experience are applicable to the world. These structures *could* simply be mental structures, characteristic of our perceptual apparatus but having no implications for realities in the world. But Husserl clearly believes that the a priority and necessity of phenomenological propositions point to their nonpsychological nature and their grounding in essences characteristic of things in the world. This suggests, instead, that Husserl intends a *metaphysically realist* account: given the determinate structure of experience, our color concepts simply amount to names for the particular, metaphysical real colors that we experience, and we generalize from this experience in order to guarantee that the concepts bear relations that mirror the relations of their objects. But such an account clearly fails to do justice to the possibility that the relations of our color concepts are (at least in part) relative to, and intelligible only in terms of, our linguistic categories or training. It is a commonplace observation of much post-positivist epistemology that the learning of a language *does* play a role in determining and structuring experiential concepts. The metaphysically realist account of color-concept formation, however, has no place for this observation. On the metaphysically realist account of color-concept formation, there is no room for a structure of concepts to evolve in anything other than strict correspondence to the underlying structures that they represent. In this sense, the contingency of our color concepts is not explained, and the metaphysical commitment of the theory cuts directly against the possibility of giving an illuminating account of the origin of these concepts that does not simply assume what is to be explained.

It is just here, indeed, that something like Schlick's insistence on a linguistic-level account might have helped. For a linguistic-level account like Schlick's plausibly explains the obtaining of the concepts and relations that we have without having to advert to their grounding in metaphysical reality. Since no particular connection between the linguistic rules of use and metaphysical possibility is assumed, a

Schlick-style account promises to remain undecided about the extent and origin of correspondence between experiential concepts and their underlying realities. An account like Schlick's, then, can both explain the necessity of our concepts of the structure of experience and allow room for the possibility that that necessity does not correspond to anything metaphysically real. Indeed, since it is offered only as an account of linguistic use, it need not venture any metaphysical theory at all.

IV

We have seen that Schlick's linguistic-level analysis, by contrast with Husserl's account, gives him a metaphysically noncommittal description of logic as exhausted by rules for the use of terms and propositions, and it is in virtue of this account that he thinks phenomenological propositions can be reduced to tautologies. Officially, then, Schlick's picture avoids the need to appeal to the particularities of experiential or nonlogical structure, and in so doing avoids the implication, present on Husserl's picture, of a grounding of phenomenological propositions in the specific structure of experience. Upon deeper examination, however, problems arise for Schlick's claim to ground phenomenological propositions in "rules of use" that are genuinely formal in the sense of being independent of the specific character of experience. This becomes particularly evident in connection with Schlick's attempt in the 1930 article to deploy Wittgenstein's developing account of formal truth and the foundations of meaning. Schlick understood that phenomenological propositions could not be tautological in the usual sense of reducing to complex propositions that would come out true under any possible assignment of *truth values* to their atomistic propositional components. It was just this feature of certain apparently logically true propositions that had led Wittgenstein to begin to supplement the Tractarian picture of meaning with the new account of logical structure that he partially developed in his 1929 article "On Logical Form." The truth of a proposition such as "X is 160 cm tall" implies not only the falsity of its direct negation, but also the falsity of any other proposition attributing to X a different height. Thus, a conjunction such as "X is 160 cm tall and X is 180 cm tall" is logically false, although the second term of the conjunction is not the truth-functional negation of the first. This means that there are logical truths that are not truth-functional truths. Such truths might be true in virtue of logical form in some extended sense, but they certainly are not true in virtue of straightforward truth-functional logic. Wittgenstein's solution to the problem was to theorize that, in Schlick's words, "such concepts as those of the colours have a formal structure just as do numbers or spatial concepts, and that this structure determines their meaning without remainder" (p. 169). In other words, the relations in virtue of which a proposition describing the color of an object excludes other propositions describing the same object as having a different color depend on the formal structure of color concepts itself. Whatever its claim to be "logical," this kind of structure, unlike the general structure of formal logic characterizing the conditions under which any proposition has meaning, is clearly particular to a specific domain of meaning. For each individual propositional type (e.g., propositions about colors, propositions about quantities, propositions about spatial objects) requires its own particular structural rules of implication and exclusion.

Like Husserl's, then, Schlick's picture requires that competent language users deploy conceptual structures somehow related to the specific possibilities of particular intuitive, factual, or formal domains. Because phenomenological propositions simply express conceptual structure in this extended sense, they might assuredly still be considered purely formal or tautological. But any attempt to describe the epistemological origin of such conceptual structures raises additional problems for Schlick's view. Doubtless, Schlick thought that the structure in virtue of which colors or quantities exclude one another conceptually could be explained simply as a matter of the actual semantic rules followed in ordinary language and practice and evidenced in the understanding of a competent speaker. A competent language speaker, simply in understanding the meaning of the terms "red" and "green," follows the semantic rule "If a surface is called 'red' it cannot also be called 'green.'" But such specific rules clearly go beyond the truth-functional rules ordinarily taken to define the sense of propositions. What, then, could explain the special status of these specific "grammatical" rules, their applicability as systems to particular intuitive or factual areas?

One possibility suggested by Schlick's remarks is a *conventional-ist* theory of the rules of use in virtue of which phenomenological propositions obtain. On such a theory, it is purely a matter of linguistic practice, owing to the stipulative adoption of a particular rule of use, that we refuse to characterize one and the same surface as being two different colors at once. A conventionalist account of analyticity was, of course, an essential component of Carnap's emerging picture of logical syntax and would become one of the central doctrines of logical positivism. The view that the grammatical structure of Schlick's phenomenological propositions is conventional, however, leads in this case to special difficulties of both historical and philosophical importance. Conventional rules of use, in order to be applied, must presumably be grasped, explicitly or implicitly; but the specificity and complexity of phenomenology bears against the prospect of handling phenomenological propositions as expressions of antecedently grasped conventional rules of use. Unlike logical truths – truths characteristic of the deductive structure of formal logic and hence evident in the deductive relationships of any inferentially linked set of propositions whatsoever – phenomenological propositions bear on *particular* domains of experience. Accordingly, the rules they express constrain only the inferential relations of particular, highly specialized sets of propositions. The phenomenological proposition stating the mutual exclusivity of red and green, for instance, has inferential implications only for the special set of propositions about red or green objects.

It follows that the special rule of use in virtue of which such a proposition holds cannot be "formal" in exactly the same sense in which a logical law might be. Whereas a logical law normally constrains a proposition's inferential relations purely in virtue of its logical form and with complete indifference to the character of its semantic referent, the phenomenological laws expressed by phenomenological propositions (on the conventionalist view) cannot be formulated on the level of general grammar and depend heavily on the specific character of the semantic referents of the propositions they constrain. By contrast with the formally specifiable rules of logic, phenomenological rules of use cannot even be *stated* without referring to a specific class of objects or states of affairs. But this poses a puzzle for the conventionalist account of their origin in that the stipulative or conventional act in virtue of which they are originally formulated can hardly be purely linguistic in the sense of concerning only the syntactic or formal characteristics of language. Whereas the inauguration of the syntactical characteristics of a language might be a matter of the stipulation of purely formal rules for the combination and interrelation of signs, phenomenological rules of use would have to be stipulated with semantic reference to their specific domains of application in view. Such stipulation would presumably require both preexisting knowledge of the real relations of objects in such domains and an explicit codification of such knowledge among the basic meaning postulates or definitions of the language. But both requirements severely threaten the privileged link between rule following and understanding that Schlick is so concerned to maintain. No matter how characteristic of ordinary use a rule may be, it still will not be purely conventional or stipulative if it makes backhanded reference to specific and preexisting relations of exclusion and inclusion among objects, properties, or experiences.

Because of the specificity of their ranges of application, then, phenomenological laws do not readily lend themselves to a conventionalist treatment. Indeed, even without prejudice to the conventionality of the rules of use for a language, it is difficult to see how they can be construed as purely syntactical (that is, as based solely upon rules governing the combinations of signs) at all. Such a construal amounts to treating an a priori proposition's apparent reference to a specific perceptual or objectual domain as a special kind of syntactic or formal feature of the proposition itself. Something like this is in fact suggested by the extension of Wittgenstein's metaphysics of meaning to the new kinds of non-truth-functional logical structure that he now (by 1929) considered to be part of the logical form of a proposition.[45] In the *Tractatus*, he had held that a proposition has meaning in virtue of the logical form it shares with a possible state of affairs. The logical form of a proposition can itself be understood in terms of the rules for its logico-syntactic use; a propositional structure's capability to have meaning applicable to a certain range of possible states of affairs depends on a formal isomorphism between that range and the possibilities of the structure's logico-syntactic employment.[46] In the *Tractatus*, Wittgenstein conceived such possibilities solely in terms of truth-functional logic. But given the newly theorized relevance of determinate conceptual structures to logical form, the account can naturally be extended to encompass a description of the specialized conditions of meaning operative in particular conceptual domains.[47] On the extended account, for instance, propositions about colors have meaning only if their rules of use – the rules establishing the consistency, derivation, and exclusion relations among them – mirror the real metaphysical possibilities of relation and exclusion among states of affairs in the world involving colors. We may take it for granted, however, that our propositions about colors *do* have meaning and that by analyzing the grammatical structure of the rules we employ, we can simultaneously clarify the actual metaphysical structure of the objects under description. Thus "grammatical" analysis on the level of language becomes, at the same time, metaphysical or phenomenological analysis of the structure of experienced qualities. Wittgenstein seems to have, in fact, taken just this logico-grammatical program of description as his own around the time of the *Philosophical Remarks*; he even used the term "phenomenology" to describe it.[48]

However, during the period of transition in which he composed the *Remarks*, a variety of difficulties had already begun to drive Wittgenstein to abandon the "phenomenological" project in favor of the more particularized descriptions of specific language games characteristic of his late work. It is clear from the *Remarks* and other writings from this period that one important source of trouble was the epistemology and metaphysics of the "grammatical" rules that he now thought capable of governing meaningful use of terms in specific conceptual domains.[49] The extension of logical form to include such rules meant that the mirroring of language and world extended far beyond the comparison of individual propositions to individual states of affairs. Determining the truth of a proposition now required that the whole *system* of propositions to which it belongs be held up to reality (like a yardstick).[50] It follows that the ability to apply such a system, even if expressed as the knowledge of linguistic "rules of use," goes beyond the knowledge of mere definitional equivalents or relations of conceptual containment. In order to apply color terms correctly, for example, one must have access to a whole multidimensional structure of relationships among terms, not just to the particular rule for the case at hand. Nor can propositions expressing rules that are "grammatical" in this extended sense be formally reduced to tautologies in the absence of the positing of logical relations that go substantially beyond truth-functional relations of implication and contradiction. The grasping of such propositions, and knowledge of the associated rules, cannot, then, be explained by any of the usual accounts of our access to analytic propositions. If there is an explanation for their a prioricity, it is not the same as the usual explanation for a tautology's a prioricity. We need, then, a substantial account of our epistemic access to them as systems after all; but one point of Schlick's linguistic account of phenomenological propositions as tautological was just to block the need for a substantial account of their epistemology.

In any case – as Wittgenstein would soon begin to realize – the characterization of "phenomenological propositions" as logically true and of their structure as just more logical form asked too much of the relatively spare and metaphysically noncommittal understanding of logical truth common to the analytic tradition. The logical positivists' account of analytic truth as "truth by convention" would soon come under fire by Quine, whose subsequent "Two Dogmas of Empiricism" would simply make, in another form, the point that the positivists had no good understanding of how a proposition could be true "in virtue of concepts." Various accounts of the partially empirical and a posteriori nature of the truths formerly thought to be analytic or synthetic a priori would follow. Seldom, however, was the alternative possibility of using a more substantial epistemological conception of logic, inclusive of description of the specific structure of experience, considered or developed in the analytic tradition.

V

Even though the dispute between Schlick and Husserl over *Wesenschau* and the synthetic a priori took place against the backdrop of a large number of shared assumptions and even substantial agreement about the proper nature of future philosophical practice as logical conceptual analysis, it nevertheless foreshadowed characteristics of each tradition that would soon divide them irreparably. Whereas Husserl's eidetic analyses remained grounded in the examination of the specific character of particular perceptual domains and regional ontologies, Schlick's spare and nominalist conception of logic and conventionalist account of logical truth eschewed the specific description of experience, preferring to operate on the level of language and understanding conceptual analysis essentially as grammatical analysis. But in connection with the nature and meaning of "phenomenological propositions," neither philosopher had an entirely satisfactory account. Whereas Schlick's account failed adequately to describe the linguistic basis of the necessity of these propositions, Husserl's failed to explain the specific connection between the understanding exhibited by competent speakers and the general *experiential* conditions for the possibility of linguistic meaning, and accordingly remained burdened with an implausible doctrine of the imaginative origin of experiential concepts and a problematic account of the relationship between imagination and experience. With these specific omissions, both traditions missed out on fulfilling one of the shared hopes that had originally sustained them: the hope of adequately characterizing the form of experience and empirical knowledge by elucidating its necessary form.

As we saw in the first chapter, the contemporary debate about the explanation of consciousness has evolved under the determinative influence of a structuralist conception of explanation that originally sought to account for the possibility of linguistic analysis by portraying meaning as structural in nature. The difficulties of explaining experience at several moments in the history of analytic philosophy can be traced to the exclusion of the content of experience from the structural picture, and historical retrospection accordingly recommends reconsideration of the structuralist picture of explanation on the ground of its methodological warrant. The historical difficulties that Husserl and Schlick faced in their attempts to explain the basis of the necessary structure of experience are, as I have argued in this chapter, no exception to the general pattern. Both failed in that they saw the necessary logical form of experience as intelligible only if underwritten by a general account of the structure of rules – whether "phenomenological" or "linguistic" in nature – that govern it. But the historical analysis also goes some way toward showing the genuine merits for improving our understanding of experience of the methods of linguistic analysis that have characterized the analytic tradition as well as those of the phenomenological tradition that it has most often refused. In raising and clarifying these questions of method, it makes available the conceptual position from which the role of philosophical methods in determining the shape of the problem of explaining consciousness can be revealed and reconsidered, allowing the debate to be reconceived in more helpful terms.

In particular, the historical analysis of the present chapter provides a methodologically sensitive means of evaluating the current popularity of calls for a rapprochement with phenomenology within the analytic discussion of consciousness. In recent years, several philosophers have called, though often cautiously, for a partial return of phenomenological or "first-personal" methods for characterizing and understanding consciousness. The call typically results from a feeling of frustration with standard scientific, physicalist, or functionalist attempts to explain it. These attempts, the usual complaint runs, fail in that they presuppose the essentially "third-person" or "objective" methods of scientific explanation. In this respect, contemporary explanatory projects are seen as sharing the methodological failings of an earlier behaviorism, which in assuming the restriction of our understanding of consciousness to the evidence of behavior, denied its reality as a field accessible to first-person introspection. Accordingly, on the standard complaint, we ought to remedy this failing by adopting the essentially first-personal methods of phenomenology, methods that clarify the structure of experience from the position of our own introspective access to it. The integration of phenomenology with the existing "third-personal" projects promises, on this view, to make consciousness intelligible by combining the two perspectives or positions from which we can view it: the exterior view accessible to the conventional means of scientific and physicalist explanation, and the "view from the inside" accessible, in the first-person case, to immediate introspection.

From the perspective of philosophical history, the underlying complaint is recognizable as an instance of the more general and recurrent complaint against the totality of structuralist modes of explanation. To say that consciousness eludes complete characterization from a "third-person" point of view is just, from this perspective, to say that it eludes explanation in the structural terms that exhaust any total physicalist description of the world. But it would be surprising indeed, in the light of the history considered here, if simply appealing to phenomenology's method of describing the structure of experience could remedy this explanatory failing. As we have seen, phenomenology failed as completely as Schlick's project to explain the structure of experience in general terms, and indeed for similar reasons. For Husserl's method of the intuition of essences, despite its apparent basis in first-person introspection and its lack of any obvious basis in reasoning about language, shared the explanatory structuralism of Schlick's project.[51] From this perspective, it could see the elucidation of the form of experience only as the description of a general structure of rules governing it, and had to, in the service of this explanatory pattern, construct an involved and implausibly specific epistemology of our knowledge of these rules.

On the other hand, there is one thought, figuring in at least some recent instances of the call for a return to phenomenology, that need not be rejected along with Husserl's original project and indeed might provide the basis for a partial reconciliation of the historical tradition of phenomenology with that of analytic philosophy, properly understood. The thought is that the typical methods of structuralist explanation fail to account for consciousness because they are best suited to the explanation of *objective* states and processes. We have seen, in the last chapter, how a structuralist picture of language continues to form the basis for the most prominent conceptions of objectivity and objective explanation within the analytic tradition; and it can accordingly seem that what makes consciousness problematic is that these forms of explanation are not appropriate to it. What emerges from the historical contrast is an alternative way of interpreting this complaint, one outside the structuralist pattern that still organizes the debate. For if the suggestion of this chapter is right, linguistic reflection on the ordinary language with which we define and articulate claims about consciousness allows the structure of our experience to show itself, in a way that reveals it as neither straightforwardly "objective" nor simply "subjective."

If the suggestion of the historical analysis is right, the structure of experience is never perspicuous from the point of view of a general explanation of language that accounts for it on the basis of a unified, objective structure, whether this structure is conceived as consisting in an abstract system of logical rules binding on all speakers of a language or, as Schlick suggested, in the conventional rules of usage that they in fact adopt. The necessity of the form of experience that Schlick and Husserl both sought to explain is immediately falsified by any account of this form as arising from sociological or empirically describable decisions or consensual patterns of behavior. It may nevertheless be perspicuous from the perspective of a carefully applied method of linguistic self-reflection that shows the commitments inherent in our linguistic practices by appealing to our *antecedent* acceptance of them. The appeal of this alternative method is, in every case, not to an abstract form of rules conceived in independence of our actual endorsement of them, but to our *recognition* of ourselves in the practice of our own language. In this sense, the method marks our understanding of the structure of our own experience as a form of *self* understanding, different from every form of "objective" explanation of states and processes in the world but nevertheless, in its inherently linguistic character, essentially distinct as well from any simple form of subjectivist, introspection-based insight.

Since Husserl wrote, the development of the phenomenological tradition itself has in fact witnessed a growing sense of the relevance of language and linguistic modes of insight while at the same time increasingly problematizing, on this basis, Husserl's original appeal to an essentially subjectivist method of insight capable of delivering the description of the objective structures of experience. This development has yielded both new insights into the ultimate basis of the language of objective description itself and the beginnings of a method of linguistic reflection that figures language, and the forms of insight that it can produce, as neither simply the subjective creation of individuals nor the objective existence of a binding form of rules. In such a method, the argument of this chapter has suggested, phenomenology might ultimately find new grounds for unity with the methodological tradition of analytic philosophy, provided that this tradition can be understood on the level of its real warrant, outside the misunderstandings to which it has been perennially and perhaps even constitutively prone.

The common object of both Husserl and Schlick's theoretical pursuits was the explanation of the *necessity* of the form of our experience, and both failed in the attempt to explain this necessity adequately in structuralist terms. Indeed, as much as our theories of experience may be constrained to respect it, there is good reason to think that there can be no general structuralist explanation of this necessity. For as Schlick realized, the possibility of experiential configurations is perfectly mirrored in the meaningfulness of the propositions expressing them. The meaningless propositions that he considered as violating the conventional rules of linguistic use are genuinely meaningless. They fail to refer to possible states of affairs at all. In this sense, the structure of experience genuinely constrains possibilities of meaning: a proposition that purports to violate it is in fact no proposition at all, but a meaningless combination of words. It follows from this, though, that any attempt to *describe* the logical form or structure of experience in general terms must fail. For such a description would amount to representing certain conditions, the failure of which would be indescribable.[52] In order to operate as a general description of the laws it elucidates, and to explain their epistemological or pragmatic basis, it would have to characterize them either as tautologies or in terms of the specific possibilities that they exclude – possibilities that, owing to the grammatical necessity of the laws, cannot be meaningfully expressed. The structuralist attempt to explain the structural preconditions for the possibility of experience, then, incoherently attempts to represent both sides of the line between the representable and the unrepresentable.

The necessity of the structure of experience, the specific character of our human form of consciousness, cannot be summarized in propositions. But it shows itself in the ordinary language of consciousness, the language that traces the contours of this form in its every expression and claim. Each of the "phenomenological propositions" that Schlick and Husserl considered has its home in this ordinary language, and the ground of the necessity they exhibit cannot go beyond the claims of this language in its everyday practice. The attempts of Schlick and Husserl to understand the form of consciousness failed in that both assumed that the ordinary language of consciousness, if it is legitimate at all, must be supported by a theoretical, structuralist explanation of the source of its claims. In this way they both missed the possibility of an alternative conception and practice of analysis, one that produces recognitions rather than theories, one that shows us the necessity of our own form of consciousness in the movement and practice of its ordinary language rather than seeking to account for this necessity in structuralist terms.

Where the *explanation* of the ineffable necessity of the form of our life must fail, the provision of linguistic reminders nevertheless suffices to bring it to self-consciousness. Historical reflection on the issues that separated Schlick's logical positivism and Husserl's phenomenology allows us to begin to anticipate a method that preserves the best aspects of each while avoiding their common structuralist assumptions, a method that integrates Schlick's recognition of the essentially linguistic form of reflection on experience with Husserl's recognition of the necessarily nonobjective character of this reflection. Combined, these methodological strands amount to a determinative recognition of the *priority* of specifically linguistic forms of investigation and insight for the elucidation of the structure and nature of experience. This methodological recognition, responsible in multiple but hitherto obscure ways for the contributions of the analytic tradition to our understanding of ourselves, might be thought of as capturing, in the context of the elucidation of experience, the priority of language for the kinds of intelligibility that we are humanly capable of. It would accomplish methodologically, in other words, the recognition that our ways of understanding ourselves are inveterately and irreducibly linguistic, that we are humanly fated to determine ourselves through the language that we use. Understanding the role of this recognition in producing the concrete insights of linguistic analysis in the twentieth century into our own form and nature would require that we understand the historical practices and methods of analysis as often opaque to themselves, perennially tempted to a theoretical form of self-description that threatens to elide and obscure their own founding insight. It would require, in other words, reading the history of the methods of analytic philosophy for the concrete insight into language that they represent in their elucidatory practice, *despite* and *against* the perennially present temptation, both within and outside these practices, to construe them as forms of explanatory insight into a general structure of meaning. In this rereading, reflection on the methods of analytic philosophy might reveal our ordinary language of experience as showing, in a way that is difficult to capture, the ineffable form of our language itself, a form that would then appear not as the present totality of a comprehensive structure but as an image constitutively elusive to us, as partial and ordinary as our everyday forms of insight into it.

4

Ryle on Sensation and the Origin of the Identity Theory

By 1950, the theory and practice of linguistic analysis had grown, from its beginnings in the philosophical projects of Frege, Russell, and Wittgenstein, to a position of unquestioned dominance within the English-speaking philosophical world. The period from 1930 to 1950 witnessed a rapid growth of interest in the Vienna Circle's logical empiricism, and the emigration to the United States during this period of key members of the Circle, and others sympathetic to its project, ensured the quick inheritance and large-scale acceptance of "scientific philosophy" and the method of logical analysis in America.[1] There, logical empiricism found common cause with native forms of pragmatism and logical inquiry, and a new generation of philosophers began to absorb the practice of logical analysis, while also subjecting it to decisive modifications.[2] A. J. Ayer's powerful *Language, Truth, and Logic*, published in 1936, put the programmatic commitments of logical empiricism in a clear and canonical form, contributing greatly to the spread of logical empiricist views and methods both in Britain and in America. Meanwhile, at Cambridge and at Oxford, a somewhat distinct tradition of analysis, tracing ultimately to Russell and Moore's decisive rejection of absolute idealism at the turn of the century, was developing throughout this period. It would culminate in the analytic practice of "ordinary language" philosophers such as Austin, Ryle, and Strawson, philosophers who, while eschewing the formal and symbolic methods characteristic of the Vienna Circle and its descendents, brought the methods of linguistic analysis to a new level of insight and capability in their application of it to the various traditional problems of philosophy.[3]

During this period, much discussion of the problems of mind and psychology focused on the application of Neurath's physicalist program of explanation to the logic of psychology and psychological descriptions. While philosophers not immediately associated with the Circle drew out some of the ontological and epistemological consequences of the linguistic doctrine of physicalism, Carnap and others explicitly drew the behaviorist consequences of linguistic physicalism for the logical status of psychology. In 1931, Carnap argued in "Psychology and Physical Language" that psychological descriptions are reducible to equivalent descriptions of behavior, in the language of physics, and that these descriptions will most often take the form of descriptions of dispositions to particular kinds of behavior. In 1935, Hempel gave this position the label "logical behaviorism," arguing that psychological sentences are translatable without remainder or loss of content to physicalist sentences characterizing the conditions of their verification, including physically describable behaviors and internal physical states of the brain and central nervous system.

Over this period, following the inconclusive results of the protocol sentence debate, some isolated challenges to the behaviorist position noted the gulf between this position and the phenomenalist one with which the Circle's hopes had begun, even suggesting that the logic of protocol sentences and other sensory reports poses special and deep problems for the Circle's underlying program of analysis.[4] But these isolated voices did not succeed in mounting any decisive challenge to the hegemony of the general methods and conception of philosophical analysis inspired by logical positivism; nor did they yet inspire any movement beyond Carnap's physicalist behaviorism with respect to psychology.

In England, the sense-datum theory of perception that had first been suggested in Russell's epistemological work was influentially defended in H. H. Price's *Perception* (1932) and Ayer's *Foundations of Empirical Knowledge* (1940). Perhaps the first definitive attack, within the analytic tradition, on this theory was G. A. Paul's influential paper "Is There a Problem about Sense-data?," written under the influence of Wittgenstein and published in 1936. In the article, Paul argued that sentences involving sense-data are logically equivalent to public-language sentences about how things seem to perceivers, but he stopped short of defending the full-blown behaviorism of Carnap and Neurath. The sense-data theory of Price and Ayer underwent a farther-ranging attack in J. L. Austin's lectures on the subject in 1947, published posthumously as *Sense and Sensibilia*. Characteristically, Austin applied to the question of sense-data his careful, specific method of linguistic reflection, considering in detail the extraordinary conceptual weight borne, in Ayer's and Price's theories, by such ordinary-language terms as "perceive," "object," "real," "material," and "seems." Austin's method additionally yielded a linguistically based refutation of the traditional empiricist's "argument from illusion," tracing to Locke and Berkeley, an argument exploited by Ayer and Price to show that sense-data are the real basis of perception. The argument from illusion trades on abnormal cases of refractions, mirages, and reflections in order to claim that sense-data, or simple perceptual data, are all that is, in normal as well as abnormal cases of visual perception, genuinely or really or primarily *seen*, and accordingly, that our knowledge of "material objects" must be based on, or inferred or constructed from, this immediate perceptual knowledge. Austin's attack on the argument and the conclusions to which it had been taken to lead displayed a keen sensitivity, reminiscent of Moore's defense of common sense, to the ordinary employment of the linguistic expressions employed by sense-datum theorists in the articulation of their philosophical claims, and his characteristic appeal to fine but significant differences in meaning between closely similar words evoked Wittgenstein's method of assembling grammatical "reminders" in order to counter the misleading effects of philosophical theorizing. Despite its significant similarities to other versions of the developing practice of "ordinary language" philosophy that exploited a linguistic method in order to dispute, in whole or in part, existing theories of mind, though, Austin's lectures did not generalize the attack beyond the sense-datum theory itself; nor did he give any general characterization of the linguistic method he employed.

Such was the backdrop of Ryle's publication, in 1949, of *The Concept of Mind*. Ryle had not conceived the project, initially, as a contribution to the philosophy of mind. His initial aim was simply to define and defend the practice of conceptual analysis, already much discussed and pursued by philosophers at Oxford and Cambridge, by exhibiting a "sustained piece of analytical hatchet-work being directed upon some notorious and large-sized Gordian Knot."[5] He initially considered the problem of freedom of will as a possible target for the linguistic method, but he soon turned to the analysis of various specific mental concepts such as those of knowledge, volition, emotion, introspection, sensation, observation, imagination, and thinking. Notoriously, Ryle aimed to defeat the "official doctrine," tracing to Cartesian metaphysics, of the "ghost in the machine," the doctrine that a person is a hybrid of a nonphysical mind and an essentially mechanistic body. He did so through a host of examples and analyses that showed how the Cartesian theory misportrays the grammatical and logical structure of our language of mentalistic description, misrepresenting the facts of mental life and the propositions that describe them as occupying linguistic categories other than the ones that in fact characterize their functioning in ordinary discourse, and so yielding descriptions of the mental that are, from the perspective of ordinary language, absurdities.

It would be difficult to overestimate the influence of *The Concept of Mind* on the literature of analytic philosophy of mind in the 1950s. During this period, scarcely a single philosophical discussion of mind omitted to address Ryle's analysis of mind and the "logical behaviorism" that it, along with Wittgenstein's *Philosophical Investigations*, was widely supposed to represent. But the vogue of Ryle's project, though deep, was short-lived. Already by the late 1950s, philosophers had begun to explore and defend an alternative approach that purported to break entirely with the method of conceptual analysis. The psychophysical "identity theory" first articulated by the Australian philosophers U. T. Place and J. J. C. Smart asserted, as an empirical hypothesis, the identity of mental states with physical brain states. It is to this theory that physicalist and naturalist theories of mind most often officially trace their own direct lineage. Today, it is customary to present Ryle's approach, where it is discussed at all, as an adventitious blind alley of behaviorism, an implausible reductionism that, in its unargued denial of both the phenomena of "inner" mental life and the inner physical or functional states that might reasonably be thought to support them, impugns not only Ryle's version of "conceptual analysis" but also the entire linguistic approach from which it arises. But historical investigation shows that both this interpretation of Ryle's project, and indeed the identity theory itself, has its historical basis in a decisive and enduring misunderstanding of it.

Ryle's masterpiece turned centrally, in many of its specific analyses of the concepts of mind, on the claim that these concepts, in their ordinary use, in fact exhibit a *dispositional* logic or grammar: that is, the grammar of tendencies, liabilities, abilities, and pronenesses rather than that of states, events, objects, and processes. In many specific cases, Ryle seemed to replace the Cartesian theory's account of a mentalistic concept with a dispositionalist account of our commitment to that concept, according to which its object is in fact a disposition to behave or respond in a certain way in a certain range of situations. This led to special problems with the characterization of our concepts of consciousness, sensation, and experience. Along with other philosophers, Place and Smart understood Ryle as claiming, implausibly, that sensations and other states of consciousness are just dispositions to behave, and they offered their own identity theory as a corrective. But Ryle's analysis in *The Concept of Mind* never in fact gave a "behaviorist" or even a "dispositionalist" theory of sensation or experience; and both Ryle's place in the history of analytic philosophy and the enduring significance of the methodological shift from Ryle's linguistic analysis to Place and Smart's empirically minded account are misunderstood if his reasons for resisting any such theory are not appreciated.

For Ryle wanted above all to apply linguistic analysis of ordinary propositions in order to illuminate and dispel the temptations that led philosophers to their presumption of being able to provide substantial theories of mind such as the Cartesian one. Accordingly, the Rylean analyst can point out the absurd consequences of philosophical theories, but he will not bring to light any philosophical or factual information that is not already present in the patterns of ordinary use. In 1962, Ryle would write of *The Concept of Mind*: "The book does not profess to be a contribution to any science, not even to psychology. If any factual assertions are made in it, they are there through the author's confusion of mind."[6] This description marks the methodological difference between Ryle's project and the project of Place, Smart, and the inheritors of the identity theory, which includes among its positive claims empirical propositions about the true, factual identity of the referents of mentalistic terms.

In this chapter, I trace this methodological shift to its roots, both in the misunderstanding of Ryle's program and in tensions inherent in Ryle's own articulation of it. In particular, Place and Smart's identity theory, I argue, rejects Ryle's project on the basis of a significant misunderstanding of Ryle's methodology, stemming from the philosophically important failure of that methodology to handle a particularly troubling special case. For Place and Smart based their reaction to Ryle on the belief that he gave a "dispositionalist" and behaviorist analysis of sensations, which they found inadequate. A clarification of Ryle's methodology shows that he did not give, and could not have given, any such analysis. But the misunderstanding traces to tensions inherent in Ryle's analysis itself. For sensation-language poses special and deep problems for the positive description of its logical structure. Concerned to show the falsity of the Cartesian theory he opposed, Ryle was led in the case of sensation to exceed the methodological warrant of his "grammatical analysis" project, giving Place and Smart the opportunity to misunderstand the project and to offer their own analysis as a corrective. The historical analysis of Ryle's real method, and the special standing of sensation-language with respect to it, opens the way to a new understanding of the relevance of linguistic analysis to the problem of consciousness, an understanding whose more or less constant presupposition within the analytic tradition has not prevented it, at the same time, from being endlessly deferred and constantly delayed.

I

A casual reader of *The Concept of Mind* will quickly notice the importance of the Rylean notion of the "category mistake" to the analyses attempted by the book. Ryle intends, he explains in the first chapter, to show that the official dogma of the "ghost in the machine" is such a mistake. Like all category mistakes, the dogma misleads in that "it represents the facts of mental life as if they belonged to one logical type or category (or range of types or categories), when they actually belong to another."[7] In order to further explain the notion, Ryle next gives some homespun examples of the "inability to use certain items in the English vocabulary" that result in such mistakes; a category mistake is committed, for instance, by the student who, having seen all the buildings and separate colleges of Oxford or Cambridge, asks after the location of the university itself, or by the foreigner who, observing a cricket match, complains of his inability to discern, in addition to the separate players and their functions, the famous element of "team spirit."[8] In both cases, the confused speaker assumes that a concept characterizes a different type of entity than it actually does, and the error furthermore rests on a misunderstanding, not merely of the place of the entity in a classification of objects, but also of the level of generality and grammatical place of its concept. The official Cartesian doctrine itself, Ryle goes on to argue, stems from such an error, originating in Descartes' desire to integrate the mechanistic description of mind that he thought necessitated by science with the religious and moral picture of human nature that he felt constrained to preserve.[9] Most often, Ryle says, this has meant that the inclination not to treat the workings of mind as mechanical or physical processes has yielded, erroneously, treatments of them as *nonmechanical* processes in some *nonphysical* domain or medium.

This general moral underlies Ryle's specific analyses of each of the various concepts of mentality. In each case, the analysis aims to show that adherents (or victims) of the general Cartesian category mistake and its specific instances misleadingly portray the logical character of one or more of our mental concepts. The Rylean analysis, then, will aim to exhibit a mental concept's *actual* conceptual logic, over against the misinterpretation of that logic that the Cartesian theory suggests. Ryle characteristically looks to ordinary language to define this actual logic. This practice justifies his methodological claim to be targeting what is, after all, only a *philosopher*'s theory of mind; typically, the conceptual practice of the layman reveals the genuine logic of a term or proposition as against the philosopher's temptation to misinterpret it. But even so, Ryle's analysis depends noticeably on some theoretical apparatus not available to the layman. For a category mistake is a failure to respect the categorial type of an ordinary-language term, but the diagnosis of such a failure will rely on some account of what it is for ordinary-language terms to *have* logical types or categories, as well as how these types can be misunderstood. Though he says little about this in *The Concept of Mind*, its specific analyses of mentalistic concepts visibly rely on such an account, one that Ryle had in fact developed in a series of articles over a period of almost two decades.

As early as 1932, Ryle had defined an early version of his analytic program in the influential manifesto "Systematically Misleading Expressions."[10] The article articulates and exhibits, through a few well-chosen examples, the possibility that an expression (a word, phrase, or sentence) may be "systematically misleading" in that "it naturally suggests to some people – though not to 'ordinary' people – that the state of affairs recorded is quite a different sort of state of affairs from that which it in fact is" (1932, p. 16). Already, Ryle focuses on the sort of misconception that arises, for instance, when a philosopher, attempting to classify states of affairs in virtue of the grammatical types of the propositions recording them, is misled by relatively superficial forms of grammar, perhaps invented for economy or ease of expression, which fail to track the logical features of the underlying states of affairs.[11] Ryle then works through several examples of problematic types of sentences, showing in each case that the sentence in question expresses a fact that may be expressed equally well by another sentence of a different, and preferable, grammatical form. For instance, a "quasi-ontological" statement of the form "x exists" or "x does not exist" where x *seems* to be a name (and the proposition, accordingly, *seems* to predicate existence or nonexistence of its bearer, leading to philosophical quandaries) in fact names nothing. Ryle relies on the familiar analysis, suggested by Russell's theory, whereby what appear to be names are actually concealed descriptions, to clarify the grammar of these propositions and to dissolve the philosophical perplexities surrounding them. Similarly, Ryle holds that statements *apparently* about universals are *really* statements, usually of a conditional form, about their instances. For example, the systematically misleading proposition "Color involves extension," which appears to describe a relation between universals, should be construed as the conditional generalization "Whatever is colored is extended," which does not.[12]

In each case treated in "Systematically Misleading Expressions," the analysis of a type of sentence shows that the type of entity apparently called for by the untreated proposition does not, or need not, exist. For the facts expressed by the untreated proposition may just as well be expressed by a less ontologically committal one. Thus, in the first case, we see that propositions of the form "x does not exist" do not in fact commit us to nonexistent objects. In the second case, we see that we need not countenance the existence of universals in addition to the existence of their instances. Finally, Ryle gives analyses of descriptive and quasi-descriptive expressions and of quasi-referential "the" phrases – including phrases such as "the top of the tree" and (portentously for Ryle's developing interest in problems about the mental) "the thought that..." – arguing that these phrases mislead by suggesting the existence of objects when in fact they stand for relational facts (e.g., that some things are higher than any other things on the tree) or conditional descriptions of actions (e.g., concrete episodes of thinking).

Though the connections shown in these examples to exist between systematically misleading propositions and the facts that they express are of various kinds, Ryle takes it as demonstrated that, at least in many cases, a fact can be expressed by any of a number of sentences of differing grammatical forms, and that some of these forms will be less misleading than others. In the specific cases he discusses, analysis clarifies a misleading proposition by showing that it does not in fact require the entities that it seems to. But Ryle says that the point of analysis is not only ontological elimination; in other cases, a successful analysis will simply show that the entities demanded by the proposition, though they assuredly exist, have a different logical form than they seem to. In general, a proposition will be free of misleading implication insofar as its surface grammar *shows* the logical form of the underlying facts.[13]

In the 1938 article "Categories," Ryle further defines the methodological basis of his style of analysis, adding to the doctrine of misleading *sentences* an account of the sense in which the grammatical behavior of individual *terms* may call for logical/linguistic analysis.[14] The claims of philosophical analysis, Ryle holds, always amount to assertions that terms belong to certain categories or types. A description of the nature of the logical categories of terms and their relation to the grammar of propositions is therefore an urgent prerequisite of the sort of analysis that Ryle defends.[15] Ryle begins this description by sketching and criticizing the Aristotelian and Kantian accounts of categories. In particular, he objects, Aristotle's eclectic and heterogeneous system of categories fails to recognize that the types of terms and other proper parts of propositions "control and are controlled by the logical form of the propositions into which they can enter" (1938,

p. 287). While Kant's system, by contrast, goes some way toward recognizing categorial form as a matter of propositions (and not only of terms), it fails to distinguish clearly between logical forms and merely natural-scientific categories of facts or propositions.[16]

In neither case is the definition of categories of terms clearly tied to the logical behavior of the types of propositions in which those terms can figure. Ryle's positive goal in the article is to articulate a conception of categories that makes this connection essential. As in "Systematically Misleading Propositions," Ryle here ties the determination of logical form closely to the conditions under which a proposition can lead to absurdity. Reasoning that type confusions show themselves by leading to absurd propositions, or to propositions whose inferential consequences include absurdities, Ryle suggests that categorial types of terms depend on the possibilities of producing absurdity when substituted into various types of sentences. Thus, two terms or proposition-parts are of different categories only if there is a sentence in which one, but not the other, can be substituted without an absurd result.[17] Owing to the diversity of possible sentence types, this definition implies that there are innumerably many categories. But analysis of specific propositions can still hope to identify the misleading consequences of the commission of type errors by exposing the tendency of misleading propositions to employ terms in such a way as to issue in, or lead inferentially to, absurdities.

By clarifying the bearing of propositional form on the logical form of terms, Ryle's doctrine in "Categories" explains the sense in which misunderstanding the logical type of an entity might yield misleading propositions about it and issue in philosophical errors of the sort that *The Concept of Mind* aims to diagnose. And, at least relative to the less comprehensive account of "Systematically Misleading Expressions," it seems to bring the philosophical presuppositions of the method of analysis closer to the cases in which analysis might actually solve philosophical problems. For, because it *defines* logical form (for terms and propositions alike) in terms of the ranges of combinations of terms and sentence frames that will or will not yield absurdity, the doctrine of "Categories" does not clearly require an independent notion of the logical form of facts of the sort that puzzled Ryle in "Systematically Misleading Expressions." On the "Categories" account, a violation of logical form will be shown straightaway by the absurdity of the violating proposition, not (as on the older account) by the recognition of a metaphysical mismatch between that proposition and the state of affairs it expresses.[18] The new definition of logical form also more readily licenses analyses of ordinary language of the sort Ryle gives in *The Concept of Mind*; for, although Ryle does not say what sort of absurdity is the target of the analysis, it seems plausible that, where a philosophical theory like the Cartesian one misunderstands the categories of our ordinary terms of description, its propositions will readily show themselves to be absurd by their deviance from, or tendency to lead to deviance from, our ordinary use of those terms. In this way, the doctrine of "Categories" leads naturally to a doctrine of category mistakes according to which nothing more than a reflection on ordinary language, and on the tendency of a specific philosophical theory to lead away from it, is needed to diagnose the error of that theory.

II

In sum, then, according to the doctrine of categories that Ryle applies in *The Concept of Mind*, a category mistake is a specific misunderstanding of the logical form of the referent of an expression revealed by the tendency of the adherents of the misunderstanding to formulate absurd propositions involving that expression. The absurdities that reveal the presence of a category mistake may be of various types, philosophical and ordinary, as is shown by the diversity of the analyses that Ryle assembles. An overriding category mistake explains, for instance, the Cartesian theory's conjunction of physical bodily processes with nonphysical mental processes, issuing in the philosophical perplexities of mind-body interaction that perennially trouble the dualistic theory. But in some specific cases, the Cartesian theory yields implications that lead to even more straightforward and obvious absurdities, quite apart from their tendency to lead to historically important philosophical problems. For example, the Cartesian theory interprets the intelligent performance of an action (for instance, playing chess) as consisting in the performance of two separate actions: one mental act of calculation or intellect, and one physical, motor act of carrying out the result, as if the two could be separated and one could be performed without the other.[19] But exposing the absurdity of this separation makes it possible to analyze the description of an act as intelligent along other lines. Ryle suggests, specifically, that such a description adverts to the skill or competence shown in the performance of the act.[20] Where the Cartesian theory absurdly calls for two separable actions – one public and observable, the other private and inward – exposure of the category mistake involved in treating them as separable clears the way for the possibility of an analysis according to which there is only one action, characterized by no special privacy or inwardness, although ascribed along with a general *capacity* of a readily conceivable kind.

The style of this analysis, shared by many of Ryle's other analyses of specific sets of mental concepts, exhibits the relevance to Ryle's attempted dissolution of the Cartesian theory of what may generally be classed as "dispositions." Whereas the Cartesian theory treats the referents of the various mentalistic concepts of intelligence, knowledge, belief, volition, and emotion as particular mental processes, states, or events, the offered analysis proposes to adhere more closely to normal use by construing these concepts as standing for "abilities, tendencies, liabilities, [and] pronenesses to react or not to react in various situations." Although not all mental concepts are dispositional – some, Ryle admits, do stand straightforwardly for particular, datable occurrences – attention to the way in which we deploy these concepts often reveals some dispositionalist account as more suitable than the Cartesian one.[21] That I know how to ride a bicycle does not mean that I am currently or even constantly in any particular mental state, but simply that I have the ability to perform in a certain way in a particular range of situations. The dispositionalist account, then, clarifies the logical grammar of the concept of knowledge (as a corrective, for instance, to the Cartesian theory's dualistic description) by revealing its close relationship to the logical grammar of other concepts that might be called "dispositional": for example, the concept of an ability. As in the case of the suggested analysis of intelligent action, to say of a mental concept that it turns out to be dispositional is, then, only to issue a reminder of plain observations about linguistic use accessible to the ordinary speaker. The reminder will show that the concept does not only refer to a state or states occurent at the time of its ascription, but also (at least in part) characterizes a background of skills, tendencies, and other standing characteristics, as they would be ascribed in ordinary language and practice.[22]

But however illuminating such analyses are in particular cases, one might naturally wonder what, in general, it means to say that a mental concept characterizes a disposition rather than an occurrence. What is the logical grammar of dispositions, and how are analyses of particular mental concepts as dispositional supposed to correct our misconception of their grammar? Ryle addresses these questions in a chapter devoted to the grammar of dispositional statements. Here, he pays special attention to the relationship between dispositions and statements of occurrent fact. To say that someone has a habit of cigarette smoking, for instance, is not to say that she is currently or constantly smoking, but that she does so at least on many particular occasions.[23] On the other hand, other dispositional properties – for example, an object's property of being "elastic" or a person's of being "greedy" – are not amenable to analysis into any particular set of behaviors or occurrences, though they will often suggest, in particular cases, the obtaining of occurrent facts.[24] In finding out that a person is greedy, I do not envision her behavior in all or even many of the cases that might provide a basis for such an ascription, or in which her behavior might be explained by it. Nevertheless, I do gain some ability to predict what will happen, given such a case.

The consideration that the dispositional terms ascribed to an object or person bear complicated and various relationships of justification and inference to the particular facts about that object or person leads Ryle to what might be called a *nonfactual* account of their meaning. This account begins, not by construing dispositional terms as *stating* facts, but by considering their complicated linguistic relationships to fact-stating terms.[25] In general, Ryle says, statements ascribing dispositions bear an analogy to statements asserting laws, in that both kinds of statement aim not to state particular facts but rather (at least partially) to "license" inferences from certain particular facts to other particular facts.[26] Just as a physical law allows the inference of one physical state of affairs from another, the ascription of a disposition (for instance, an ability) to a person will allow certain sorts of inferences to be drawn about the person's behavior or verbal responses under particular conditions. For instance, to ascribe to a person the ability to speak French is just to allow certain inferences: if addressed in French, he will respond correctly; if given a French newspaper, he will be able to read it; and many others of this type.[27] But it would, again, be quite incorrect to suppose that such an ascription adverts to any fixed or definite range of facts; the inferences it licenses will be as diverse and unlimited as the range of situations in which the ability to speak French has any bearing at all.[28] Just as misleading would be the supposition that the ascription of a disposition states the obtaining of *one* normally unobserved "behind-the-scenes" fact in order to explain all the particular inferences it licenses:

Naturally, the addicts of the superstition that all true indicative sentences either describe existents or report occurrences will demand that sentences such as "this wire conducts electricity," or "John Doe knows French," shall be construed as conveying factual information of the same type as that conveyed by "this wire is conducting electricity" and "John Doe is speaking French." How could the statements be true unless there were something now going on, even though going on, unfortunately, behind the scenes? Yet they have to agree that we do often know that a wire conducts electricity and that individuals know French, without having first discovered any undiscoverable goings on. They have to concede, too, that the theoretical utility of discovering these hidden goings on would consist only in its entitling us to do just that predicting, explaining and modifying which we already do and often know that we are entitled to do. They would have to admit, finally, that these postulated processes are themselves, at the best, things the existence of which they themselves infer from the fact that we can predict, explain, and modify the observable actions and reactions of individuals.[29]

Ryle's objection to a construal of disposition statements as factual, then, rests on the observation that ordinary linguistic practice neither requires nor includes reference to any of the further facts that such a construal would give. Ordinary practice already suffices to negotiate the complicated and diverse relationships that dispositional terms bear to particular facts; it would be misguided to suppose it possible to discover the backing of these relationships by some *further* set of esoteric facts not already evident to the ordinary speaker.

In the special case of the Cartesian theorist's misapprehension of the logic of mental concepts, the Rylean analyst reminds the theorist of the adherence of ordinary language to a dispositional (rather than factual) grammar for these concepts. The analysis will suggest that the obscure and occult occurrent facts suggested by the Cartesian theory do not actually obtain, although the ordinary occurrent facts among which dispositional statements (now rightly construed) operate certainly do.

A proper appreciation of the nonfactuality of Ryle's account of dispositional language substantially clarifies the often-assumed relationship of Ryle's program to behaviorism, showing that, as Ryle himself protests at the end of *The Concept of Mind*, that relationship is much less direct than has been supposed.[30] It is true that the Rylean account of the logic of a particular dispositional concept often consists of adducing reminders of its relationship to occurrent facts and episodes (for instance, the particular episodes of smoking that make someone a smoker, or the particular episodes of greed that make someone greedy), and that most such instances are publicly observable. But the emphasis of Ryle's account on the linguistic performance of terms ascribing dispositions shows that his reasons for assembling such reminders were not at all behaviorist. For the point of a Rylean analysis of a dispositional term is not to dissolve it into descriptions of behavior, but rather to clarify its logical function by revealing its relationships to terms of a quite different logical category: namely, statements of fact. Ryle does not imply that, at the conclusion of the analysis of a dispositional term, that term will be eliminated or eliminable from ordinary language or even from any specialized language. What will have been clarified is, rather, its legitimate place in the logical geography of our ordinary descriptions of the mind. Nor will the analysis reveal the dispositional term as redundant or elliptical with respect to any set of occurrent fact-terms. For a dispositional term such as "greedy" does not refer to, and does not require explanation by, any particular totality of occurrent facts. It will be ascribed on the basis of, and used to make inferences with respect to, facts in an unspecifiably wide and vague range of situations. The Rylean analysis, officially at least, does not seek to delimit this range. It aims only to reveal the patterns of ordinary use that specify it, and in so doing to dislodge a misleading philosophical theory that gets its grip on our imagination in part by ignoring these patterns.

Officially at least, then, Ryle's program of analysis favors no category of facts – inner *or* outer, private *or* "behavioral" – as epistemologically or methodologically privileged over any other.[31] Its aim is quite a different one: to remind us of the logical interrelationships of the concepts that we use, as shown in the ways that we use them. Accordingly, his method gives Ryle neither the inclination nor the ability to attempt an investigation of what the objects of mental concepts really *are*. All he can claim to do is to defuse a misleading theory by providing some clarification of how these concepts themselves interrelate. Ryle's dispositional analyses of various mentalistic concepts can claim, then, only to offer clarifications of how those concepts operate anyway. Indeed, the temptation to treat a dispositional analysis of a concept as revealing, or depending on, further occurrent facts about the object of the concept is itself one source of the Cartesian myth and its related category mistakes.[32]

III

In the specific case of sensation, Ryle applied his linguistic methodology in order to provide a far-ranging analysis of the logical behavior of sensation-language and to motivate the claim that sensation-language does not characterize or describe irreducibly psychical items, as the Cartesian theory supposes that it does. In so doing, Ryle anticipates or inaugurates a number of specific strands of the analytic approaches that would characterize philosophy of mind over the next several decades. But he also goes beyond the ambit of philosophically diagnostic grammatical reminders, for he gives at least the outline of a positive, descriptive theory of the meaning of sensation-language. This deviation from his own method in the special case of sensations led to the circumstances under which his analysis of sensations, and indeed his analysis of mental concepts overall, would be misunderstood, with decisive consequences for the subsequent development of the methodological assumptions of analytic philosophy of mind.

One of Ryle's chief aims in the chapter in *The Concept of Mind* devoted to "Sensation," and probably the aim for which it is today most often remembered, is to dislodge the "sense-datum" theory of perception. According to this theory, Ryle says, to have a visual or olfactory sensation is to catch a momentary glimpse or whiff of something private or proprietary; it is these somethings – whatever they might be – that are in the strictest sense, or most directly or immediately, seen, or smelled, or sensed.[33] Characteristically, Ryle analyzes the whole theory as resting on a category mistake that he calls a "logical howler," namely the mistake of assimilating sensation to observation. For the connection between the concept of sensation and the concept of observation is not at all what the sense-datum theorist supposes:

> As has been shown earlier, there is an important logical connection between the concept of sensation and that of observing or perceiving, a connection which by itself entails that they are concepts of different kinds. There is a contradiction in saying that someone is watching or peeping at something, but not getting even one glimpse of it; or in saying that someone is listening to something, though he gets no auditory sensations. Having at least one sensation is part of the force of "perceiving," "overhearing," "savouring" and the rest. It follows that having a sensation cannot itself be a species of perceiving, finding, or espying. If all clothes are concatenations of stitches, absurdity results from saying that all stitches are themselves very tiny clothes.[34]

In normal parlance and practice, the making of an observation always, and with logical necessity, involves the having of at least one sensation. But the sense-datum theorist completely reverses this legitimate logical relationship with his suggestion that having a sensation somehow involves *observing* a private, proprietary entity. Such entities are, in turn, made the basis of the sense-datum theorist's entire account of knowledge. Ryle dispels the underlying error of this account by pointing out the salient differences between the grammar of verbs such as "observe" and that of verbs such as "sense." An act of observation, for instance, may depend on or show the observer's skill or patience, but an act of sensing can do neither. Observations, again, may be deliberately suspended or refrained from, but pains and tingles cannot be. All of these differences suggest, Ryle concludes, that to observe is, but to sense is not, to be in some relation to a sensible object. To have a sensation is not, by itself, to stand in any relation to anything, even if the having of sensations very often plays a part in the sorts of relationships to things that we occupy in the course of observing, checking, verifying, watching, and listening.

So far, Ryle's attack targets only the sense-datum theorist's conception of sensations as inner *objects of observation*; but as an immediate consequence, Ryle's analysis of sensation-language and the allied attack on the sense-datum theory tends to show that the sense-datum theorist's favorite epistemological model, according to which sensations are not only inner entities but also epistemically foundational ones, derives from an entirely wrongheaded conception of the logical form of sensation-language as well. According to Ryle, proponents of this traditional model rightly discern that, although knowledge about a public state of affairs depends in part on simply observing that state of affairs, it also depends on the satisfaction of further conditions, which may in some special cases fail to obtain. But they mistake these *standing* conditions for occurrent processes, said to accompany the observation as it happens, or very soon afterward:

When a person is described as having seen the thimble, part of what is said is that he has had at least one visual sensation, but a good deal more is said as well. Theorists commonly construe this as meaning that a description of a person as having seen the thimble both says that he had at least one visual sensation and says that he did or underwent something else as well; and they ask accordingly, "What else did the finder of the thimble do or undergo, such that he would not have found the thimble if he had not done or undergone these extra things?" Their queries are then answered by stories about some very swift and unnoticed inferences, or some sudden and unrememberable intellectual leaps, or some fetching up of concepts and clapping them upon the heads of the visual data. They assume, that is, that because the proposition "he espied the thimble" has a considerable logical complexity, it therefore reports a considerable complication of processes. . . .

   Certainly a person who espies the thimble is recognising what he sees, and this certainly entails not only that he has a visual sensation, but also that he has already learned and not forgotten what thimbles look like. He has learned enough of the recipe for the looks of thimbles and to recognise thimbles, when he sees them in ordinary lights and positions at ordinary distances and from ordinary angles. . . . [35]

Where the traditional theorist assumes that some implicit or explicit process of inference must bridge the gap between noninferential perception and full-fledged conceptual knowledge, Ryle proposes to analyze the gap as a fiction and to account otherwise for the facts that generate the traditional theorist's assumption. In particular, Ryle suggests that when a sensation occurs without leading to full-fledged conceptual knowledge, it is not the failure of some process of inference, but rather the absence of standing abilities of thought and recognition, that accounts for the situation. In this sense, the full story of perceptual knowledge involves not just states and processes, but dispositional concepts as well. Ryle replaces the traditional theorist's occurrent "leap of inference" with the dispositions that normally characterize a person who we will describe as capable of such a leap. To observe a thimble ordinarily suffices *by itself* to know that the thimble is there.

The possibility of cases in which it does not suffice does not demonstrate the existence, in general, of a gap between the observing and the knowing, but only the abnormality of such cases.

In addition to diagnosing the category mistake at the basis of the sense-datum theory, though, Ryle also sketches what can easily be construed as the outline of a positive characterization of the logical behavior of the concept of sensation. Unsurprisingly, the characterization aims to legitimize normal talk of sensations without giving it objects of an irreducibly mentalistic or private sort. It begins with a far-reaching observation about ordinary language, one that would play a central role in a number of subsequent theories of mind.[36] Ryle observes that we do not possess a "neat" vocabulary for the description of sensations; that is, we learn our terms for describing sensations, as we learn all of our language, in a public context, and our language for the description of sensation bears the mark of its origin in that we describe sensations, if at all, in terms that apply as well to public objects and events.[37] For instance, we describe the putative colors of visual sensations using just the same color terms we use to describe public objects – "red," "blue," and so on. This observation bears "great theoretical importance," Ryle says, because it shows in just what sense there is a problem concerning the logical nature of concepts of sensation. Whereas sensation-talk is supposed to refer to inner, proprietary objects, our language for describing such objects depends essentially on our language for the description of outer objects that can be observed by anyone. Ordinary talk of sensations typically and paradigmatically treats of "sensations of . . ." or "sensations that . . ." where the ellipsis can be filled by a straightforward description of a publicly accessible object or state of affairs. Even when we describe sensations directly, we do so in terms that are noticeably dependent on such constructions. For instance, a "stabbing pain" is really a pain like that of being stabbed.[38]

This, together with the already-noted relevance of sensation to observation, suggests an account of sensation-language that construes it as elliptical for observational language and that at the same time accounts for the typical reasons cited in favor of construing it as having a nonobservational use in particular cases where observational conditions are recognizably not ideal. Our terms for description of sensations, Ryle says, derive from "referring to how common objects regularly look, sound and feel to any normal person" (p. 203). Characteristically, Ryle explains this analysis by way of a story about how they were subsequently misconceived as referring to special inner objects:

> It was half-correctly observed that when a common object is described as green, bitter, chilly, pungent or shrill, it is being characterized as looking, tasting, feeling, smelling or sounding so and so to a sentient observer; it was correctly noticed, too, that conditions which affect his sensitivity make a difference in how the things look, taste, feel, smell, or sound to him. . . . From such facts the theoretical jump was made to the doctrine that to say that an object is green is to say something about the visual sensations of the particular observer who reports that it is green. It was supposed that "green," "bitter," "chilly," and the rest are adjectives which properly apply to sensations and are only improperly applied to common objects. And then, as it is obviously absurd to say that a sensation is a green thing, or an elliptical thing, or a chilly thing, it seemed necessary to allot to sensations their own peculiar objects, so that "green" might be suitably applied not to the having of a sensation but to a peculiar object internally nursed by that sensation. . . .
>
> But when I describe a common object as green or bitter, I am not reporting a fact about my present sensation, though I am saying something about how it looks or tastes. I am saying that it would look or taste so and so to anyone who was in a condition and position to see or taste properly. Hence I do not contradict myself if I say that the field is green, though at the moment it looks greyish-blue to me; or that the fruit is really bitter, though it appears to me quite tasteless. And even when I say that the grass, though really green, looks greyish-blue to me, I am still describing my momentary sensation only by assimilating it to how common objects that are really greyish-blue normally look to anyone who can see properly.[39]

The Rylean analysis of sensation-language, then, explains it as constitutively and essentially derivative of ordinary terms of public observation. It allows that sensation-language, at least occasionally, has its own legitimate function: that of standing in for observation-language when the speaker wants to recognize the nonveridicality of a particular observational act, an observation that the observer wants to flag as probably or certainly incorrect. This, anyway, explains the ordinary speaker's occasional recourse to descriptions of how things look or seem as opposed to how things are. And though this sort of talk may slide into quasi-objectual talk of sensations, its semantic value remains unchanged even when it does so. The further thought that there are special internal objects called sensations, then, is a philosopher's fiction, an invention for particular theoretical purposes, and one that, upon analysis, actually provides no help for the psychological or epistemological problems it was designed to solve.[40]

IV

The first philosophers to define the identity theory, J. J. C. Smart and U. T. Place, construed Ryle as defending the substantive claim that reports of mental states, including sensations and mental images, are to be analyzed simply as behaviors or dispositions to behave; and they took it that, however adequate this analysis might be in the case of knowledge, volition, and emotion, it would not do in the case of sensations and images. But as physicalists, Smart and Place wanted least of all to return to the Cartesian dualist theory that was the main target of Ryle's attack. Accordingly, Smart and Place advanced the view that sensations and images are *in fact* internal brain processes, or that they may one day be shown to be such by advancing science. But Ryle had not intended for his analysis to make any contribution to the empirical demonstration of scientific claims, or even to the conceptual investigation of which scientific claims might someday be demonstrated. For, as we have seen, the Rylean analysis of a mental concept as dispositional, officially at least, has no tendency to establish anything about the factual characteristics of the object of the concept that is not already evident in ordinary patterns of use. The Rylean program would have construed the Place/Smart claim, accordingly, as more meaningless than false. Since our ordinary concepts of sensations and images, shown in the language with which we describe and evoke them, give us no clear understanding of *how* sensations and images *could be* brain states, the philosophers' theory according to which they are brain states must inevitably lead, like the Cartesian theory itself, to insuperable absurdities.

In 1956, U. T. Place first offered what would become known as the identity theory: the theory that, as a matter of scientific fact, consciousness is a brain process. Place introduced his theory as a corrective to a dispositionalist behaviorism that fails, Place thought, in the special case of the notions surrounding consciousness and experience:

Modern physicalism... unlike the materialism of the seventeenth and eighteenth centuries, is behavioristic. Consciousness on this view is either a special type of behavior, "sampling" or "running-back-and-forth" behavior as Tolman has it, or a disposition to behave in a certain way, an itch, for example, being a temporary propensity to scratch. In the case of cognitive concepts like "knowing," "believing," "understanding," "remembering," and volitional concepts like "wanting" and "intending," there can be little doubt, I think, that an analysis in terms of dispositions to behave is fundamentally sound. On the other hand, there would seem to be an intractable residue of concepts clustering around the notions of consciousness, experience, sensation, and mental imagery, where some sort of inner process story is unavoidable.[41]

Place goes on to describe the sort of process that sensations and mental images might be: namely, physical brain states. As offered, Place says, the claim of the identity theory is a straightforward empirical hypothesis about the identity of a certain kind of entity, and therefore neither logically true nor necessarily false. Place speculates that "there is nothing that the introspecting subject says about his conscious experiences which is inconsistent with anything the physiologist might want to say about the brain processes which cause him to describe the environment and his consciousness of the environment in the way that he does" (p. 36). If the identity hypothesis is true, every introspective description of consciousness will be explained in the physiologist's terms, adverting to the brain processes that cause the introspector to issue that description.

In 1959, J. J. C. Smart reviewed and updated Place's thesis, attempting to clarify it and to answer certain natural objections left unanswered in the original treatment. Smart, like Place, began by sketching what he took to be the prevalent behaviorist and dispositionalist account of mental states. Specifically, Smart begins by discussing what he supposed to be Wittgenstein's view that the linguistic expressions of sensations, for instance the linguistic expression of pain, are replacements for primitive, "natural" expressions.[42] On this view, the expression of a pain or a visual sensation does not report the existence or properties of some inner item or state. Instead, it is simply the vocalization resulting from a standing behavioral tendency or temptation:

Suppose that I report that I have at this moment a roundish, blurry-edged afterimage which is yellowish towards its edge and is orange towards its center. What is it that I am reporting? One answer to this question might be that I am not reporting anything, that when I say that it looks to me as though there is a roundish yellowy orange patch of light on the wall I am expressing some sort of temptation, the temptation to say that there is a roundish yellowy orange patch on the wall (though I may know that there is not such a patch on the wall). This is perhaps Wittgenstein's view in the *Philosophical Investigations*.... Similarly, when I "report" a pain, I am not really reporting anything (or, if you like, I am reporting in a queer sense of "reporting"), but am doing a sophisticated sort of wince.[43]

Smart admits to finding this analysis in some ways "congenial" to a physicalist perspective. Because it effectively eliminates sensations by treating them as behaviors and behavioral dispositions, it need not give a Cartesian characterization of them as nonphysical. And it provides, at the same time, a natural account of our linguistic *expressions* about sensations, according to which they do not report, but only replace or express, natural tendencies or dispositions. But despite its acceptability to the physicalist, Smart concludes that the behaviorist/dispositionalist account simply will not suffice. For our reports of sensations *do*, after all, report something:

Maybe this is because I have not thought it out sufficiently, but it does seem to me as though, when a person says "I have an after-image," he *is* making a genuine report, and that when he says "I have a pain," he *is* doing more than "replace pain-behavior," and that "this more" is not just to say he is in distress. I am not so sure, however, that to admit this is to admit that there are nonphysical correlates of brain processes. Why should not sensations just be brain processes of a certain sort?[44]

Both Place and Smart recognize that their thesis differs somewhat from the usual sort of thesis that until then had been offered by analytic philosophers. For their thesis is not the *conceptual* thesis that talk of mental states is really talk of internal brain processes, but the *empirical* thesis that at least some mental states – what we talk about when we refer to mental states – *really are* internal brain processes. Smart, in particular, answers several possible objections to the identity theory that have their basis in the observation that the properties ascribed to sensations in normal discourse are not at all like the properties ascribed to brain processes. In each of these cases, he replies that since his claim does not assert any identity of meaning, and since the conceptual logic of two expressions may be quite different, even when both turn out to refer to the same object, the objections have no force against the offered theory.[45]

Nevertheless, it is significant in the larger history of the development of analytic philosophy of mind that the change of subject thereby effected results in a theory of a quite different shape than anything that Ryle, or any "ordinary language" analyst, could have produced. First, by tying the theory to an empirical thesis about the possible identity of the referents of sensation-language, Place and Smart broke the *necessary* connections between the terms of the theory and their referents that a linguistic-level account would provide. For the Place/Smart theory, the identity between brain states and sensations does not characterize the logic of our concepts or of anything else, but simply (as Smart admits) a contingency that, like our other theoretical identifications in science, has no particular logical force or necessity.[46] This involves the philosophical proponent of the claim of identity in a quite different project than previously had been entertained. In particular, the analytic philosopher's traditional task of "conceptual analysis" now cedes to a project involving, at least in part, the investigation of empirical contingencies. Second, the Place/Smart claim about sensations inevitably commits itself to their existence in a way that a linguistic-level theory could avoid. For the claim that our ordinary sensation-talk refers to something that may in fact turn out to be brain processes requires that our ordinary sensation-talk indeed refers, and does so even when employed by speakers quite innocent of neurophysiology.[47] But this demands of the identity theorist an account of the pretheoretic meaning of sensation-terms, and because he has no place for such mentalistic or irreducibly psychical items as might be thought by the plain man (perhaps under the sway of Cartesian metaphysics) to be the referents of sensation-talk, this account will inevitably involve additional theoretical sophistications.[48]

Place and Smart thus misunderstood Ryle as offering an inadequate positive account of the nature of sensation rather than an ontologically innocuous analysis of sensation-language. But this misunderstanding itself arose from a second, deeper misunderstanding. For they construed Ryle as holding a dispositionalist theory of sensations, and they construed this dispositionalism as, at least implicitly, inviting a causal analysis. Just as the properties in virtue of which a glass is brittle are its microphysical, microstructural properties, they took it that a dispositional description of the mind promises to yield some microstructural description of the properties of the brain in virtue of which it has the disposition in question. In a later article critical of Ryle, Smart took the microstructural description of mental states to be an implication of Ryle's "dispositionalist" treatment of them, and wondered at Ryle's refusal to consider such a description:

Ryle's idea that (as far as normal behaviour is concerned) psychology does not go deeper than our ordinary commonsense explanations is evidently connected with the view that if it did give causal explanations these would be para-mechanical ones, based on the Cartesian "two-worlds" myth. It looks as though he cannot see a third possibility beyond either behaviourism or Cartesian dualism. He seems strangely reluctant to allow the identification of "mental" causes with structures or processes in the central nervous system, whether these are described neurophysiologically or functionally. Neglect of this possibility indeed clouds his whole concept of a mental disposition. Thus vanity can naturally be taken as the structure which explains typically vain behaviour. No adequate translation into hypotheticals about behaviour can be produced. Similarly for physical dispositions. We cannot translate "This glass is brittle" by "If a stone hits it then it breaks," because conditions can exist in which the stone hits the glass without breaking it. We can, however, identify brittleness with an inner structure which explains typically brittle behaviour of the glass. This strategy of identifying dispositions with physical structures is as efficacious as Ryle's in disposing of "ghosts" and it avoids obvious difficulties in Ryle's account.[49]

But as we have seen, Ryle was not "strangely," but for reasons internally connected to his entire methodological program, reluctant to identify the objects of dispositional mentalistic concepts with brain structures. The sort of "explanation" that Smart imagines it possible to give of a disposition has no relevance to Ryle's analysis of logical geography, and the multiplicity of application and openness to new contexts of most of the mentalistic terms that Ryle treats as dispositions provides additional reasons to suppose, in many particular cases, that the wanted explanation will not even be possible. For to be a chess player or a speaker of French is to have properties meaningful only against a social and contextual backdrop that has nothing to do with a neurophysiological description.[50] Ryle's reminder that concepts like these have a dispositional logic calls attention to their having the role of characterizing people against backdrops of this sort. An immediate consequence is that they do not, as Smart supposes, stand for inner mental items or structures of a physical, or any other, kind.[51]

V

The early identity theorists misunderstood Ryle's theory, in part, because they missed its central methodological sophistication, namely its conception of the philosopher's task as a kind of negative conceptual analysis that would investigate ordinary language in order to diagnose the failings of specific philosophical theories. This led them to misconstrue Ryle's theory as aiming to show that expressions of mental states reduce to behavioral dispositions, and accordingly to object that the theory provided an implausible account of sensation. But there is a more specific and philosophically revealing source of Place's and Smart's misunderstanding in Ryle's theory as well, one that can be seen in the partial failure of Ryle's analysis of sensation itself.

Recall that Place and Smart *accepted* what they took to be Ryle's dispositionalist theory in the case of most mental concepts; they objected only in the special case of sensation. It is particularly significant, therefore, that Ryle concludes his chapter on "Sensation" by expressing certain large-scale doubts about the analysis offered there, and by suggesting that these doubts trace to a failing in the ordinary speaker's (viz., *not* the philosopher's) understanding of how to use the concept of sensation:

As I said in the Foreword, there is something seriously amiss with the discussions occupying this chapter. I have talked as if we know how to use the concept or concepts of sensation; I have spoken with almost perfunctory regret of our lack of "neat" sensation words; and I have glibly spoken of auditory and visual sensations. But I am sure that none of this will do.[52]

The analyses of the chapter, even though they expose the absurdity of supposing that sensations, or sense-data, are directly or immediately seen or observed, still concede to the official theory that visual and auditory sensations are items that we *have* when visually or auditorially perceiving. But Ryle notices that the sense in which we, perhaps being "conversant with modern physiological, neurological, and psychological hypotheses," treat visual and auditory sensations as items or events caused by other items or events, of a sort whose nature could be clarified by experimentalists, is quite logically distinct from another, "unsophisticated" use of "sensation" that relates primarily to the tactile sense and to verbs such as "feel."[53] In the unsophisticated use, sensations are always locatable in a particular part of the body. For instance, I may have a tingling feeling in my arm or a burning sensation in my foot. As Ryle points out, I will not, by contrast, say that I have feelings or sensations *in my eye* when I am perceiving something visually (unless, perhaps, I am perceiving a painfully bright light). When the unsophisticated use attributes properties to sensations, these properties are straightforwardly dependent on objective properties of external objects and events: a "burning sensation" is not something that burns, but a case of feeling as if something burns.[54]

This clarifies the fact that the unsophisticated use of "sensation" does not give us even the beginnings of an autonomous language for the description of sensations but instead remains semantically dependent on straightforward occurrences of tactile and kinesthetic sensing. Matters are, however, quite different with the special notion of "sense-impressions," invented, Ryle says, to serve a para-mechanical theory of mind. For the notion of "sense-impression," borrowed from the sense in which objects impress wax, was invented to subserve a philosophical theory according to which perception of objects depends on causal connections with them. It was only for the purposes of this theory, Ryle suggests, that the ordinary notion of "sensation" was generalized from its originally tactile and kinesthetic sense to cover all modalities of perception.[55]

But the target of this criticism of the "sophisticated" use of the concept of sensation actually differs importantly from the usual target of Ryle's attacks elsewhere in *The Concept of Mind*. Here, Ryle alleges that the ordinary speaker does not, after all, "know how to use" the concept of sensation. And he flatly admits that the para-mechanical theory embodied in the sophisticated use of the concept has infected – albeit only by "hearsay knowledge of physiological, psychological or epistemological theories" (p. 242) – ordinary practice and understanding. Accordingly, Ryle cannot be construed here as offering what he usually offers: a diagnosis of, and alternative to, the *philosopher's* misconstrual of the logical grammar of language. His analysis of the language of sensation must operate on a different level, and its relation to his usual methodology accordingly becomes problematic. Ryle objects to the "sophisticated" ordinary use of the concept of sensation because it gives comfort to the Cartesian theory and its mechanistic counterpart. But in so doing, he is constrained to recognize that it has a naturalness revealed both in its various scientific contexts and in the unavoidability – even for Ryle – of speaking as if we *do* have auditory and visual sensations. This naturalness betrays the fact that, as Ryle admits, the suggested analysis, according to which we should *never* (strictly speaking) consider that we have auditory or visual sensations, will not quite suffice.

The reason for this insufficiency explains in part the unacceptability to Place and Smart of what they took to be Ryle's dispositionalist account of sensation. Smart's particular reason for suggesting an inadequacy in what he took to be Ryle's behaviorist account was that a report of a sensation is genuinely a *report*: that is, a *description* of some object or state of affairs with genuine properties, and not just a reaction or response. Though Smart happily admits, for instance, that the properties we ordinarily ascribe to the after-image will not be its *real* properties – the *brain process*, after all, is not yellow or red, blurry or sharply defined – still he takes it that our ability to ascribe these properties shows that something genuine is being reported on. Even aside from the determinate representational properties ascribed to sensations in specialized discussions of physiology, Smart's intuition shows particularly clearly what is wrong with Ryle's eliminative attempt to theorize sensation-language as parasitic on observation-language. For ordinary discourse quite often includes (what appear to be) immediate descriptions of the properties of felt sensations (this is particularly clear in the case of pains), descriptions that are not obviously epistemically dependent on descriptions of the properties of external objects. To say that I have a stinging pain may indeed be to say that I have a pain, as if something is stinging me; but I still say that I have something, and I ascribe to it a property.

The main observation that provided the basis for Place's and Smart's replacement of what they took to be Ryle's theory was, therefore, itself a piece of reflection on the grammar of ordinary language. In ordinary usage, the report of a sensation implies the existence of its object; and this fact of ordinary use shows the inaccuracy of any account that takes sensation-reports to be anything other than directly referential and descriptive. Ironically, Ryle's account of sensation-reports as specialized instances of observation language meant that he missed this point, and so was constrained to falsify the grammar of ordinary language in order to justify his eliminative conclusion about sensations. This eliminativist conclusion, together with their confusion about the significance of Ryle's dispositionalism, led Place and Smart to construe Ryle as adhering to the "replacement" view that they thought he shared with Wittgenstein, according to which sensation-reports are just replacements for more primitive kinds of verbal behavior. In a 1962 article about *The Concept of Mind*, in fact, Ryle recognizes and admits the tendency of his account to support this construal:

In my book I half-assimilated avowals to the yawns which manifest the sleepiness of which they are signs or to the oaths by which the angry man vents his rage and shows others how angry he is. As an oath is not a report of anger, so, I was inclined to say, an avowal of depression is not a report of depression but an ejaculation of depression. It is exempt from uncertainty only for the reason that an ejaculation or a complaint cannot be qualified by "perhaps" or "indubitably." But it is clear that this assimilation of avowals to ejaculations or complaints will not do. An avowal may be a reply to a question; it may even be meant to provide a doctor or an oculist with the information that he requires for his diagnosis. If I say "I have a shooting pain in my eyes," while I may be complaining, I am also reporting. Avowals seem then to be like reports, and yet not to be reports of anything discovered or established, to merit being received as incontestable and yet not to issue from any kind of certitude on the part of their authors, or of course of incertitude either.... Here, then, we have another puzzle or trouble-spot in the philosophy of mind. These first-person, present-tense declarations refuse to behave either like ebullitions of mental states or like testable reports of ordinary matters of fact. Above all they refuse to behave like infinitely well-certified reports of matters of solipsistic fact. Their conceptual location is not yet fixed; so the locations of the concepts of consciousness and self-consciousness remain unfixed; so what is conveyed by "I," "you" and "he" remains unfixed. But perhaps we are clearer than we were about the sort of position-fixing that we desiderate.[56]

By 1962, therefore, Ryle felt constrained to recognize the grammatical observation that was the main basis of Place's and Smart's suggestion of the identity theory, and to recognize the inadequacy of his *Concept of Mind* account on this point. By Ryle's own admission, even his sophisticated account of sensation-language as dependent, where meaningful, upon observation-language could not adhere, insofar as it established his eliminativist conclusion, to the grammar of ordinary language that was the only possible basis and resource of his philosophical method. In the perspective of philosophical history, this failing on Ryle's part invites explanation, in a way that sheds further light on the legitimate and illegitimate uses of the method he had developed, in connection with the language of consciousness.

A main theme of early commentaries on Ryle's book was already the objection that he mistook our ordinary commitments for a special philosophical theory, which he then set out to refute on the basis of the logical analysis of ordinary language, whereas the actual ordinariness of the commitments that he attacked make this methodology ill-conceived. For instance, Stuart Hampshire (1950) notes that many European languages systematically, and apparently independently of any philosophical theory, connect words like "ghost" with words concerning the mind. This habit can be traced, for instance, to the Greek *psyche* and *pneuma*, and to the Latin *anima*. Hampshire concludes that Ryle's method is misdefined:

> Professor Ryle throughout represents philosophers as corrupting the literal innocence of common sense speech with alien metaphors. In this he not only greatly exaggerates the influence of philosophers, and particularly of Descartes, on the forms of common speech, but (more seriously) neglects the fact, or rather the necessity, that the forms of common speech and its modes of description should be permeated with such metaphors, most of which can ultimately be traced back to underlying myths and imaginative pictures.[57]

Along somewhat similar lines, John Wisdom (1950) objects to Ryle's "insufficient explanation of the purpose of his demonstration of the omnipresence in our minds of the model of the hidden stream, his insufficient explanation of the purpose and merits of that model, and the consequent insufficiency of his explanation of the defects of that model" (p. 51). Wisdom emphasizes the ordinary-language role of the temptations that lead us to think, and talk, of mental states as private:

> My point is that, though the sources of solipsism are also sources of doubt about the minds of others, there is also a source of this doubt other than those sources of it which also lead to solipsism. And this source lies in the facts covered by the words "The soul is visible only to one." . . . What are these facts? They are the facts which lead people to say that a person has a way of knowing how he feels which no one else has, has a right to say what he does about how he feels which no one else has ever had or ever will.[58]

If the philosophical theory stems in part from nonphilosophical temptations, both Hampshire and Wisdom conclude, the diagnosis of the philosophical theory will not wholly address these temptations. If there is an analysis, or an analytic practice, that can begin to dislodge the temptations themselves, it will function on the level of quite ordinary propositions and situations, and without alleging that these propositions owe their attractiveness to a bad philosophical theory. Wisdom in fact begins such an analysis, an analysis of the sorts of reasons for which, and contexts in which, we are tempted to say that "The soul is visible only to one." Hampshire's and Wisdom's general point is that Ryle's analyses rely on ordinary language to combat the philosophical theorizing sometimes involved in it, with prejudice to the correctness of ordinary language, whereas a more methodologically sound style of analysis would not assume that the temptations that lead to philosophical theorizing of an objectionable kind are not already fully present in ordinary language itself.

Hampshire's and Wisdom's complaints challenge Ryle's presupposition of a clear and distinct line between ordinary and philosophical reasoning, and in so doing they problematize his ability to draw substantial philosophical conclusions, even of an eliminative kind, from the grammar of ordinary language itself. According to the objection, Ryle's tendency to portray his analysis as bearing decisively and univocally against philosophical theories such as the Cartesian one elides his sensitivity to just the sort of commitment of ordinary language that Place and Smart recognized: a commitment to the reality of sensations underlying our reporting and description of them. That this commitment can be interpreted as providing partial support, *within* the context of substantial philosophical theorizing, for a Cartesian theory of mind (or, indeed, as Place and Smart would show, for a physicalist one) should not have led Ryle to falsify the grammar of ordinary language by denying its commitment to sensations. Had he adhered more consistently to the method that he himself had defined, Ryle would have had to recognize this commitment of our ordinary language of consciousness, along with others evident in its use, as defining a concept of sensation that is complex and in many ways philosophically ambiguous, one providing definitive resistance *but also* (at least occasionally) partial support to the Cartesian theory. The further analysis of the ordinary concept of sensation would elaborate these complicated and contradictory implications, focusing in each case on the *specific* use of the language of consciousness in the context of a *specific* situation. Such elaboration can defeat general theories of consciousness by showing how they falsify the grammar of ordinary language in these specific cases, but it cannot hope (as Ryle himself most often understood) to establish any general philosophical conclusion, even the negative one that sensations do no* in fact exist. His taking himself to be entitled to this conclusion provided whatever warrant there was for Place and Smart to judge Ryle's theory inadequate, and to insist upon the grammatical observation upon which they based their articulation of the Identity Theory.

Of course, that Place and Smart, in this case, improved upon Ryle's analysis by accommodating an important grammatical observation – that of the referentiality of sensation-reports – did not prevent them from immediately misconstruing the significance of this observation in their construction of a positive theory of mind around it. It is one thing to recognize that ordinary sensation-reports typically, and as a matter of grammar, imply the existence of their objects, and quite another to propose, as Place and Smart immediately did, a specific theory of the nature of these objects that goes far beyond the properties ordinarily ascribed to them in discourse. That the bare grammatical observation of the referentiality of sensation-reports could appear to provide decisive support for the Identity Theory's assertion of contingent psychophysical identity was itself just a consequence of Place and Smart's own lack of sensitivity to the methodological status of the grammatical datum that they introduced. Seeing this datum as a contribution to the total description of the objective world by scientific theory, rather than as the grammatical observation that it was, they construed it as providing support for the identification of mental states with physical brain states in the context of a complete physicalist description of the world. The possibility of such a complete description was itself not questioned, and neither was the structuralist picture of language that provided the historical basis for its interpretation of the significance of grammatical investigation.

VI

As we have seen, Place and Smart misunderstood Ryle as advancing a positive, dispositionalist, eliminative theory of sensation-language, and this misunderstanding was the immediate basis for their own advancement of the Identity Theory. But with Ryle's method clearly in view, we can see that the grounds of the Place/Smart misunderstanding of it were not completely alien to Ryle's own understanding of its implications. Ryle's own positive characterization of sensation-language as elliptical for, and reducible to. special applications of the ordinary language of observation provided sufficient ground for construing his theory of sensation (albeit by a route more circuitous than Place and Smart perceived) as a reductive and eliminative one, amounting to the claim that talk of sensations is reducible without remainder to behaviors or dispositions to behave. We have seen that this reductive and eliminative claim could not have resulted from a consistent application of Ryle's real linguistic method, confined as it was to the identification of category mistakes in official philosophical doctrines, including the Cartesian theory. That Ryle in fact exceeded the warrant of his own method in the case of sensation is witnessed both by his own doubts about his theory of its concepts and by his unusual animadversions against the *ordinary*, and not just the Cartesian's *philosophical*, uses of these concepts. Even if it were right to suppose, as Ryle suggested, that in the case of the concepts of sensation, ordinary language had come under the illicit influence of the Cartesian theory, these animadversions could not have been justified by the Rylean practice of analysis. For as we have seen, this practice of analysis has no source of evidence, no ground of insight, other than reflection on the ordinary uses of ordinary concepts. Since its definitive resource was no positive source of theoretical insight, but rather the detection of the absurdity of philosophical claims *by comparison to* ordinary grammar, Ryle accordingly did not provide – nor could he have, consistent with his own method – any methodological ground for construing the commitments of our ordinary linguistic practice as false, deviant, or misconceived in a comprehensive or wholesale way.

Even so, to analyze the ordinary commitments of our language in terms of the linguistic functioning of the concepts that they support is not necessarily to construe these commitments as fully consistent, clear, or mutually reconcilable. The conceptual analysis of ordinary language, even if limited to the investigation and clarification, in particular cases, of the claims of our practice, provides ample and deep ground for insight into the nature and meaning of our language of consciousness. And it is in this respect that we can see most clearly, in retrospect, how to prize the legitimate use of Ryle's method apart from the additional warrant that he sometimes claimed for it, and that led most directly to the early identity theorists' misunderstanding of it. Most often, Ryle's analysis of sensation points out grammatical connections, unimpeachable on the level of ordinary use, that show that the language of sensation has neither the distinctive epistemological status nor the primacy and autonomy that the sense-datum theorist characteristically claims for it. Thus, for instance, the observation that many instances of sensation-reporting are importantly conceptually similar to, and often restateable in terms of, special applications of observation-language, suffices by itself to show that the sense-datum theorist's claim to base the epistemology of observation entirely on a supposedly prior and autonomous stratum of sensation is a nonstarter. On the other hand, though, to move from this observation about practice to the positive claim that sensation-language is, in each case and without remainder, *definable in terms of,* or *eliminable in favor of,* observation-language is to move decisively beyond the ambit of ordinary-language reflection and into the realm of positive philosophical theory. From this general claim of reducibility, it is but a short step to the positive description of the language of sensation itself as reducible, saving the truth of everything that it ordinarily says, to some set of behaviors or dispositions to behave. And it is only on the basis of *this* misunderstanding, as we have seen, that Place and Smart were able to offer the Identity Theory as a corrective to Ryle's account.

The ultimate roots of Ryle's tendency occasionally to overstep the warrant of his method may perhaps be located in the sometimes ambiguous suggestions of his methodological doctrine of categories itself. We have seen that, following out the implications of the practice of analysis developed by Wittgenstein, Moore, and others, Ryle developed the doctrine of "category mistakes" as a way of characterizing the kind of systematic infelicity in the description of the logical place of our concepts to which philosophical theories unconstrained by linguistic reflection are prone. The point of identifying a "category mistake" is always to mark such an infelicity by contrasting the aberrant locutions and descriptions suggested by a philosophical theory with the ordinary use of the same concepts. The characteristic sign of the category mistake is absurdity, perspicuous from the perspective of ordinary language, and it requires nothing more for its proof than the identification of such absurdities. But given the description of philosophical errors of logical geography as mislocations of the categories of particular concepts, it can easily seem as if the practice of analysis depends on, or tends to articulate, a *general* theory or description of the categorical *structure* of the language as a whole. The traditional application of doctrines of categories, whether in an ontological mode or a linguistic one, is after all to produce a comprehensive picture of the overall nature of things or words, and Ryle's own applications of the notion of categories do not always completely avoid the suggestion that he has such a picture in view.

It is true that, as we have seen, Ryle's own explicit statements about categories moved from the substantialist conception of "Systematically Misleading Expressions," rooted in the notion of "logical form" that he drew from the early Wittgenstein, to the much less substantialist usage of *The Concept of Mind*. Here, though Ryle describes category mistakes as misattributions of the logical category of a term, he does not generally use the notion of "category mistakes" in such a way as to suggest that, when one is detected, it makes sense to say in general terms *which* category the term belongs to or has been misattributed to. Still, talk of rectifying the logical geography of concepts can easily suggest, what is not licensed by Ryle's method itself, that he pictures the philosophical analyst as having access to a comprehensive overall picture of this geography, perspicuous in terms of an overall, systematic characterization of the norms of practice or rules of use definitive of the language. To take the suggestion is to interpret the method of analysis as moving beyond the introduction of specific grammatical reminders, bearing in specific ways against positive philosophical theories, to show or describe the overall grammatical or conceptual structure of language. And it is within the scope of such a suggestion that any claim to the effect that our sensation-language *really is* observation-language, or is reducible to behaviors or dispositions to behave, must arise. For only a general picture of the logical structure of language as a whole could license this claim, insofar as it falsifies rather than respects the grammar of ordinary language. To point out the error of a philosophical theory's construal of the logical status of a particular kind of term, evident in the absurdity of the statements it makes using that term, is to apply Ryle's method consistently. But to offer, on the supposed basis of this method, a characterization of what a particular region of language *really* means or represents, over against what it appears to

mean or represent ordinarily, is to go essentially beyond this method –
though in ways that Ryle himself did not always explicitly disclaim – to
a general picture of the overall structure of language. The linguistic
method of detecting category mistakes in no way provides or supports
such a picture, nor does it ever license any positive determination
that the real or genuine meaning of a specific region of language is
different from what ordinary language supposes. It was only Ryle's occasional temptation to move beyond the warrant of his own method
to a positive, structuralist conception of language and of the form of
reflective insight into it that led him to this determination in the case
of sensation.

In any case, it was only on the basis of their own underlying structuralist picture of explanation that Place and Smart could themselves
offer the Identity Theory as a corrective. The basis they cited for their
own antibehaviorist theory of the mind – that sensation-language has
a genuine *reporting* status – is itself, on its own terms, simply a "grammatical" or linguistic remark about the use of certain terms in the
language. To say this much, and from this perspective, is simply to remind us of the ordinary locutions that describe such things as pains,
after-images, and tickles, and to show from the perspective of ordinary
use the absurdity of any philosophical theory – Ryle's included, if it in
fact did so – that denies the reality of such things. Within the ambit
of Place and Smart's physicalist structuralism, however, this linguistic
reminder appears to necessitate a positive theoretical description of
the *nature* of the reference of sensation-terms – a reference that, given
antecedent physicalism, can now only seem to be physical brain states.
Thus was the identity theory born as a positive theoretical claim about
the reference of a particular area of ordinary language.

Insofar as it is discussed at all in contemporary contexts, both the
downfall of Ryle's theory and its replacement by the Identity Theory
are usually ascribed to the failure of a linguistic method. But if the
suggestion of the current analysis is correct, Ryle failed, not by applying a linguistic method insufficient for explaining the mind, but
rather by failing to apply his linguistic method consistently enough.
Had he stuck with the conceptual analysis and clarification of particular ordinary concepts and not succumbed, even if only occasionally, to the temptation to characterize the results of this analysis in
terms of a more general structuralist picture of language overall, he

would never have involved himself in the contentious denials of the referentiality of sensation-language that Place and Smart would seize upon as offering an occasion for their own, more thoroughly structuralist theory. In historical retrospect, however, it is possible to distinguish the legitimate use of Ryle's linguistic method to produce insight into the meaning of our language of experience from the structuralist implications that he was sometimes tempted to draw from it, and that provided the occasion for Place and Smart's decisive misunderstanding. Drawing this distinction in the specific context of Ryle's theory points the way, in turn, to a more comprehensive understanding of the way in which the distinctively linguistic methods characteristic of the analytic tradition can operate to produce insight into our language of experience, even outside the structuralist pictures of explanation that have so often gone along with them.

In the last two chapters, we have seen how the language of consciousness posed unique and historically decisive problems for the structuralist analytic project of logical positivism. This project saw itself as requiring, for the possibility of its analytic methodology, a general conception of meaning as logical structure. Given this conception, the sentences, such as protocol sentences, that directly report experience could only seem to be outside the system of empirical meaning they were called upon to authorize. But this structuralist preconception did not entirely prevent the practice of logical analysis itself from producing, at least occasionally, genuine insights into the meaning of sentences reporting immediate experience. Such insights were captured, for instance, by the logical positivists' sense of these sentences as providing an ultimate source of the verification of empirical claims, as well as by Schlick's identification of certain of them as expressing the necessity of our particular form of experience for us. These positive insights do not, admittedly, go beyond the identification of features of our ordinary use of the concepts of experience, recognizable at the level of ordinary practice; but they do exhibit the way in which the method of linguistic analysis can be applied positively in order to render features of our language of experience without employing the support, or encountering the problems, of a general structuralist *picture* of language overall. Ryle's project, in its orientation toward ordinary language, amounts to a more self-conscious and sustained application of the same method of insight, and it encounters distinctive difficulties with the language of experience only when it imposes upon this method a structuralist picture.

Ryle's linguistic method, the practice of conceptual analysis that produces insight into the meaning of our mental concepts by exposing the category mistakes of philosophical theories, nevertheless produces no theory of its own. Confined to its proper application, it can do no more than point to logical features of the use of our concepts that are themselves wholly recognizable from within this use. And this lack of theoretical import might seem to suggest a decisive objection against the project, even if it makes for the possibility of pursuing the method outside the structuralist picture of language that renders consciousness especially problematic. For do we not want our philosophical methods to produce an understanding of the phenomena they consider that goes beyond our ordinary, commonsense understanding of them? And do we not, in the specific case of the explanation of consciousness, want an account that responds to a particular kind of question, quite possibly unanswerable from the perspective of common sense: the question of *how* consciousness can be physical? But as we have seen, the question *itself* imports a substantial conception of the nature of explanation – namely, the structuralist one that takes a phenomenon to be explained only if it can be located within a structure of relations. This conception provides the question with whatever determinate content it has, specifying, through the structuralist explanatory pattern of physicalism, the desired intelligibility of consciousness as an explanation of its physical nature. And it is not obvious – particularly in view of the consistent failure of the structuralist picture to accommodate consciousness – that *this* particular kind of intelligibility is the sort that we need, or even ought to, expect.

If the suggestion of this chapter is right, Ryle's linguistic method, in its legitimate nonstructuralist use, effectively produces *another* kind of insight into the nature of consciousness: a kind of insight that operates consistently by appealing to what we ordinarily say, but that also moves beyond what we ordinarily (or anyway, commonsensically) *understand* about what we say about consciousness. It does so by showing us similarities and differences, unnoticed points of contact and points of tension, in our own concepts – not indeed in order to produce a comprehensive, schematic total picture of them, but rather in order to produce the perspicuity that allows us, faced with philosophical problems or theories, to find our way about with them. Should this be thought a task unworthy of philosophy, it ought to be asked what makes the structuralist theoretical project any more dignified. And should it be asked what recommends Ryle's alternative method, it ought to be asked in response what other form of method a consistent nonstructuralist investigation into consciousness might possibly take. Ryle's "ordinary language" philosophy is among the last in the history of the analytic tradition to consistently recognize, and to use as its chief methodological asset, its own linguistic character and form. But the accounts and projects that followed Ryle's, I argue in the next two chapters, retained this linguistic character and basis even in their growing ignorance and disavowal of it. In the self-reflexive appeal of Ryle's linguistic method, then, we can see a detailed and suggestive example of the sort of understanding that the analysis of language can produce. This, in turn, offers a model that might be thought to capture what is really characteristic and decisive about the analytic tradition's linguistic turn, even against its constant tendency to misunderstand itself in structuralist terms.

The structuralist assumptions of Place and Smart, both in interpreting Ryle's remarks on sensation as they did and in offering their own empirical theory as a replacement, have left their mark, in multiple ways, on the subsequent history of analytic philosophy of mind and on contemporary discussion of the problem of explaining consciousness. From the perspective of Place's and Smart's physicalism, the grammatical observation that sensation-language is reporting language could only seem to be legitimated by an account of sensation-language as in fact *caused by* real happenings, intelligible in physical terms. The ultimate and genuine referents of the language of experience could only be, given antecedent physicalism, physical brain states of one or another kind, comprehensible to structuralist explanation. The Place/Smart suggestion of an *empirical*, rather than a purely conceptual or logical, subject matter for the philosophy of mind thus traded on a picture of the progress of science as a process of increasing explanation and theoretical unity through increasing structuralization that had already been operative in Carnap's own explanatory physicalism. The root of both projects was the structuralist physicalism they shared. If Place and Smart recognized more fully the ultimately empirical nature of the investigative project licensed by structuralist physicalism, they also perceived less clearly its underlying linguistic basis. Physicalism subsequently appeared to be an essentially ontological or metaphysical doctrine. But the deepest source of evidence for its positive claims, and the most determinative factor in its subsequent development, remains the evidence of the language of experience.

Like Carnap and Schlick's structuralism before it, the physicalism of Place and Smart attempted to integrate consciousness within the structure of the world, at the same moment denying it any special ontological or semantic status. It counted on the future progress of empirical science to bridge the theoretical gap between the apparent commitments of our ordinary language and the real place of consciousness in the natural order. But the underlying source of its plausibility, as against Ryle's theory, was not an empirical claim or any evidence for one, but rather a grammatical remark about the logical status of our language of experience: the recognition that sensation-reports are genuinely reports. Thus was the evidence of language appropriated for the motivation of an explanatory project ultimately arising from the investigation of language, but unclear in itself about its own pragmatic and linguistic dispensation. At the same time, the possibility, exhibited by Ryle's method, of a nonstructuralist use of linguistic analysis and reflection to render the language of consciousness intelligible was forgotten and largely abandoned under the overwhelming force of the strengthening claims of structuralism. From this point forward within analytic philosophy of mind, to make consciousness intelligible would be to make it intelligible structurally, to locate it within the total causal network of nature or the semantic web of behaviorist or functionalist analysis. At each stage of the subsequent dialectic, the language of consciousness would resist this structuralization, speaking its claim to be understood, in each case, from a problematic position *outside* any total pattern of the relation of elements or totality of structure, even when this totality seemed to be the objective world itself: a position that structuralization, in each of its subsequent theoretical moments, would again strive to appropriate, or dissimulate.

5

Functionalism and Logical Analysis

Thirty-five years after its initial development, the *functionalist* theory of mind today remains the most popular general position on consciousness among analytic philosophers and scientists alike. The functionalist theory has remained popular, in large part, because it seems to integrate a plausible empirical research program for the investigation of the mind with a wholly physicalist or materialist ontological outlook. But although it is often presented as a metaphysical or empirical position on the nature of the mind, philosophical history shows that functionalism is in fact the latest and most consistent application of an essentially semantic structuralism to the theory of mind. Both in its underlying method and in its fund of decisive arguments, functionalism makes detailed and essential use of reflection on, and reasoning about, the logical and semantic form of language about immediate experience and states of consciousness. Like other theories before it, though, it interprets this reasoning about the language of consciousness as part of an overall theory of mind that *explains* consciousness by locating it within a total pattern of logical and causal relations.

Viewed in the perspective of philosophical history, the problem of explaining consciousness, as it is currently discussed, arises primarily from the recurrent resistance of consciousness to structuralist programs of explanation. Philosophical history shows the origin of the functionalist theory of mind in a structuralist program of semantic analysis and thereby shows its continuity with the older forms of structuralist explanation we have explored in earlier chapters. This identification, at the same time, helps to define a new perspective from which to understand the contemporary problem of explaining consciousness. Because of the prevalence of functionalist forms of explanation, this problem is today most often stated as the problem of the *resistance* of consciousness to functionalist explanation. Whatever the successes of functionalism in theorizing the other phenomena of behavior or intentionality, it is often suggested, functionalism cannot account for the presence of qualia, raw feels, or phenomenal states. As we saw in the first chapter, further specification of the complaint often cites the *structural* nature of functionalist explanation and the seeming intrinsic or nonstructural character of consciousness. But exposing the historical reason for the formulation and prevalence of functionalism also shows the complaint to be but the most recent version of a historically recurrent one: that consciousness consistently resists otherwise successful forms of explanation in terms of logical or linguistic structure. Showing the continuity of functionalism with these basically linguistic forms of explanation has the effect of exposing the depth and decisiveness of functionalism's own appeal to the language of consciousness, as well as the profound ambiguity of this appeal within the scope of structuralism.

When Place and Smart suggested the Identity Theory of mind in the early 1950s, they presupposed in detail the physicalist ontology that had originally been suggested, in a semantic mode, by Neurath and had more recently been defended, in a less obviously semantic register, by philosophers of science such as Hempel, Putnam, and Oppenheim. Its physicalism was in fact the largest recommendation of the Identity Theory for Place and Smart, and its amenability both to a physicalist worldview and to empirical projects of inquiry probably accounted for its quick and widespread popularity among analytic philosophers. This popularity was further aided, as we saw in the last chapter, by a misinterpretation (sometimes aided by Ryle himself) of Ryle's program of analysis as suggesting a physicalist, reductive behaviorism, akin to the logical behaviorism that Carnap and Hempel had in fact earlier suggested on physicalist grounds. Place and Smart had, indeed, offered their Identity Theory more as a corrective to logical behaviorism than as a replacement for it, and as their initial articles show, there was certainly no feeling of any great methodological tension between the ontological outlook of logical behaviorism, as they understood it, and that of their own theory.

But philosophers soon began to recognize that there were genuine and unresolved tensions, both methodological and thematic, between the two strands of structuralism represented by the Identity Theory and logical behaviorism. Place's and Smart's empirical claim of identity, to be established conclusively by future science, could not plausibly offer itself (as the claims of a dispositionalist logical behaviorism still could) as an instance of the analysis of ordinary language, at least as it is currently spoken; but if the hypothesis was to be taken as coherent at all, it had to be understood as at least potentially meaningful, given the expected progress of future empirical investigation. These tensions led philosophers, extending a suggestion already made by Smart, to undertake a detailed new consideration of the logic of claims of identity in empirical science, especially as these claims operate diachronically in the development of new theories and in the reduction of theories to one another. The ultimate outcome of this consideration was the hybrid theory we know as functionalism, and the rudiments and remnants of the inquiry into the semantics of scientific theory that it suggested still figure prominently in contemporary discussions about the "reducibility" of consciousness. But the historical analysis exposes both the more general structuralist form of the functionalist theory and its detailed dependence on linguistic and semantic methods of reflection and analysis. In so doing, it offers the hope of a new approach to the language of consciousness that preserves the positive insights of functionalism about this language while nevertheless avoiding the problem of consciousness that arises from resistance to the structuralist assumptions that have organized the functionalist theory.

I

In the last chapter, we saw that the Identity Theory, as Place and Smart articulated it, could avoid what they took to be the logical behaviorist's implausible implication that there really are no such things as sensations, feelings, pains, and inclinations, while still avoiding any commitment to irreducibly mental or nonphysical items. The methodological key to this possibility was that the claimed identity of mental states with brain states could not be a straightforward *analytic* identity.[1] Thus defined, the identity theory does not imply that statements about sensations are translatable into statements about brain processes, or that the logic of sensation-statements is in any sense the same as the logic of descriptions of brain processes.[2] Instead, as a *synthetic* claim of identity, Smart suggested, the identity thesis is evidentially and semantically akin to other theoretical identifications between the objects of semantically distinct terms in the empirical sciences. For instance, in claiming that lightning is electric discharge, we do not claim that "lightning" *means* the same as "electric discharge." We can even imagine, Smart points out, coming to abandon the electrical theory of lightning according to which the two are identical. Nevertheless, assuming the truth of the theory, there is but one phenomenon that we can call "lightning" or "electric discharge" indifferently.

Smart's treatment of the identity thesis as synthetic allowed him to answer a number of traditional objections to theories asserting the identity of mental and physical states as an *analytic* claim. Given the syntheticity of the identity thesis, for instance, the observation that a person may know a great deal about mental states without knowing anything about neurology or brain states has no force against the theoretical identification of the two. The neurophysiologically naïve ordinary speaker and the trained scientist simply speak about the same thing using different concepts, or under different modes of presentation.[3] Similarly, the ordinary speaker does not ascribe spatial or physical properties to the sensations that he reports having. But this does not prevent his reports and descriptions from referring to brain processes that do in fact have such properties.[4] Finally, we can admittedly *imagine* that someone might have sensations and pains without having any particular brain states (or even any brain states at all), but this simply shows again that the terms "sensation" and "brain state" do not have the same meaning.[5] As in the case of the identity of lightning and electric discharge, the conceivability of the situation in which the identity comes apart does nothing to establish that the identity does not, in fact, obtain. In all three cases, Smart appeals to the possibility of referring to one and the same process using different concepts in order to account for the prima facie counterintuitiveness of the identity thesis. As long as the identity claim is understood as a synthetic one, we can easily accept that its assertion may initially seem counterintuitive from the standpoint of purely philosophical or conceptual evidence, and that no amount of "meaning analysis" alone will suffice to make it plausible. As in the case of other synthetic identities, whatever plausibility it gains will derive from the progress of empirical investigation within the special fields of science concerned with the objects identified.

Following Smart's suggestion, philosophers of mind became newly concerned with the results and practices of empirical inquiry, and it became less and less apparent that any substantial results in the philosophy of mind could come from a priori conceptual or linguistic analysis alone. At the same time, though, Smart's argument left open a great number of properly philosophical questions and objections concerning the meaning of his thesis itself. In particular, despite its utility in answering traditional objections to materialist theories of mind, the innovation of treating the identity thesis as synthetic raised a host of historically decisive questions about the structure of scientific innovation and, in particular, about the kind of changes likely, or at least foreseeable, to occur in our ordinary psychological language under the pressure of new scientific results. In answering these questions, philosophers sought to clarify the proper relationship of philosophical or conceptual investigation of the logical structure of our ordinary psychological descriptions and explanations to the empirical results of the specialized sciences of neurophysiology and cognitive psychology. This new kind of methodological self-concern would lead, in turn, to the first formulations of the hybrid doctrine, part empirically minded identity theory and part conceptually minded meaning analysis, known as functionalism.

As Smart left it, the synthetic identity thesis stood open to objections on at least three general fronts. First, as Max Black objected, it was not at all clear that the thesis is even meaningful.[6] Even the synthetic claim that mental states could be (for all we know) brain states must be rejected if that claim is not only implausible or unproven but *meaningless.* And there is reason, Black suggested, to think that this is so, insofar as we have, at least at present, *no idea at all* how mental states *could* be brain states. A sentence like "Pain is identical with the stimulation of C-fibres" is, Black claimed, so unusual as to have no use in any normal context. Given this, Black argued, any sentence asserting the general identity of the two kinds of states or the particular identity of one kind of mental state with one kind of brain state must be considered so linguistically deviant as to have no clear meaning; the philosopher who asserts psychophysical identity is giving words new meanings, rather than describing an actual or possible discovery.

Second, even if one considered the synthetic identity thesis meaningful, one might question the extent of its theoretical utility. As Brandt and Kim objected in 1967, it is unclear how the synthetic identity thesis represents any explanatory improvement over the thesis of psychophysical *parallelism*, according to which nonphysical mental states are correlated one-to-one with physical states.[7] Even if mental states are identified with physical states, Kim and Brandt pointed out, mental states are still not ontologically eliminated; they are simply redescribed. (It was, after all, part of the original motivation of Smart's claim to show that certain mentalistic language *really does refer* to the objects that it seems to.) And because identity is symmetrical, even if the synthetic identity thesis allows the "reduction" of mental states to physical states, it just as easily allows the opposite "reduction" of physical states to mental states.[8] For all of these reasons, Kim and Brandt objected, it is not clear in what way the identification of mental states with physical states could be required by, or even particularly helpful to, the empirical investigation of the nature of the mind.

Finally, a third source of possible objections to Smart's view was its *underspecification*. As it stood, the identity thesis asserted the identity of mental states with brain states, but it gave no specific characterization of *which* brain states might be identical to mental states, or even of what kind of consideration would count as establishing particular identities. Smart provided no reason to believe that semantically relevant types of mental states (as defined, say, in ordinary discourse, or in descriptive psychology) would, or even should, correlate with neurophysiologically perspicuous types of brain states. But if no such correlations were available, the identity thesis would fail to define any realistic research program beyond a general physicalism with no particular empirical consequences. More generally, Smart's formulation of the identity thesis omitted any account of the relationship between the ordinary logic of psychological description and explanation – the logical structure of psychological terms, their roles in the prediction and explanation of behavior, and the criteria on the basis of which they are normally ascribed and deployed – and the logical structure of the neurophysiological description of physical states of the brain. Such an account would be needed in order for the identity theory to stand any chance of empirically earning the particular identities that would justify its general claim, but such an account would also require all of the resources of a thoroughgoing conceptual investigation of the logical structure of psychology. Justifiably, philosophers wanted to know not only *that* mental states could be physical states, but also *how* they could be and *what* it would tell us if they were.

II

With many of these concerns in mind, Hilary Putnam began in 1957 to articulate a new way of looking at the relationship between psychological and physical terms, as this relationship might develop diachronically under the influence of the growth of empirical discovery. Aided in part by related developments such as Quine's repudiation of the analytic/synthetic distinction, Putnam's investigation of the diachronic meaning of theoretical terms and the implications of theoretical identifications would define an influential program of semantic analysis in its own right, playing a role in such innovations as Kripke's modal semantics, the increased attention to "direct reference" in the philosophy of language, "externalism" in the philosophy of intentionality, and the predictive account of the relationship of mentalistic terms to future neurophysiological descriptions that came to be known as "eliminative materialism." But Putnam's goal in his first paper on the mind-body relationship, "Psychological Concepts, Explication, and Ordinary Language," was simply to defend the identity theory against some natural objections traditionally made against it from the standpoint of meaning analysis. In particular, Putnam sought to show how a term such as "the sensation blue" could *refer* to a physical state, even if it does not *mean* anything like a physical state. Like Smart, Putnam treated the identity thesis as a synthetic one and used this to motivate the thought that a mental and a neurophysiological term might refer, using different concepts or under distinct modes of presentation, to one and the same item. But by considering the conditions under which theoretical identifications such as the one asserted by the identity thesis become possible at all, Putnam also could suggest a more complete account of the semantic reason for this situation. The behavioral and semantic evidence on which we base our ordinary ascriptions of mental states and discussions of psychology might play a role, Putnam suggested, akin to that of the *symptoms* of a disease whose underlying nature is, as yet, unclear. The symptoms are neither logically identical to, nor necessarily concomitant with, the disease. Still, before we understand the nature of the disease, its symptoms function as more or less reliable *indicators* on the basis of which we can determine its presence:

> By way of comparison, let us consider the case of polio. Let us say that we are pretty sure that polio is caused by a virus, but we cannot say at present which particular virus. Then it makes sense to say that by polio we now mean the disease caused by a certain unspecified virus, and not the simultaneous presence of a certain group of symptoms. Even if a person has all the symptoms of polio, if it later turns out that he does not have the virus which is normally the cause of those symptoms, we should say that we had been mistaken in thinking he had polio.[9]

As in the case of polio, Putnam suggested, even though we do not yet know which underlying physical states are identical to particular mental states, we might now be using more or less reliable indicators of these physical states – in particular, behaviors and linguistic expressions – to support our reference to them.[10] Our ordinary terms of psychological description, deployed on the basis of these indicators, would then refer to the underlying physical states, even if we do not yet know which states these are. As theoretical progress began to demonstrate the truth of the identity thesis, we would gradually replace our current partial definitions of psychological terms, by means of the indicators, with full definitions referring to the physical states they designate. But retrospectively, we would still treat our original indicator-based descriptions as having referred to the very underlying states that we would now be able to display. If descriptions of sensations and other mental states are indeed analogous in this way to descriptions of diseases, therefore, the analogy gives the identity theorist a principled reason to believe that they may indeed, even now, refer to yet-unknown physical states, even if we will not be in a position to see *which* states these are for some time to come.

As Putnam realized, the structure of his suggestion for the semantics of mental-state terms also gives the identity theorist a new and compelling argument against the logical behaviorist doctrine that propositions describing mental states reduce to propositions describing behavior and behavioral dispositions.[11] For the logical behaviorist, so construed, must claim that it is *conceptually* or *logically* impossible that a person should manifest the symptoms and characteristic behaviors of being angry, and pass all behavioral tests for being angry, yet still not be angry. For the thoroughgoing logical behaviorist (as Putnam construed him), because to be angry *just is* to manifest the behavioral symptoms of anger, there is simply no possibility that such a person might, despite all possible behavioral evidence, really not be angry. By contrast, Putnam argued, the identity theorist need not deny the coherent-enough possibility of a person's being in a particular mental state despite all behavioral indications to the contrary. Just as someone might exhibit many or all of the characteristic symptoms of polio without actually having the disease, a person's behavior has, on Putnam's view, no necessary or logical link to the underlying mental state or states that cause it. Behavior and tendencies and dispositions to behave are at best good, but defeasible, indicators of the presence of the underlying state. Given the applicability of Putnam's analogy, the identity theorist could therefore avoid the logical behaviorist's implausibly strong identification of mental states with behavioral effects while nevertheless allowing for the real strength of the *causal* connections that normally exist between the two.

In the 1960 article "Minds and Machines," Putnam further develops this account of the diachronic change in reference of psychological terms, tying it to a more explicit consideration of the success conditions for the identification of terms within a theory and portentously suggesting, for the first time, an analogy between the logic of human psychological descriptions and the abstract computational or functional description of a computational machine. As in the earlier article, Putnam argues that the theoretical identity between mental states and brain states could become more and more plausible with the future progress of empirical investigation.[12] As theory develops over time, what began as mere correlations between mental states and physical states might become identities. But having considered in more detail the nature of diachronic theory change, Putnam is now more willing to admit that this development could importantly change the way in which scientists describe mental states:

I do not deny that today any newly-discovered "correlation" of the form: "One is in mental state ψ if, and only if, one is in brain state ϕ" would at first be a mere correlation, a pure "empirical generalization." But I maintain that the interesting case is the case that would arise if we had a worked out and theoretically elaborated system of such "correlations." In such a case, scientific talk would be very different. Scientists would begin to say: "It is impossible in principle to be in mental state ψ without being in brain state ϕ."[13]

Such an identity, Putnam goes on to argue, could attain the status of a conceptual necessity; scientists might even come to find its denial inconceivable.[14] Under these conditions, whatever deviance had originally characterized an ordinary-language sentence asserting the identity of a particular mental state with a particular brain state would vanish, and such assertions could become a legitimate and meaningful part of scientific discourse. Essential to Putnam's argument for this position is the observation that, as scientific theories develop, terms are often used in new ways, not because they change their meanings, but because they take on new uses in the new contexts revealed by new pieces of theory. This becomes particular clear in cases of *theoretical identification*. For instance, the claim that "Water is H_2O," advanced on the basis of empirical results in chemistry, does not so much change the meanings of the terms "water" and "H_2O" as give them a new cluster of theoretically advantageous uses.[15] If mind-brain identity is akin to water-H_2O identity, then the new use according to which identity statements become conceptual necessities, similarly, need not represent a change of meaning so much as an extension of old meanings to new uses on the basis of new empirical discoveries.

In this way, Putnam's attention to the way in which empirical discovery can change the uses of scientific terms gave him a ready and compelling answer to Black's "incoherence" objection to the Identity Theory. If theoretical identifications represent empirically justified extensions in the uses of terms without implying any great change in the underlying *meanings* of those terms, then the identity theorist can both admit that mental state/physical state identifications are today "deviant" and describe conditions under which the very same identifications could become nondeviant and indeed necessary. And Putnam's consideration of the special character of the "is" of theoretical identification also gives him the ability to suggest, at least in outline, what these conditions might be. The theoretical identification of mental states with physiological states, Putnam suggests, will begin to make sense when we understand not only how the two kinds of states are correlated, but also how physiological states themselves *cause* behavior. Were physical science capable of describing the causation of behavior by physiological states, the identification of physical states with mental states would subsequently have two theoretical advantages:

1) It would be possible . . . to derive from physical theory the classical laws (or low-level generalizations) of common-sense "mentalistic" psychology, such as: "People tend to avoid things with which they have had painful experiences."

2) It would be possible to predict the cases (and they are legion) in which common-sense "mentalistic" psychology fails.[16]

This account of the conditions under which the theoretical identification of mental states with physical states might be justified gives Putnam an answer to another of the prima facie objections to the Identity Theory: that its thesis, even if correct, has little theoretical utility. For both the derivation of classical or commonsense psychology from physical theory and the prediction of cases in which commonsense psychology fails would extend and improve our understanding of human thought and behavior. Moreover, as Putnam realizes, at least the first of the two advantages could not be secured by any theory of psychophysical "correlation" weaker than the Identity Theory. Given the physical identification of the role of physiological states in causing behavior, the derivation of psychological laws from physical ones requires identity in the subject matters of the two domains. If it is indeed, or may someday be, possible to identify the causal roles of physiological states, the two advantages Putnam cites appear to provide a powerful pragmatic argument for the utility of the identity thesis.

In recommending the identity thesis partially on the basis of its ability, given the contemplated identification of the roles of physiological states in causing behaviors, to reduce commonsense psychology to physical theory, Putnam relied upon a broadly physicalist and reductionist picture of unification and explanation in science, according to which explanation in a specialized scientific field is unified with other fields of scientific explanation to the extent to which the special entities of that field can be shown to reduce to, or be composed of, entities treated by another, more basic, specialized field. For instance, biological entities reduce mereologically to chemical entities, and chemical entities reduce mereologically to physical entities. Science as a whole is unified as the entities of "higher-level" sciences such as psychology and sociology are reduced to those of lower-level sciences such as biology and, ultimately, physics. This picture of explanation has long been a familiar component of discussions of reduction and defenses of physicalism, and as we saw in Chapter 2, Putnam himself had, together with Paul Oppenheim, forcibly defended it in a 1958 article.[17] On the most familiar version of the picture, the possibility of unified science depends not only on the mereological composition of entities by other, more basic entities, but also on the existence of a unified causal order relating all scientifically explicable phenomena, in virtue of which it becomes possible to reduce causal laws in higher-level domains to those of lower-level domains. In the 1960 article, Putnam emphasizes the parallel between the mental-physical case and other cases in which theoretical identifications have simplified the structure of scientific explanation by allowing the derivation of higher-level from lower-level causal laws. For instance, the identification of light with electromagnetic radiation allowed the derivation, at least up to a first approximation, of optics from the more basic physical laws of electromagnetism and thereby simplified the overall explanatory structure of science.[18] Given the correctness of the underlying picture of scientific explanation that Putnam presupposes, then, the discovery of the causal roles of physiological states in producing behavior would allow the explanatory unification of psychology with the more basic areas of unified science, as well as the more accurate prediction of cases of deviation from the already-understood laws of psychology. The possibility of this gain in unification and accuracy would itself then justify the identification of the well-known psychological states with the newly discovered physiological states.

Putnam's 1960 article, then, defends the Identity Theory as an empirical program of research based in the hope that the recognition of the causal powers of physiological states could enable the reduction of psychology to physics and thereby facilitate the total unification of science. But Putnam's concern in the article is not only to define such a program, but also to suggest its almost total lack of important philosophical consequences. In contemplating the possibility of reducing psychological theory to physical law, Putnam had also begun to think about the logical structure of commonsense psychological description itself, as well as about its relationship to the traditional philosophical problems of mind-body identity. This led him to the most historically significant suggestion of the paper. In 1936, A. M. Turing had given an abstract description of a kind of computing machine that could implement any logically well-defined function or program whatsoever, what came to be called a "Turing machine." Turing's aim had been to solve, with this abstract description of computability, an important problem of Hilbert's in the foundations of mathematics, but philosophers and scientists soon saw that Turing's abstract description provided a general logical form for the description of the behavior of any actual computing machine.[19] In 1950, Turing famously speculated that a machine that could not be distinguished from a human being in dialogue would actually possess intelligence.[20] Now, in 1960, Putnam argued that a sufficiently complex computational machine with certain abilities of self-description and theory building could serve as a rough analogue of a human's psychological organization, and that in so doing, it would develop strict analogues of *all* of the traditional philosophical problems about mind-body identity:

> In particular, if the machine has electronic "sense organs" which enable it to "scan" itself while it is in operation, it may formulate theories concerning its own structure and subject them to test. Suppose the machine is in a given state (say, "state A") when, and only when, flip-flop 36 is on. Then this statement: "I am in state A when, and only when, flip-flop 36 is on," may be one of the theoretical principles concerning its own structure accepted by the machine.... Now all of the usual considerations for and against mind-body identification can be paralleled by considerations for and against saying that state A is in fact identical with flip-flop 36 being on.[21]

Given only the possibility that such a machine can issue reports of its abstract or computational states that do not immediately expose their relation to the *physical* states underlying them, such a machine would be justified in wondering, just as a person might, about the identities between the two kinds of states. The machine could have the same questions that a human might about whether identifying the two kinds of states would unify theory or eliminate unnecessary entities. It could even make the "dualistic" argument that state A *could not be* identical with the state of having flip-flop 36 on because the one is, while the other is not, an "immediately observable" or apprehensible state. The possibility of such concerns arises, in the case of the machine at least, from the distinction between two levels on which it might seek to describe itself: in terms of its abstract functional or logical states, on one hand, and in terms of the underlying physical states that realize these, on the other:

> When a Turing machine is described by means of a "machine table," it is described as something having a tape, a printing device, a "scanning" device...and a finite set (A, B, C, etc.) of "states."...Beyond this it is described only by giving the deterministic rules which determine the order in which the states succeed each other and what is printed when.
>
> In particular, the "logical description" of a Turing machine does not include any specification of the physical nature of these "states" – or indeed, of the *physical nature* of the whole machine. (Shall it consist of electronic relays, of cardboard, of human clerks sitting at desks, or what?) In other words, a given "Turing machine" is an *abstract* machine which may be physically realized in an almost infinite number of different ways.
>
> As soon as a Turing machine is physically realized, however, something interesting happens. Although the machine has from the logician's point of view only the states A, B, C, etc., it has from the engineer's point of view an almost infinite number of additional states (though not in the same sense of "state" – we shall call these structural states).[22]

Putnam notes that this situation gives the machine a strict analogue of the distinction between "mental" and "physical" as it usually operates in *our* discussions of the mind-brain question. The machine's directly apprehensible and self-evident *logical* states seem, to the machine at least, to be categorically different from its nonobvious and mostly unknown physical states. Putnam even suggests that the distinction between the two levels in the machine case parallels two approaches that one can take toward human psychology: the logical-level description of the machine parallels classical psychology's intuitive description of human thoughts as impressions, ideas, and other rationally organized "mental" states, whereas the physical-level description of the machine parallels the physicalist's description of human behavior in terms that connect it to base-level physical and chemical theories.[23] Just as in the case of human psychology, the logical-level description can be given entirely independently of the physical-level one; but also as in the case of human psychology, the physical-level description explains such deviations from the laws established by its logical-level description as may appear in the machine's behavior.

The 1960 paper, then, already articulates the roots of the functionalist doctrine that we know today. Putnam suggests the analogy between the Turing machine and human psychology as one with broad application to the clarification of issues in the metaphysics of mind, and he already clearly distinguishes between the abstract or functional organization of such a machine and its physical-level realization. He even suggests that the functional description of a Turing machine might, in principle, provide a model for everyday psychological theory and, at least implicitly, that such a model might be the first step toward the contemplated reduction of commonsense psychology to a physical-level theory. Still, Putnam's use of the Turing machine case in this article is theoretically and rhetorically far from the full-blown functionalism that he would articulate several years later. At this point, no *identification* of our mental states with functional states of an abstract computational order is considered or contemplated; there is no evidence in the article that Putnam considers the relationship between a machine's functional description and our psychological organization to be anything more than an illuminating analogy. And although Putnam clearly distinguishes between a machine's abstract functional states and its underlying physical states, there is no clear account of the nature of the relationship between the two kinds of states, or of the way in which information about one level might lead to insight on the other.

Perhaps most importantly, though, Putnam does not yet see the machine analogy as recommending any distinctive philosophical theory of mind on the level of the Identity Theory or its philosophical competitors. Instead, he uses the analogy between functional descriptions of systems and commonsense psychology to suggest that the philosophical question of mind-body identity is, in a certain sense, empty, and the decision among its possible answers inconsequential. It would be pointless, Putnam concludes, to puzzle over the identity or nonidentity of a Turing machine's logical and physical states, for no matter of fact and no concern of theoretical importance turns on the answer. If the analogy is good, the philosophical question about the identity of our own mental and physical states is empty in just the same way. "It is quite clear," Putnam concludes, "that no grown man in his right mind would take the problem of the 'identity' or 'non-identity' of logical and structural states in a machine at all seriously – not because the answer is obvious, but because it is obviously of no importance what the answer is" (p. 384). That the machine could raise the same – or the precisely analogous – question shows, in particular, that the correct answer to the identity question has nothing to do with the supposedly special nature of our subjective experience.[24]

This result clearly sits in some tension with the other main result of the paper, its defense of the meaningfulness of the identity theory on the basis of a consideration of theoretical identification and diachronic theory change. If the question about mind-brain identity is as empty as the machine analogy suggests, then there seems little need to defend the Identity Theory or to articulate the specific theoretical conditions under which it might become more plausible. Behind this thematic tension, moreover, lies a recognizable methodological tension: where Putnam's treatment of the diachronic semantics of theoretical reference suggests a significant role for philosophical investigation and clarification in rendering particular empirical hypotheses meaningful and coherent, his machine analogy simultaneously argues that philosophical considerations have little or no bearing on the progress of *any* empirical theory of mind. The resulting doctrine of the nature of commonsensical psychological descriptions and everyday ascriptions of mental states has a curiously hybrid flavor: according to the machine analogy, commonsense psychology characterizes the autonomous logical-level description of our mental life as ordered cognitively and rationally, but according to Putnam's reductive description of theoretical identifications, it simply redescribes the underlying physical states of affairs responsible for the causation of behavior.

To some extent, of course, both strands of argument grow from Putnam's ongoing concern to show that "ordinary language" investigations of the logic of behavior do not somehow rule out a priori the empirical discovery of mental-physical identities; and it is possible to interpret Putnam's considerations about diachronic theory change simply as comprising an argument in favor of the feasibility of this purely empirical project. But even if Putnam's goal was simply to defend the integrity of an empirical search for psychophysical identities against a priori semantic and behaviorist objections to any such program, his own development of the machine analogy into a self-standing metaphysical description of the nature of mind would soon deepen these tensions and endow the question of the relationship between philosophical analysis of the logic of psychology and empirical discovery of psychophysical correlations with a new urgency. For while the reduction of psychological descriptions to physical descriptions suggested by Putnam's account of the utility of theoretical identification fit well enough within the reductive, causal picture of physicalism, the suggestion of an analogy between commonsense psychology and the abstract functional organization of a Turing machine argues, somewhat contrarily, for the self-sufficiency and autonomy of psychological description and explanation with respect to this reductive picture. Where the physicalism of the unaugmented Identity Theory had explained too little about the specific nature of the identities that it contemplated, the greater psychological plausibility of the functional-level description now threatened to leave psychological theory floating free of a reductive basis.

III

At the beginning of the 1960s, then, what would become the functionalist theory of mind still consisted of nothing more than a suggestive analogy, one invoked, moreover, not in order to establish any new result in the metaphysics of mind but rather to show the emptiness of any philosophical description of the mind-brain relation. In a series of papers written over the next few years, however, Putnam would develop the analogy into a full-blown metaphysical description of mind, culminating in the decisive suggestion that our mental states simply *are* abstract states within our total functional organization.

In the 1963 article "Brains and Behavior," Putnam gave a new, and stronger, argument against the logical behaviorist identification of pains and other mental states with behaviors and behavioral dispositions. In order to show that there is no logical link between mental states and behaviors, Putnam suggested the example of a race of people who, owing to restrictive social conventions, never describe or otherwise express their feelings of pain. These "super-Spartans" would exhibit no pain behavior. Yet it is, Putnam argued, still meaningful to say that they feel pain. For instance, it might well be possible to detect within them a distinctive neurological configuration similar to ours when we are in pain.[25] Given this, it would make sense to conclude that they were indeed in pain. Even if their neurological states were, in general, different from ours, we could still come to conclude that they were in states enough like ours in relevant respects to be called pains.

This argument's more explicit consideration of the relationship between behavioral evidence and empirical discovery gave Putnam new resources against the logical behaviorist, but it still depended on the thought that mental states ultimately are brain states. Putnam still treats states such as pains as the *causes* of the behaviors that express them, and he repeats the suggestion that the grammar of pain ascriptions is controlled by behavioral criteria that function as "symptoms" of an underlying structure. The Turing machine analogy makes no appearance in the article, and there is no suggestion that mental states such as pains are in any sense functional or logical states distinct from underlying physical states.

The first impetus for Putnam's development of the Turing machine analogy into functionalism, and indeed much of the theoretical apparatus of functionalism itself, would come, instead, from the articulation of a new antireductionist description of psychological explanation by the young philosopher Jerry Fodor. In the 1964 article "Explanations in Psychology," Fodor argues for the independence of psychological explanations from physicalist descriptions on the basis of an extended application of the functionalist model that Putnam had suggested in 1960. Arguing from assumptions strikingly unlike those of Putnam's original reductionist picture of the unity of science, Fodor suggests that the characterization of psychological states as functional states offers a reasonable model of both the logic of psychological theory and the relationship that we can expect to find between it and lower-level physiological and physical descriptions.

Much of Fodor's argument for this position depends on a sophisticated consideration of the structure of psychological explanation and prediction, on the basis of which he argues against an oversimple and naïve reductionist view of the relationship of such explanation and prediction to lower-level causal explanations. Psychological theory, Fodor argues, intends to explain and predict behavior. But it is misleading to suppose that this explanation and prediction can be reduced to terms any more basic or primitive than the terms of psychology themselves.[26] Even the simplest notions of psychological description – for instance, the behaviorist notion of a "response" – resist reduction to a physicalistic description purely in terms of physical motions. For there is no way even to characterize the set of possible physical movements that can count as a simple behavioral response without using the psychological predicate that characterizes them all as the same "response" to begin with. The psychological description in terms of responses is not elliptical for an underlying physicalist description, but rather an autonomous functional description in its own right:

In laboratory situations, an organism is said to have mastered a response when it regularly produces any of an indefinite number of types of functionally equivalent motions under the appropriate stimulus conditions. That some reasonable notion of functional equivalence can be specified is essential, since we cannot in general require that two motions manifesting the same response be identical either in their observable properties or in their physiological basis. Thus, a rat has "got" the bar pressing response if and only if it habitually presses the bar upon food deprivation. Whether it presses with its left or right front paw or with three or six grams of pressure is, or may be, irrelevant. Training is to some previously determined criterion of homogeneity of performance, which is to say that we permit variation among the motions belonging to a response so long as each of the variants is functionally equivalent to each of the others: *viz.* so long as each of the motions is correctly related to the bar, to the general stimulus situation, and to the history of the organism.[27]

Even in the simple case of Skinnerian behaviorism, the grammar of psychological explanation makes ineliminable use of terms that cannot be defined physicalistically. Even if explanation on this level is in part causal, what is important in understanding its logic is not definitional reduction of psychological to physical predicates but a functional characterization of the relations of definition and causality *among* psychological terms and their referents.[28]

But what, exactly, is a "functional" characterization, and what is the relationship between a "functional" description and a straightforward causal description if one does not reduce to the other? Picking up on Putnam's suggestion, Fodor argues that psychological explanation has two levels or "phases."[29] On the first level, corresponding to classical psychology, mental states are characterized in irreducibly psychological terms according to their roles in producing behavior. Importantly, at this level of explanation, the explanatory use of descriptions of mental states requires no reference to the underlying physical mechanisms that correspond to or realize them:

It should be noticed that explanations afforded by phase one theories are not causal explanations, although a fully elaborated phase one theory claims to be able to predict behavior given sufficient information about current sensory stimulations. Phase one explanations purport to account for behaviour in terms of internal states, but they give no information whatever about the mechanisms underlying these states. That is, theory construction proceeds in terms of such functionally characterized notions as memories, motives, needs, drives, desires, strategies, beliefs, etc. with no reference to the physiological structures which may, in some sense correspond to these concepts. Now, if I say "He left abruptly upon remembering a prior engagement" I am giving an explanation in terms of an internal event postulated in order to account for behaviour (including, perhaps, behaviour which consists in his telling me why he left). . . . Yet, it is not a causal explanation in the sense in which that term is usually used. That is, it is not at all like a reflex-arc explanation of a knee-jerk response or an explanation of the trajectory of a billiard ball; no causal laws are invoked, nor is any notion of a causal chain at issue.[30]

By postulating intuitively described inner states such as motives and memories, phase-one explanations, Fodor suggests, allow us to predict and explain behavior in a wide variety of situations; all that is required to formulate them is the observations we make of the behavior that people and other organisms produce in response to stimulations. Still, they give us no insight into the underlying physiological mechanisms that are literally responsible for causing the behavior in question. For this, we need a second level of explanation, on which we specify the *mechanisms* that actually underlie our functionally defined phase-one states. Applying Putnam's machine analogy again, Fodor notes that any given functional-level explanation corresponds to *indefinitely many* mechanical-level explanations:

In a phase one explanation, we picture the organism as proceeding through a series of internal states that terminate in the production of observable behaviour. But we make no attempt to say what these states are states of: what internal mechanisms correspond to the functionally defined states we have invoked. Now, the set of mechanisms capable of realizing a series of such functionally defined states is indefinitely large. Only our ingenuity limits the number of mechanisms we could devise which, upon exposure to the relevant stimulations, would go through a sequence of internal states each functionally equivalent to a corresponding state of an organism and would then produce behaviour indistinguishable in relevant respects from the behaviour of the organism.[31]

The character of the relationship between mechanical-level explanations and functional-level ones has a number of significant consequences for the growth of psychological theory. First, Fodor suggests,
mechanical-level explanations may help to suggest new functional-
level ones. For instance, speculations about the neurology of memory
might lead to new functional-level characterizations of memory in
terms of familiar psychological notions. Second, mechanical-level explanations constrain functional-level ones; though each functional
system has an indefinite number of mechanical realizations, any
functional explanation that is *inconsistent* with the mechanical-level
explanation of the same system can be dismissed.[32] Additionally, the
one-many relationship between functional-level and mechanical-level
explanations implies a nonreductive picture of the relationship of
mental to physical states. If psychological explanation really does have
the two-phase structure of Fodor's account, then "reductions" (if there
are any such) from the mental to the physical are not, as Oppenheim
and Putnam had supposed, mereological decompositions of higher-
level entities into their lower-level parts. Instead, they correlate *functions* with *mechanisms*, explaining the functional role played by a mental
state by referring to the mechanism enabling it to play that role. To
look for a functionally characterized mental state such as a motive or
a hope within a mechanistic description of the mind, Fodor suggests,
would be just as misguided as looking for a "valve lifter" in a mechanistic description of an automobile. The autonomy of functional-level
descriptions is, however, preserved, in a way that is nonthreatening to
physicalism, when we realize that, at least in standardly constructed
automobiles, camshafts *are* valve lifters (although something else, a
mechanically different structure, certainly *might have* served this functionally characterized role).

Beginning with considerations of the logic of psychological theory
and the unlikelihood of its reduction to physical theory, then, Fodor's
article succeeded in defining "ordinary" or classical psychology as the
functional description of internal states of an organism, a description
that, in each case, may correlate with any number of mechanical-level
descriptions of the same organism couched in the language of neu-
roscience and physiology. This suggestion led Putnam to define and
articulate, over the next five years, the thesis that a mind might simply
be a system of functional states realized physically. In his articles defining and defending functionalism, Putnam significantly extended and

developed Fodor's consideration of the logic of psychological explanation and drew out its consequences for the philosophical question
of the mind-body relation. These consequences would lead Putnam
to move decisively beyond the Identity Theory as well as to repudiate
much of the semantic argument that he had formerly deployed in its
defense.

Putnam went on to define the functionalist theory of mind in three
articles: "Robots: Machines or Artificially Created Life?" (1964), "The
Mental Life of Some Machines" (1967), and "The Nature of Mental
States" (1967). In these articles, Putnam's arguments for functionalism
fall into four main types.

First, there are arguments, akin to Fodor's, from *the logic of psychological terms*. Psychological terms, if they are definable at all, are only
*inter*definable; there is no hope of "unpacking" the definitions of psychological terms into behaviors or behavioral dispositions that are not
themselves psychologically described.[33] This suggests that psychological descriptions do *not*, as the identity theory had held, covertly or
elliptically refer to physical internal states, and indeed that the hope
of defining a physicalist research program culminating in the identification of the physical referents of ordinary psychological description
is largely misguided.

A second sort of Putnamian argument for functionalism grew from
his earlier arguments against logical behaviorism, particularly the argument that there is no logically necessary link between behavior and
mental states.[34] Because the functional states of a Turing machine
need not necessarily correspond to, or even be determinable on the
basis of, behavior, it is possible to construct a machine analogue of
the "super-Spartans," a machine that is often in a particular functional
state but will not express that it is. Because formal rules govern the
transitions between a Turing machine's logical states, it is possible to
implement rule-governed "preference-functions" for the Turing machine. These rules can govern the self-expression of the machine's
states, so that, given an abnormal preference-function (for instance,
one that places an infinitely high disvalue on expressing that it is in the
state functionally defined as "pain"), the Turing machine could "experience" functional states that it does not behaviorally express. Thus,
functional states, like our mental states, need not be logically linked
or interdefined with behavior. This recommends the functionalist

account and shows that it survives at least one of the objections that had doomed logical behaviorism.

This argument shows the depth of the logical difference between functionalism and behaviorism. But a third sort of argument for functionalism that Putnam uses actually suggests a surprising amount of commonality in philosophical motivation between the two theories. Even if functionalism allows that functional states – and hence mental states – need not be identifiable with, or logical constructions from, behavior, nevertheless the consideration that our *criteria* for the everyday ascription of mental states are largely behavioral provides an argument in favor of functionalism:

> Turning now to the considerations *for* the functional-state theory, let us begin with the fact that we identify organisms as in pain, or hungry, or angry, or in heat, etc., on the basis of their *behavior*. But it is a truism that similarities in the behavior of two systems are at least a reason to suspect similarities in the functional organization of the two systems, and a much *weaker* reason to suspect similarities in the actual physical details. Moreover, we expect the various psychological states – at least the basic ones, such as hunger, thirst, aggression, etc. – to have more or less similar "transition probabilities" (within wide and ill defined limits, to be sure) with each other and with behavior in the case of different species, because this is an artifact of the way in which we identify these states. Thus, we would not count an animal as *thirsty* if its "unsatiated" behavior did not seem to be directed toward drinking and was not followed by "satiation for liquid." Thus any animal that we count as capable of these various states will at least *seem* to have a certain rough kind of functional organization.[35]

Even if mental states are not logically dependent on, or identifiable with, public behavior, it nevertheless remains a philosophically significant feature of the logic and grammar of our commonsense and classical psychological theories that we *ascribe* mental states on the basis of publicly observable behavior. Moreover, the connection between the observation of behavior and the ascription of a mental state is, as Putnam realizes, closer and tighter than the connection between evidence and theory. For as a matter of logical necessity (at least in an extended sense of that term), we will not ordinarily be prepared to *call* an organism "thirsty," "hungry," "enraged," and so on if it does not exhibit *any* of the behavior that is criterial for that particular ascription. Under normal circumstances, the proposition that Jones is angry, if he exhibits *none* of the usual behavioral signs of anger, will at least call for further clarification. As Putnam had earlier argued, the logical behaviorist takes this kind of logical connection between behavioral evidence and the determination of mental states to be stronger than it is, forgetting that there are, after all, *some* conceivable circumstances under which mental states might reasonably be ascribed in the absence of their usual behavioral symptoms. Still, its behavior is prima facie good evidence for an organism's having a particular functional organization, and many, if not all, functional states are primarily characterizable in virtue of their logical relationships to publicly observable behaviors.

Finally, the observation that functional states are in part characterized by their relationship to, and ascribed on the basis of, behavioral evidence suggests what is Putnam's most oft-used and characteristic argument for functionalism, what has been called the "multiple realization" argument.[36] It begins as an argument *against* the Identity Theory. The identity theorist, Putnam argues, is committed to the *identification* of a particular mental state – say, pain – with a particular neurological or neurophysiological structure found in all and only those organisms that are currently feeling pain. Moreover, this identification, if the identity hypothesis has any explanatory force, must be at least nomologically necessary. Whatever state is to be identified with pain must exist, then, in mammalian and molluscan, human and extraterrestrial brains alike, and moreover must be correlated, as a matter of scientific law, with the behavioral manifestations of pain in all of these species. Of course, it is extremely unlikely that any such state exists. What all and only organisms that are in *pain* do share, though, is a certain *functional* state that can be characterized by its logical and causal interrelationships with other functional states (moving away from a particular stimulus, acting as one has acted when physically damaged in the past, etc.). Where the identity theory necessarily posits an underlying state that could hardly exist (or, anyway, be theoretically useful; we could, of course, refer to all of the biologically distinct states that realize pain in various organisms as a single, wildly disjunctive state), the functional-state theory uses what we already know about the logical criteria on the basis of which mental states are ascribed and discussed to characterize them as functional states that *could* be held in common by a wide variety of possible organisms and systems.

The multiple realization argument has often been considered a decisive argument in favor of functionalism, but it is important to be clear on just what sort of argument it is. Even if the Identity Theory fails because it requires nomological connections between mental states and (possibly hugely disjunctive) brain states, the functional-state theory improves upon it in this respect only because the specification of a functional state has no particular consequences for the identity of the underlying physical states. The thought that a given functionally characterized system can be realized by any of an indefinite number of possible physical systems had been suggested in passing in Putnam's 1960 article, and Fodor had made it the basis of his antireductionist picture of the relationship of phase-one to phase-two psychological explanations. Following Fodor's suggestion, Putnam clearly thought of the one-many relationship between functional and physical descriptions as one of the most crucial recommendations of the functionalist program. Unlike the nomological identities required by the Identity Theory, the one-many structure of functionalist explanation allowed that the meaning of ordinary psychological descriptions does not depend, overtly or covertly, on their reference to esoteric neurological or physiological facts. On the level of functional explanation, at least, the functional-state theory defines a much more plausible research program: rather than having to determine the underlying physical "identities" of the entities invoked in our psychological explanations, we treat these entities as well defined from the outset and simply attempt further to characterize their functional roles, employing only such evidence as is available publicly and prior to the detailed investigations of the brain sciences.

The force of the multiple realization argument, then, does not arise as much from the failure of the identity theory to handle species-specific mental-physical correlations as from the ability of functionalism to define a program of psychological investigation that takes much greater and more sophisticated account of the evidentiary and causal logic of traditional psychological explanation. Were it only the first kind of argument, defenders of the identity theory could simply respond, as Kim (1972) in fact did, that even if pain is realized in *various* ways in *various* different species, species-specific identity laws are enough to prove the identity theorist's case. Putnam resisted this position not because he thought it would be impossible to identify the species-specific physical "correlates" of pain in each particular case, but because he thought such identification would have little relevance on the level of traditional psychological explanation and, accordingly, little to do with defining the *identity* of pain.

As Putnam began to define and articulate the view that mental states simply *are* functionally defined states, the one-many character of the functional-state/physical-realization relation became central to his thought about the metaphysical status of the mind, causing him to abandon some of the most important parts of his earlier picture of explanation and reduction. Significantly, the thought that a functional description of the psychology of an organism has *no* consequences for the nature of its realization led Putnam to doubt traditional materialism itself:

Traditional materialism (which is pretty much of a philosopher's straw man by now) holds that mental conduct words are definable in terms of concepts referring to physical-chemical composition. If this is right, then the predicate "T prefers A to B" should be definable in terms of the physical-chemical composition of our Turing Machines. But in fact there is no logically valid inference from the premiss that one of our Turing Machines has a certain physical-chemical composition to the conclusion that it prefers A to B, in the sense explained above, nor from the premiss that it prefers A to B to the conclusion that it has a certain physical-chemical composition. These are logically independent statements about our Turing Machines even if they are just machines.[37]

Since the functional-state hypothesis, as Putnam understood it in 1967, defines a mental state *simply* in terms of an abstract functional description, it has no consequences whatsoever for the nature of the medium realizing it. Functionally defined states are completely logically independent of their realizers. This gives the functionalist reason to doubt not only the identity theorist's "definition" of mental states in terms of physical states but even materialism itself, as Putnam shows with another argument arising from the possibility of multiple realization:

Indeed, there could be a community of robots that did not all have the same physical constitution, but did all have the same psychology; and such robots could univocally say "I have the sensation of red," "you have the sensation of red," "he has the sensation of red," even if the three robots referred to did not "physically realize" the "sensation of red" in the same way. Thus, the attributes having the "sensation" of red and "flip-flop 72 being on" are simply not identical in the case of the robots. If Materialism is taken to be the denial of the existence of "nonphysical" attributes, then Materialism is false even for robots! (Putnam 1967a, pp. 392–3)

The lack of inferential relationships between functional states and physical states shows the logical distinctness of the two types of states. Indeed, there is no reason to believe that functionally defined states must be *physically* realized at all. As Putnam remarks elsewhere, the functional-state theory is not even incompatible with dualism: even a nonphysical "soul" could perfectly well "implement" any given functional organization, as long as it had a number of logically distinct and temporally successive states. And even in the case of an actual, material Turing machine, its functionally defined states are logically distinct from, and not derivable from, *any* of its physical states or attributes. In this respect, at least, they are genuinely "nonphysical," defining real and ascertainable attributes above and beyond the set of all of the machine's physical attributes and all of their logical consequences.

Putnam's goal in making these points against materialism, of course, was not to argue for dualism or for some new account of the metaphysics of mind, but to suggest the emptiness, given the functionalist picture, of all traditional philosophical descriptions of the mind-body relation. If materialism is "false" even in the case of a purely physical machine (one constructed, anyway, only from physical parts), then this kind of falsity probably has no metaphysically interesting consequences. Still, even if its original intent was to show the emptiness of all traditional metaphysical positions on the mind-body relation, it can hardly be denied, in the wake of thirty-five years of philosophical history, that the functional-state theory raises a host of new metaphysical questions and issues of its own. And it even seems difficult, in historical retrospect, to deny that his thinking about the metaphysics of functionalism had significant effects on Putnam's own constellation of concerns. Most importantly, it caused him, following Fodor, to repudiate the reductionist picture of explanation that he had earlier advocated and to abandon as irrelevant the entire account of diachronic theory change that he had previously developed. In 1967, Putnam used yet another version of the "multiple realization" argument to show that, given the functional-state theory, the special character of theoretical identifications provides no help for the progress of empirical research:

I cited in [Putnam (1960)] the "is" of theoretical identification (i.e. the "is" exemplified by such statements as "water is H_2O," "light is electromagnetic radiation") and I suggested that some properties might be connectible by this kind of "is." But this would not be of help to the identity theorist. (This represents a change of view from my earlier paper.) Even if we are willing to say "being P is being Q" in some cases in which the designators "P" and "Q" are not synonymous, we should require that the designators be equivalent and that the equivalence be necessary, at least in the sense of physically necessary. Thus, if one particular physical-chemical composition should turn out to explain all cases of solubility, it would not be a wholly unmotivated extension of ordinary usage to say that solubility is the possession of this particular physical-chemical composition. There is an argument in my earlier paper for the view that this would not necessarily be a "change of meaning." This sort of thing cannot happen in the present case. We cannot discover laws by virtue of which it is physically necessary that an organism prefers A to B if and only if it is in a certain physical-chemical state. For we already know that any such laws would be false. They would be false because even in the light of our present knowledge we can see that any Turing Machine that can be physically realized at all can be realized in a host of totally different ways.[38]

Even if the semantics of the "is" of theoretical identification retains some relevance to the description of diachronic theory change generally, Putnam here abandons the hope that it has any significance for the semantics of psychological theory and neurophysiological description. For by this time, Putnam had come to think that the functional-state theory simply provided a more plausible account of this semantics. With the functional-state theory in mind, Putnam no longer saw it as necessary to preserve ordinary psychological description by construing it as covertly, or anyway eventually capable of, referring to underlying physical states in the context of an emerging reductionist description of the mind, for he came to think that ordinary psychological description *already* characterizes its functionally defined states as readily, and completely, as could ever be needed or hoped. Given the logical independence of mental and physical states on the functionalist model, the autonomy of psychological description poses no threat to its inclusion, *even taken at face value*, in a total description of the world that (if not exactly "materialistic") makes no appeal to mysterious nonphysical states or processes. This clearly involves, however, a substantially different picture of reduction and explanation than the one that Putnam had originally defended. On the new picture, physicalism neither requires nor implies the microphysical reduction of mental states to physical ones. On the other hand, the irreducibility of functional-level description on the level of psychology suggests a considerably broader and more nuanced picture of the varieties of scientific explanation than the physicalist reducibility picture would imply.

Despite, therefore, Putnam's own suggestion of the irrelevance of the functionalist theory to philosophical descriptions of the metaphysics of mind, his articulation of it caused a substantial change (if only a negative one) in his own thinking about explanation and reduction. Additionally, in the perspective of the subsequent historical development and articulation of the functionalist theory, it seems reasonable to wonder whether, even given the functionalist model, the relationship between physical and functional states is really as metaphysically innocuous and uninteresting as Putnam maintained that it was. If functional states, even for a mechanically realized Turing machine or a physical computer, are, as Putnam sometimes suggests, genuinely "nonphysical" in the sense of being irreducible to physical states or properties, then their compositional and microstructural nature is prima facie mysterious, and may stand in need of further philosophical investigation. The functional-state theory provides a model, it is true, for the straightforward "arising" of functional states from physical ones, but the ontology and metaphysics of this "arising" remains somewhat puzzling. Putnam took it that the machine analogy would dissipate any special sense that the mysteriousness of the mental arises from the particular characteristics of *human* mentality (for instance, "subjectivity" or consciousness), but his passing remarks about the nonmateriality of functional states and their consistency with nonmaterialist pictures of mind might easily be taken to suggest a broader metaphysical investigation of mentality that comprehends both humans *and* physically realized Turing machines.

The question left open about the nature of the relationship between functional and physical descriptions suggests, as well, an objection to Putnam's functionalism as it now stood. For Putnam's lack of concern for the metaphysics of the physical state/functional state relationship left functionalism, as so far defined, open to a charge of *underspecification* much like the one that had earlier troubled the Identity Theory. If there are indeed *no* inferential relationships between functional and physical states, then whatever its plausibility as a description of the logic of ordinary psychological explanation, the functional-state theory provides no guide whatsoever for the empirical investigation of the nature of the physical and physiological states that are supposed to underlie our mental states. There is no guarantee that a functional-level description will correspond in any sense to a perspicuous division of biological-level states into types relevant to their roles in the causation of behavior. Indeed, in this respect the functional-state theory is seemingly even worse off than the Identity Theory. For according to the Identity Theory, there is only *one* correct description of the mental states of an individual (the correctness of any mentalistic description depends on the extent to which the entities it postulates *really exist* as brain states); but the functional-state theory leaves open the possibility that *any number* of possible functional descriptions of the same individual may equally well explain and predict its behavior. Absent a more specific and metaphysically committal description of the relationship between functional and physical states than Putnam was, at this point, prepared to give, the functional-state theory seemed in danger of losing whatever theoretical advantage it had hoped to gain with its assimilation of the mental-physical distinction to this relationship.

Functionalism earned its plausibility from its closeness to the logic of ordinary and classical psychological explanation. But, at least as it stood so far, it had bought this closeness at the price of the kind of metaphysical specificity that would have been needed in order to clarify fundamentally the relationship between philosophical description of mental states and empirical discovery of their physical correlates. Methodologically, it rewrote the traditional analytic project of logical analysis of mental states in an idiom that avoided the excesses of logical behaviorism, but in so doing it lost the empirical-mindedness of the identity theory. Despite years of concerted thought on the part of functionalists and their predecessors, the semantic analysis of the logic of mental states still threatened to float free of any clear application to the newly developing cognitive sciences of mind and brain. At the same time, the question of the metaphysical nature of the relationship between mind and brain, while certainly transformed by the functionalist model, was, at least from a certain perspective, less clear than ever before.

IV

In 1966, in a brief and crisply argued *Journal of Philosophy* article, David Lewis proposed a philosophical innovation that, when added to the functional-state theory as Putnam had defined it, completed the theory from a logical (if not a chronological) point of view, effectively ended the further metaphysical speculation that might otherwise have been engendered by the unclarity of Putnam's account, and defined much more specifically the kind of relationship between philosophical analysis and empirical discovery that could be expected on a functionalist account. Despite its functionalist motivation, Lewis called his article "An Argument for the Identity Theory," and his argument indeed succeeded in making the physicalistically described world, once again, uncompromisingly safe for functionalism, thus quieting the doubts expressed by Putnam about the cogency of a materialist outlook given the functionalist model. However, its central innovation was essentially a semantic one: the suggestion that mental states, and in particular "experiences," are defined by their causal roles, their pattern of typical causes and effects. With this innovation, Lewis made it possible to maintain that the *functional* roles definitive (according to functionalism) of mental states are at the same time *causal* roles, and therefore that the placement of a mental state in our ordinary and classical psychological descriptions adverts to, and locates it in the total theory by means of, the *same* properties and features that locate it in the total causal web of physicalistically described nature.

If the suggestion is accepted, the logical analysis of the grammar of the ordinary description of mental states will henceforth be an *integral part* of the empirical analysis of the underlying physical states, for the semantic features of mental-state terms will mirror the causal roles in virtue of which their bearers can be identified with physical states. What had seemed to be purely "philosophical," "logical," or "grammatical" analysis will then have a new richness of empirical relevance; the structure of the traditional philosophical investigation of the relational logic of mental states will be mirrored as the empirical investigation of the causal relations of functionally defined states.

Thematically and methodologically, the innovation of Lewis's account would add to Putnam's functionalism the most philosophically compelling features of Smart's physicalism: its explanatory and metaphysical economy; its sensitivity to the possible philosophical relevance of new discoveries in the brain sciences; and its congeniality to an uncompromisingly physicalist picture of the world with no suggestion of esoteric nonphysical or mental facts, properties, or entities.

Lewis gives three arguments for the advantage of the identification of experiences with their causal roles over previous accounts of their nature. Together, these arguments demonstrate the physicalist and functionalist motivations of Lewis's suggestion as well as the originality of his own account. First, Lewis repeats Smart's argument for the advantage of the Identity Theory over logical behaviorism: experiences are real and are really "the effects of their occasions and the causes of their manifestations, as common opinion supposes them to be" (p. 21). Like the Identity Theory, Lewis's suggestion allows this to be the case, whereas logical behaviorism is constrained to deny the reality of experiences as causally efficacious items. Second, Lewis gives a version of Putnam's argument from the interdefinability of psychological terms.[39] Experiences, he argues, are interdefinable only with each other. There is no hope of defining them in more basic terms that do not refer to experiences at all. But if Lewis's suggestion is correct, an experience is defined in terms of its causal role, including its role in causing, and being the effect of, other experiences. The definitions of experiences therefore make ineliminable reference to other experiences; there is no need to eliminate this reference in order to make experiences physicalistically respectable. Finally, Lewis suggests that if his suggestion is correct, functionalist analysis need not establish *necessary and sufficient* behavioral conditions for the presence of a particular mental state.[40] For if experiences are defined by their causal roles, they nevertheless need not be identified with *all* of their possible causes and effects. It suffices that they be defined by their *typical* causes and effects, the events that cause them and that they cause in most normal circumstances. If this is correct, then cases like Putnam's "super-Spartan" case, where behaviors come apart from mental-state ascriptions, call for no specially involved analysis. It is no objection, on Lewis's view, to the functionalist description of a mental state on the evidentiary basis of observed behavior that this description might mislead in a case of highly abnormal behavior. All that is needed is that our descriptions of mental states advert to their most typical causes and effects.

Together, these arguments recommend a position that recognizably combines the two distinct levels of analysis that Fodor had originally suggested: experiences are defined, Lewis suggests, by their causal roles, and particular physical states, as a matter of contingent fact, are the *occupiers* of those causal roles. Experiences are defined, and spoken of, by way of the patterns of what causes them and what they cause, but it is ultimately particular physical states of the brain that are doing the causing. Thus, the contingent identities of the identity theory fit right alongside the analytic, or near-analytic, explanations of functional description. One side of the account constrains the other in that only something that really can do the causal work of a particular experience is a candidate for contingent, species-specific identity with that experience. By articulating this connection between the functional level of analysis and the physical level, though, Lewis suggests a new kind of answer to Putnam's "multiple realization" argument: the identity of particular experiences with particular brain states is the contingent and species-specific *occupation* of a particular causal role (definable without reference to any particular species or biological configuration) by a particular physical configuration. In a 1969 commentary on Putnam's 1967 article, Lewis urged that a reasonable identity theorist can therefore avoid the multiple realization problem, given only that he recognizes that the fixed concept "pain" – defined as a causal role – varies in denotation from species to species.[41]

In 1968, David Armstrong would make much the same suggestion of identity between functional roles and causal roles the centerpiece of his influential *A Materialist Theory of Mind*. Like Lewis, Armstrong aims to defend a sophisticated version of Smart's Identity Theory. But he argues that the identity theorist's identification of mental states with brain states ought to be augmented by specific analyses of our mental concepts, much like the analyses suggested by logical behaviorists. The two strands of theory can be joined, Armstrong suggests, by recognizing that "the concept of a mental state is primarily the concept of a state of the person apt for bringing about a certain sort of behaviour" (p. 82). On Armstrong's suggestion, then, mental states are identified in terms of the types of behavior that, under ordinary or appropriate circumstances, they normally cause.[42] As on Lewis's view, this allows the proponent of the identity theory to accept much of the logical behaviorist's analyses of mental concepts into behavioral facts, without denying that the objects of mental concepts are brain states:

> I have emphasized that the argument put forward for a Materialist theory of mind involves two steps. In the first place, it is argued that a mental state is a state of a person apt for the bringing about of behaviour of a certain sort. This is intended to be a piece of logical analysis. In the second place, it is argued on general scientific grounds that this inner cause is, as a matter of fact, the brain.[43]

To motivate the first component of the argument, Armstrong goes on to offer logical analyses of the concepts of willing, knowledge, perception, and mental images into the kinds of behavioral and public facts apt to cause them and be caused by them.[44]

With the Lewis/Armstrong suggestion, logical-level functional analysis and empirical-level discovery of psychophysical identities fall cleanly into their relative places in a comprehensive program of jointly functional and causal analysis. In addition to defining a realistic research program combining logical and causal analysis, moreover, the suggestion effectively quells any remaining doubts about the extent of functionalism's compatibility with physicalism. Citing Putnam and Oppenheim's 1958 article, Lewis argues that physics must at least be *explanatorily* adequate: that is, every event must be explicable physically. But if experiences are defined by their causal roles, then we need nothing more than the nonexistence of nonphysical causes or physical causes of nonphysical events to guarantee that experiences will be physically explicable. From this perspective, there is no danger that functionally defined states, because *logically* distinct from their physical realizers, will be in any interesting or relevant sense "nonphysical" or that they will represent any obstacle to a materialist description of the world. But at the same time, Lewis's suggestion, because it depends only on the physical explicability *in principle* of every physical event, does not obviously demand or imply the oversimple reductionist picture of psychological explanation that Fodor had originally resisted. The relationship between a causal role and its contingent occupier, unlike the compositional relationship between a macro-level object or process and its micro-level constituents, is plausibly a relationship characterized by some degree of explanatory autonomy. Because various structures may instantiate one and the same causal role, the explicability in principle of each physical event does not demand, on this picture, that there be, in general, any univocal or nomological relationship of explanatory reduction between an experience and the physical state with which it is (contingently) identical.[45]

It is important to note the extent to which Lewis's suggestion represents a genuine improvement over Fodor's original two-level treatment of psychological explanation. For recall that Fodor had *not* considered functional-level description to be, in any real sense, causal description. Though the explanatory relations among functionally described mental states might superficially *resemble* causal relations, the real causes of behavior would be evident, according to Fodor, only upon the completion of the "phase-two" mechanistic redescription. For Fodor, phase-one descriptions constrain phase-two descriptions in the weak sense that any mechanism *incapable* of accomplishing the function called for by a phase-one description of the same system can be ruled out. But on Lewis's picture, the relationship between the two levels of explanation is much more direct. For on Lewis's suggestion, the mechanism offered as a realizer of a given functional state must have the *very same* causal powers as does that state. It remains a possibility that many different sorts of mechanisms may have the same causal powers, but the antecedent, functional-level specification of a functional state in terms of its causal role places a powerful and determinative, though not unique, constraint on the range of structures that may realize that role. In his 1968 book *Psychological Explanation,* Fodor repeated and expanded his earlier suggestion that the logic of psychological explanation, at least initially and prior to the investigation of neurophysiological mechanisms, is functional. But he corrected his earlier view with a new account of the nature of functional explanation that accommodates Lewis's suggestion that functional description is already causal description:

To say that, in the first phase of psychological explanation, the primary concern is with determining the functional character of the states and processes involved in the etiology of behavior is . . . to say that, at that stage, the hypothesized psychological constructs are individuated primarily or solely by reference to their alleged causal consequences. What one knows (or claims to know) about such constructs is the effects their activity has upon behavior. It follows that phase-one psychological theories postulate functionally equivalent mechanisms when and only when they postulate constructs of which the behavioral consequences are, in theoretically relevant respects, identical.[46]

In the context of the 1968 book as a whole, the new thought that functional description is already causal description gives Fodor both a new argument for functionalism and a more specific account of the relationship between functional and mechanistic description. For Fodor now argues that much commonsensical psychological description *is* causal description. If functional roles are already causal roles, individuated by their role in causing behavior, then functional description need not deny that explanations of behavior often do advert to underlying psychological causes such as beliefs and desires. If these causes are inferred entities, postulated in order to explain behavior, Fodor reasons that it must make sense to imagine observing the entities that they in fact are, and neurophysiological states and processes are prima facie good candidates. Moreover, Fodor now suggests a more definite kind of relationship between functional and mechanistic descriptions than on the earlier account: if ordinary mentalistic language *identifies* inferred mental causes in virtue of a functional description of their behavioral causes and effects, then functional descriptions can *individuate* the internal mechanisms that it is the task of the second-phase mechanistic description to analyze. Given that a functional-level psychological description is already a description of an inferred mental state's typical causes and effects, a functional characterization of the entire organism will usually divide it into functionally distinct mechanisms that can fruitfully be considered individually for purposes of the mechanistic analysis. Lewis's suggestion, then, clarifies the relationship between functional and mechanistic analysis suggested by Fodor's earlier account, bringing the two phases of explanation together into a single program, a program both amenable to physicalism and faithful to the logic of ordinary psychological description, unified by its identification of the position of mental states in the causal order.

Much of the subsequent discussion of functionalism over the last thirty-five years can be traced to issues left open in the final configuration comprised by the combination of Putnam's functional-state theory and Lewis's suggestion. If functional roles are causal roles, then how should these roles be characterized? Philosophers soon noticed that even if experiences are defined by their causal roles, they might be described in a number of very different ways. Their description in terms of causal roles might portray them as caused by, and responsible for, environmental stimuli and behavior described on the ordinary, commonsensical level of psychological explanation. Alternatively, it might ultimately require their description in the sparer resources of some restricted language of neuroscientific, computational, or cognitive-scientific description. Again, the causal roles that experiences are might "reach out" to include stimuli and behavioral effects outside the organism, or they might be limited to causal chains beginning with irradiations of the senses and ending with motor effects on the body; thus the issue of "externalism" versus "internalism" has characterized much subsequent discussion. In addition, philosophers have sought clarification of exactly what is said of a physical state when it is "functionally" defined in terms of its causal role, and in particular, the extent to which such descriptions must be considered ineliminably teleological; and Lewis's suggestion that experiences be defined in terms of their "normal" set of causal roles has invited the accusation that no defensible criterion of such "normalcy" may be available.[47]

But aside from all of these issues in the philosophy of intentionality, functionalism has encountered its greatest obstacles in its description of the nature of *consciousness*. In 1972, together with Ned Block, Fodor first expressed cautious doubts about the ability of functionalist description to explain subjective, phenomenal, or conscious states, and in recent years these doubts have grown into a widespread position of resistance among philosophers who doubt that a functionalist explanation of consciousness can be correct.[48] This situation cannot be viewed without a certain level of historical irony, as for Putnam and Lewis alike it was the facility of functionalism in describing the nature of subjective states such as pains and other experiences that had first, and most primarily, recommended it as a systematic description of the mind. Yet the history of the development of functionalism from Putnam's first suggestion of the machine analogy, through Fodor's characterization of the logic of psychological description as functional, to Lewis's conclusive innovation of identifying functional with causal roles, can lend significant insight into why functionalism should still have a problem with consciousness, and into where a resolution to this ongoing problem might be found.

V

In suggesting causal-role functionalism, Lewis exploited a structuralist view of the semantics of intertheoretic reduction that had in fact originated within the analytic tradition decades earlier, in F. P. Ramsey's 1929 consideration of the semantic relationship between the statements and axioms of an empirical theory and the nontheoretical factual sentences that they summarize.[49] In "Theories," Ramsey had suggested a logical method by means of which sentences in the theoretical language could be construed as definitionally related to statements of fact, even if there were no direct definitions available to connect theoretical terms to terms of the factual language. The solution turned on the possibility of rewriting a theoretical sentence by construing its theoretical terms as existentially quantified bound variables. Given the set of postulates of a theory T, we can rewrite them as the *Ramsey sentence* for T: the sentence that results when each of the theoretical terms in the set of postulates is replaced with a unique existentially quantified bound variable. The Ramsey sentence of T says, then, that there is some set of entities that *realizes* T: some set of entities that makes its set of postulates true. More generally, given any theoretical story sufficient to designate uniquely the entities that it concerns, we can replace the theoretical story (we can imagine it as a single, long, conjunctive sentence) with its Ramsey sentence: the sentence that says that there are unique entities that realize the theoretical story, that stand in just the relations that it specifies in theoretical terms.

In its conception of intertheoretic reduction as requiring a single, comprehensive characterization of the reduced theory, articulated purely in terms of the relations that it asserts to hold, Ramsey's suggestion both espouses the semantic structuralism that (as we saw in Chapters 2 and 3) was the basis of the Vienna Circle's contemporary attempts to understand experience and anticipates the subsequent application of the structuralist picture to the question of the explanatory relationships between theories. In the 1970 article "How to Define Theoretical Terms," Lewis noted explicitly that Ramsey's account of theoretical terms offers a substantially new conception of the relationship of reduction between an old and a new theory. For whereas it had standardly been assumed that reduction, if the reducing theory involves terms not directly definable in terms of the reduced theory, must involve the positing of additional substantial "bridge laws" to connect the old theory and the new one, Ramsey's innovation showed how new terms could be introduced without direct definition, but without requiring new bridge laws either. On Lewis's account, reducing a theory means discovering the entities, written in terms of a second, reducing theory, that satisfy the reduced theory's Ramsey sentence. Once this occurs, the sentences of the reduced theory can be seen to be straightforward logical consequences of the sentences of the reducing theory, even though they are not linked to them by relations of direct definition. The situation is rather that the entities of the reducing theory *realize* the reduced theory by satisfying its Ramsey sentence. If this is a good model of reduction, though, it also follows that there is no need for additional substantive "bridge laws" to link the two theories. All the laws of the reduced theory follow directly from the reducing theory, given the way in which the theoretical terms are introduced.

The upshot for the logic of psychophysical identity is straightforward. If Lewis's model of reduction is generally correct, then the identity between mental states and physical brain states need not be *posited* independently of the implicit theory that governs ordinary mentalistic discourse. Instead, this identity is a definitional *consequence* of the everyday mentalistic theory: given the theory's descriptions of mental states and their realizations, the identity hypothesis says only that the theory is realized. Given this, all that is needed for the completion of the Identity Theory is the determination of which particular brain states realize it. The ordinary-level mentalistic theory already sufficiently determines the identities, provided only that the ordinary-level theory itself defines the objects of its mentalistic terms as the occupants of the causal roles that it specifies:

I shall uphold the view that psychophysical identifications thus described would be like theoretical identifications, though they would not fit the usual account thereof. For the usual account, I claim, is wrong; theoretical identifications in general are implied by the theories that make them possible – not posited independently. This follows from a general hypothesis about the meanings of theoretical terms: that they are definable functionally, by reference to causal roles.[50]

The direct descendence of Lewis's suggestion from Ramsey's original suggestion about intertheoretic reduction shows the depth and extent of its roots in the structuralist picture of language, definitive for the methods and conceptions of analysis that both Ramsey and Lewis presupposed. By showing how functional analysis could at the same time be causal analysis, Lewis effectively allowed the traditional analytic program of logical analysis to continue in a new – and newly empirically respectable – form, while guaranteeing the amenability of functionalist description to the prevailing physicalist picture of explanation and ontology. In this respect, Lewis's suggestion ameliorated the fundamental unclarity of Putnam's and Fodor's unaugmented picture on the relationship of functionally defined states to their physically defined realizers. But viewed historically, his suggestion has something of the character of a solution by fiat, a pragmatic suggestion that allowed philosophical discussion to continue in an empirical domain but left many outstanding, and important, philosophical issues internal to its doctrine unresolved. From a semantic point of view, at least, the underlying suggestion that experiences are defined by their causal roles offers little improvement, as Lewis himself recognized, over the logical behaviorist's claim that mental states are logical constructions from publicly observable behaviors or dispositions to behave.[51] It shares with this claim the problematic inference of semantic facts about the definition of terms from epistemological considerations about the justification of our ascription of them, and it does even less justice than its predecessor theories to the logical features of our use of experience-terms that do *not* relate directly to our positioning of them in a unified causal order. (For instance, it seems plausible that *descriptive* uses of experience-terms – their uses to rank and evaluate the quality of experiences, for example – have some bearing on their definition. But if so, their definition can hardly be *simply* a matter of their place in the causal order.)

Methodologically, the historical investigation reveals functionalism as a hybrid doctrine, born of the competing demands of traditional, linguistic-level analysis, on the one hand, and allowance for specialized empirical discovery, on the other. But as long as the functionalist model leaves the hypothesized relationship between functional states and physical states unclear, the program, as so defined, is at best a combination of two logically and conceptually distinct components.

Lewis's suggestion, it is true, succeeds in unifying the two into a single program, blending conceptual research into the causal roles definitive of experiences with empirical research into the identity of their contingent occupiers. Still, if the *identification* of experiences with their causal roles is not recommended by some more fundamental and semantically perspicuous argument connecting commonsense-level causal roles with physical-level ones, the resulting doctrine of functionalism remains a hybrid that fails to define a clear and comprehensive investigative program. In particular, the identification of experiences with their causal roles does not, at least immediately, determine the conditions under which a logical-level analysis of the causally descriptive function of an experience-term could be defeated by a specialized neurophysical or physiological investigation (or vice versa). Nor does it give any account of the *criteria* for the identification of causal roles described on the level of commonsensical psychological description with causal roles described on the neurophysiological level. This unclarity has continued to trouble the logic of the investigation and reporting of results within the cognitive sciences, and it seems unlikely to be resolved without the deployment of a new level of explicit philosophical attention to the sometimes conflicting methodological claims of meaning analysis and empirical research within the context of the progress of those sciences.

Lewis's solution effectively inaugurated functionalism as a unified theory by unifying the logic of behaviorist explanation with the logic of causal explanation. The innovation solved the problems that had puzzled Putnam and Fodor about the relationship between functional descriptions and underlying causal ones. But the core of its suggestion was by no means unprecedented in the history of philosophy of mind. For the two explanatory structures that Lewis integrated were, in reality, siblings, joint offspring of the structuralist picture of explanation that consistently recurs in analytic philosophy of mind.

The historical analysis shows that both the underlying inspiration of functionalism and its most essential source of evidence over the course of its development arose from considerations of the logic of language. Both the Identity Theory and logical behaviorism, which functionalism united, themselves arose, as we have seen, from considerations of the logic of our language of consciousness. And it was to this language that functionalism most determinatively looked for inspiration

over the period of its development. It was, after all, the consideration, already suggested by Smart, that the references of psychological
terms could remain fixed even while their senses changed that led
Putnam to his decisive reconsideration of the diachronic logic of theory change and to the first suggestions of functionalism on its basis.
The suggestion operated at first, as we have seen, within the thoroughly reductionist picture of theoretical interrelations that Putnam
initially presupposed. But Fodor's more sophisticated consideration
of the logic of psychological description soon suggested trouble for
the integration of psychology into the unreconstructed reductive picture, and thereby led to a more nuanced consideration of the logic
of reduction. It was on the basis of this consideration that Lewis, in
1965, offered what was in effect a semantic solution to the problem of
the reducibility of functionalist descriptions: his proposal that psychological terms, as ordinarily used in intersubjective language, could be
defined in terms of causal roles occupied contingently by particular
physical brain states.

Lewis's solution, like the innovations that preceded it, thus traded
decisively on a suggestion about the logic of our language of experience. In this case, the suggestion was that this logic is essentially a
causal logic: that is, that the terms by means of which we describe and
relate sensations and other experiences define them by reference to
the total pattern of causes and effects in which they figure. The suggestion depends to some extent on features of the logic of mentalistic
explanation and description already noted by Fodor; but it gains most
of whatever plausibility it has from the antecedent presupposition of a
structuralist picture of explanation, according to which explaining the
terms of mentalistic description ultimately amounts to locating them
within a total relational structure in terms of which they are defined.
That the relevant structure would be a structure of physical causes
and effects had already been suggested by Neurath's original semantic
version of physicalism, and Lewis's suggestion just drew out the consistent implications of this doctrine, given the subsequent identification
of problems with the reductive model of the unity of science that it
had initially seemed to suggest.

The historical analysis reveals functionalism as the consistent, and
probably the ultimate, expression of the structuralism that has organized inquiry in the analytic tradition's consideration of experience

since its inception. Like its antecedents, functionalism exploits particular features of the language of experience in order to present this language as explicable insofar as it can be located within a total, relational description of the world. At the same time, it inevitably ignores other important features of the logic of the language of consciousness, leading to the recurrence of the complaint that experience resists structuralist explanation. For decades, the puzzles and thought experiments that have problematized the claim of functionalism to be able to explain subjective experience have turned on the general objection to structuralism that has repeatedly recurred, and driven theoretical innovation, at several stages of the history of analytic philosophy of mind. Examples, like Block's, that picture a functionally characterizable system isomorphic to the organization of a human individual simply provide vivid illustrations of the underlying objection: that no general structuralist account can adequately explain experience.

Exhibiting the real linguistic provenance of the theory of functionalism has the effect of exposing its seldom-understood methodological basis and thereby opening it to criticism on methodological grounds. In particular, decisive theoretical innovations like Lewis's can then be reevaluated in terms of the extent of their real grounding in the evidence to which they appeal. As we have seen, the essentially semantic investigations of theorists such as Putnam and Fodor showed that important logical features of the ordinary practice of psychological description and explanation are indeed similar, wholly or in part, to logical features of causal explanation in other domains. And here, as elsewhere, focusing attention on the semantics of diachronic theory change is a legitimate and helpful way of recognizing that ordinary descriptive practices can change under the influence of new empirical discoveries, and of making room in one's analysis for this possibility. But the recognition of instructive partial parallels between two discursive practices is obviously far from providing a warrant, by itself, for assimilating the logic of one of them wholly to the logic of the other; and to recognize that ordinary explanatory practice often changes under the influence of new empirical results clearly is not, by itself, to provide reason to believe that it *must* change in any particular way, given any particular result. These further general conclusions could in fact seem justified only in that they seemed obligatory within an antecedently assumed structuralist picture of explanation, a picture that is itself not supported by any particular result of linguistic reflection. It was only the assumption of such a general picture that could seem to necessitate that ordinary psychological descriptions must in fact characterize causal roles, or that the real reference of descriptive sensation-terms must ultimately be revealed to be the contingent physical occupants of these roles. Both claims trade on considerations about the meaning of psychological terms of description in ordinary, intersubjective discursive practice, but they result only from the imposition upon these considerations of a global picture of explanation ultimately rooted in structuralist assumptions about meaning.

As we have seen in the preceding chapters, the causal physicalist picture of the world that Lewis applied in his ultimate solution ultimately arose from semantic structuralism, the doctrine that meaning is a matter of logical structure. Place and Smart had themselves presupposed physicalism when they appealed, against what they supposed to be Ryle's theory, to the referential character of sensation-terms as establishing the physical nature of their ultimate referents. Each of the reflective discoveries that led to the development of functionalism out of the Identity Theory concerned some aspect of the language of psychology. But as had repeatedly happened in the past, these discoveries of meaning were taken as discoveries of aspects of a general logical structure. Taken in this way, their real significance could not appear. Instead, they were interpreted as providing evidence for the structuralist theory of functionalism, and the complaint that experience cannot be explained in these terms remained and reoccurred.

6

Consciousness, Language, and the Opening of Philosophical Critique

The contemporary discussion of the problem of consciousness, interesting in itself, conceals what might prove to be the most important contribution of analytic philosophy to philosophical history. This contribution is the explicitly *linguistic* development of a philosophical understanding of ourselves through reflection on the language of consciousness. The tradition of analytic philosophy has comprised a set of characteristically linguistic practices and programs of explanation and analysis, programs that make sense of and support our ability to understand the world and ourselves by clarifying the concepts, terms, and propositions with which we do so. As I have attempted to show in the last four chapters, the contemporary discussion of the problem of explaining consciousness manifests an enduring and repeated problem for these methods as they have ordinarily been understood, a problem that can be clarified only by examining the methodological presuppositions that have dictated the specific forms of analysis characteristic of analytic philosophy at several moments of its history. The investigation of philosophical history reveals the genuine sources of the contemporary problem of consciousness in the analysis of the language that expresses it. This paves the way, in turn, for a future discussion that better satisfies the actual needs that have historically generated and continue to drive the current debates.

In the history I have related, the discussion of conscious experience has consistently taken the form of a dialectical oscillation between the explanatory claims of theories of experience, grounded in particular analytic projects, and forms of resistance to these projects that cite it as unexplainable in their terms. The general sources of this resistance have most often been obscure, because the general problem with explaining consciousness has figured in the philosophical discussion only as an objection to *particular* theories and programs of analysis. But the historical interpretation identifies the more general and underlying form of the problem by focusing attention on the consistent *methodological* assumptions that run through the particular theories and programs.[1] The historical analysis reveals the contemporary problem of explaining consciousness, in particular, as the consistent outcome of the methodological assumptions that have governed analytic philosophy's encounter with the human self-image, assumptions that have portrayed language as a unified structure of meaning and that have constrained the discussion of the language of consciousness to the description of structure. Within the ambit of these assumptions, consciousness consistently seems inexplicable. By reopening the question of the methods of interpretation that have yielded analytic philosophy's insights into consciousness, however, the historical analysis allows these assumptions to be reconsidered, and eventually to be replaced.

As the historical analysis shows, the real philosophical point of insisting on consciousness as insuperable to conceptual or logical explanation is not to manifest some unexplained phenomenon, state, or process that is part of the objective world, but rather to resist an assumption that has been implicitly accepted mostly because it has been obscured: the assumption that structuralist forms of explanation can adequately account for *everything* that we ordinarily say about ourselves. The historical investigation conducted here shows how to develop the contemporary debate into a more reflective discussion that takes this complaint seriously at its actual level of generality – in particular, to develop an explicitly *critical* discussion that recovers for the philosophical future the underlying meaning and continuing suggestiveness of the analytic tradition's century-long investigation of language and experience.

I

At the center of each of the moments of theoretical change we've investigated in the last four chapters is a single underlying problem: the intractability of experience to logical, linguistic, or structural analysis or description. I have argued that the problem of the intractability of consciousness to objective explanation – today often discussed as *the* most interesting and difficult problem in philosophy of mind – is more than simply another special problem. Instead, it has been, in its various forms, the central theoretical impulse driving changes in the investigative practices that have characterized analytic philosophy of mind. In this tradition, the attempt to explain the mind has consistently been the attempt to describe, using the conceptual tools of a linguistically informed investigation of meaning, the structure of experience. The philosophical problems involved in doing so have recurred again and again, even as philosophers of mind have altered their investigative practices in the attempt to solve or dismiss them. In the history of analytic philosophy of mind, conscious experience has been both the recurrent site of an intractability that consistently problematizes the totality of structuralist explanation and, in structuralism's various attempts to handle or dissimulate these problems, the most significant source of its methodological innovations.

The investigations of the preceding four chapters have suggested that the problems of explaining consciousness, at each important stage of the analytic project, have been, in the most general terms, problems of the relationship of *content* to *structure*. The forms of explanation and analysis characteristic of the analytic tradition have consistently been *structural* in that they have attempted to explain the nature of the referents of our terms of self-description by elucidating the logical, conceptual, or functional structure of those terms or of the claims that we make with them; and the complaint that consciousness is unexplainable has recurrently represented a form of protest against the totality of these structural methods. The close parallels between contemporary formulations of the recalcitrance of consciousness to objective explanation – such as Chalmers's – and older formulations, such as Carnap's, of the relationship of consciousness to structurally described objectivity already suffice to suggest the existence of a continuous philosophical problem underlying the debate at each of its intervening stages.[2] The four specific historical investigations support this suggestion by clarifying the nature of the underlying problem and its role in driving philosophical discussion at each of the moments we have examined.

To interrogate structuralism as such is, among other things, to question the comprehensiveness of the forms of explanation and analysis of *objectivity* that have defined the analytic tradition. The special link between the analysis of linguistic structure and the description of objectivity, generally characteristic of the analytic tradition's approaches to explanation, has taken various forms over the course of the history investigated here. We have seen that the link first figured in the logical positivists' attempt to explain the possibility of locating a basis of objectively articulated knowledge in subjective experience. The investigation of Husserl's and Schlick's different attempts to characterize the logical structure of experience considered the philosophical sources of a related structuralist idea: that conceptual analysis of the structure of our experience ought to be able to clarify the way in which the a priori possibilities of experience constrain the possibilities of meaning for objectively descriptive language. Ryle's project of conceptual analysis took the nature of our public and intersubjective concepts of mind to be characterizable in terms of the grammatical structure of interrelationships allowed by ordinary language and description for our claims about mental life. Finally, the functionalism of Putnam, Fodor, and Lewis explains our language of mentalistic description as specifying functional roles in virtue of the relational logic of ordinary psychological description, roles that are themselves characterizable as causal roles in the context of a total description of the causal structure of nature. Over the course of these developments, the claim of structural forms of analysis to elucidate has consistently resulted from the inclination to make the structure of *objectivity* intelligible through an investigation of the logical or conceptual structure of objectively meaningful language. This inclination has itself been one of the most central and continuous methodological tendencies of analytic philosophy, subsuming both the older reductive and atomistic forms of logical analysis and today's broader and more holistic investigative practices. The recognition of conscious experience as posing a constant and recurring problem for the methodologies of analysis that share this tendency, however, recommends that structuralism be reconsidered on the ground of the theory of language that it presupposes and depends on, even where its explanatory conception of objectivity takes forms that are not explicitly linguistic, but ontological or metaphysical in character.

II

Because it identifies the conceptual determinants of the contemporary problem on the level of permanent methodological features of the practices of analytic philosophy, the historical analysis developed here does more than just exhibit the continuity of these practices and the recurrence of the underlying problem. It additionally suggests a consistent *historical dynamic* that reveals the philosophical sources of some of the most important historical positions in the philosophy of mind.

We have seen that a structuralist conception of *meaning* has supported a variety of analytical projects and approaches throughout the course of the history here investigated. In each case, this conception of meaning additionally has implied a structuralist conception of *explanation*. For all of these approaches, to explain is to describe logical, conceptual, causal, or functional structure, and the promise of analysis is that our concepts of mentality and consciousness can be elucidated in just this way. But this invites a very general and comprehensive kind of protest to the explanatory project: the objection that consciousness will involve some feature or set of features that must be left out by any structural explanation of meaning or objectivity.[3] So far, the protest is a general one: experience has its essential meaning for us, not in virtue of the structure of objectively descriptive language, but on its own terms and somehow prior to such structure. Accordingly, it is tempting to conclude, there will be some aspect or feature of experience left out of even the best description of the logical structure of objectivity. But the protestor will soon, naturally enough, face the demand to *describe* the recalcitrant feature or property that he cites. He will be asked, in other words, to say which particular feature or property of consciousness it is that he thinks makes it resistant to forms of explanation that seem otherwise exhaustive. To satisfy the demand, the protestor can cite some range of facts, or some bit of ordinary description of the mental, that is left out of the current structuralist explanation.

But it is clear that once the protestor can cite such a fact or piece of language, it will itself be subject to the explanatory powers of a (possibly expanded) structuralist form of analysis. For it will itself be cited and described in effable terms of public discourse, exhibiting the very kinds of logical structure and interrelationships that generally make structuralist explanation possible. Under the admitted pressure of the demand to explain the recalcitrant phenomena of consciousness, the structuralist explanatory project has several times undergone extensive alterations in its specific character, transforming itself from the logical analysis of Carnap and Schlick, to the "logical geography" project of Ryle, to the functionalism of today. At each stage, the new form of analysis accommodates some of the facts of consciousness that could be cited as problems for its predecessor. But each transformation in the nature of structural analysis eventually prompts a renewed version of the general complaint that consciousness must escape it, and hence another iteration of the dynamic.

Thus it is not surprising that Schlick's foundationalism about experience was replaced by Neurath's coherentism, or that the failure of Ryle's project in the description of sensation reports led to the Identity Theory, or that questions about the Identity Theory's explanation of conscious states suggested functionalism as a successor theory (see Figure 1.1, page 23). In the recent discussion of consciousness, the dialectic has tended to repeat itself again. Functionalist theories of mind offer structuralist descriptions of consciousness that treat it as a set of information-processing capacities, prompting, naturally enough, the antistructuralist response that they leave out or disregard consciousness *itself*. But the positive concepts with which what has been left out is then characterized – concepts such as "quale" and "phenomenal content" – leave themselves open to a familiar objection. These concepts remain fundamentally unclear, the functionalist objector can point out, unless their advocates can point to the features or phenomena that they refer to.[4]

But if these features or phenomena are just objective properties of conscious beings, then the functionalist has already, at least in principle, explained them. Since the functionalist can account for any positive phenomenon that the antistructuralist cites, the *positive* characterization of consciousness as involving subjective qualia or phenomenal contents misses its mark and falls into incoherence. But since the protest is actually, at its basis, a more general one, against the totality of structuralist explanation itself rather than against any of its specific versions, its underlying philosophical sources remain in place.

It is important to understand the underlying form of the recurrent critique at its real level of philosophical generality. In each case,

(A)

Views about meaning *determine* → Analytic programs *determine* → Results about experience

(B)

Views about meaning *determine* → Analytic programs   Problems with experience

determine

FIGURE 6.1. The form of the discussion. The form that the discussion of experience in philosophy of mind has taken in (A) its normal moments and (B) some of the extraordinary moments of methodological change that I have discussed.

the complaint against structuralist explanation cites some particular feature or phenomenon of experience that the particular structuralist projects currently on offer leave out. But the enduring motivation of the critique does not depend on any particular feature or phenomenon of experience. Most generally, the complaint is just that structuralist forms of explanation fail to explain *everything* that figures in our ordinary linguistic practices.

The historical dynamic that I have described has been possible only because critical attention to specific philosophical results has usually rendered invisible the determination of those results by the presuppositions of particular programs of analysis. Specific programs of analysis have ordinarily insulated the general views of meaning that underlie them from the particular philosophical results that they determine (Figure 6.1a). Even at the exceptional moments (some of which I have examined in Chapters 2–5) when the recalcitrance to explanation of phenomena of experience and consciousness has caused new programs of analysis to arise, they have not done so by putting any direct pressure on the views about meaning that they presuppose (Figure 6.1b). With the continuity of structuralist forms of explanation in the analytic tradition revealed as such, however, the programs of analysis that they have supported can be explicitly reconsidered on the ground of the conceptions of meaning that those programs have presupposed. In this way, the exposure of structuralism to philosophical critique makes possible an explicit discussion of the way in which the language of consciousness problematizes or contests the totality of structuralist methods.

III

Although the historical investigation thus supports the notion of a systematic elusiveness of consciousness to the forms of objective characterization developed in the analytic tradition, it provides no support for any of the standard *positive* accounts of consciousness as a phenomenon recalcitrant to forms of explanation that work for most of the natural world. The most usual of these accounts remains *dualism*, and among those who take seriously the thought that consciousness cannot be explained in the usual structuralist ways, a historically retrograde dualism has sometimes seemed the only way to accommodate this failure of explanation. Thus Chalmers, for instance, after developing the "hard problem" in a comprehensive and compelling form, argues that it might be solved by a "naturalistic dualism" that seeks new natural laws, perhaps at a basic level, linking nonphysical consciousness with physical states and events.[5] But by missing the critical level of reflection on methodology that the historical investigation suggests, these attempts repeat the perennial theoretical failure of dualism. Seeking to accommodate the thought that subjectivity cannot straightforwardly fit into the objective physical, spatial world – but missing that the underlying reason for this lies in the distinctiveness of our ways of talking about subjectivity itself – the dualist makes the experiencing subject a *nonphysical, nonspatial* entity that is nonetheless, ontologically and semantically, as much an objective constituent of the world as any spatial and physical state, process, or event.[6]

There is little reason, therefore, to suppose that a dualist solution can solve the problem of explaining consciousness, for any such solution simply invites a recurrence of the underlying complaint that originally prompted it. The dualist's nonphysical subject of experience would participate in the same network of causal and explanatory relations that support physicalist explanation. If the problem of explaining consciousness is, as has been argued, the problem that *no* explanation of this relational form can suffice, then the dualist "explanation" of consciousness is no better off than the physicalist one.

More generally, the historical investigation suggests that the debate about the explanation of consciousness has been possible only because both sides of the debate – both structuralists who assert the explainability of consciousness and their opponents who deny it – have adhered in their philosophical practice to a common assumption, one that the historical investigation exposes and shows us how to resist. The assumption is that our ability to talk about experience, if it is legitimate, *must* be supported by a philosophical or scientific *description* of consciousness as a state, phenomenon, or process. This assumption has supported both the structuralist's reductive and deflationary analyses of consciousness and the usual antistructuralist responses that point to positive features and phenomena supposedly left out of the structuralist's analysis, leading to the consistent historical dynamic already discussed. But the historical investigation shows that, if we want to escape this dynamic and understand the real form of the problem, we ought to avoid the assumption. We should not think that, in order to *legitimate* or *understand* consciousness, we need to *theorize* it as a state, phenomenon, or process. We should, instead, recognize that any positive antistructuralist theory of consciousness – for instance, any positive theory of qualia or "raw feels" – will fail to preserve the complaint that motivates it. By articulating a positive vision of the special nature of consciousness that supposedly accounts for its unexplainability, it will invite rather than resist structuralist critique, inviting appropriation by structuralist methods where it points to facts of the familiar, structurally comprehensible kinds, and lapsing into incoherence where it points to facts of other supposed kinds.

The structuralist theories and pictures that we have examined here share more than just the commitment to a common style of linguistic analysis. They additionally make for this style a claim of *comprehensiveness*: a claim that *all* meaningful linguistic utterances are explicable by structuralist means. This structuralist claim of explanatory totality originates in the structuralist's claim to capture the necessary preconditions for the possibility of linguistic meaning overall, but it survives in each of the particular structuralist attempts to theorize consciousness examined here. Its totalizing character is evident in each theoretical appeal to a totalizing structure that we have examined: it shows up, for instance, in each of the Vienna positivists' characteristic appeals to the logical structure of language as the necessary form of communication; in Schlick's claim to theorize language as the total structure of conventional rules of use; in Ryle's occasional references to the "logical geography" of our concepts; in Place's and Smart's conception of the "physical world," later developed as the physicalist worldview; and in the early functionalists' references to "the logic of psychology." Even those philosophers in the tradition, such as Schlick and the early Carnap, who think of consciousness as ineffable content "outside" the total field of structuralizable language presuppose the claim to explanatory totality in their conception of the ineffability of whatever lies outside this field and in their analyses of our reference to experience as involving ostension or bare presence. The claim to explanatory totality, indeed, provides the only significant warrant there is for subjecting the language of consciousness to structuralist analysis. Without it, there would be little or no reason to think that the ordinary language of consciousness requires or even admits of such an analysis. Indeed, in the absence of the claim of explanatory totality, it seems singularly implausible that the specific kind of self-understanding that we want out of our investigations of consciousness, an investigation of the language in which we express what is in each case idiosyncratic, particular, and self-reflexive, can be produced by reference to a structure of relations that is itself universal and objective.

Even aside from the specific kinds of resistance that philosophical descriptions of consciousness have offered to it, the structuralist claim to explanatory totality ought to seem dubious as soon as it is exposed by methodologically sensitive analysis. It amounts to the assertion that particular forms of explanation and analysis that have been clarificatory for some areas of language are in fact applicable to *all* areas and, moreover, that their explanatory abilities in each of these areas are *comprehensive*, that they leave out nothing that we should want to understand about why we talk in the ways that we do. Only this latter claim of comprehensiveness could issue in the suggestion that a structuralist analysis can show that some or all of our ordinary talk of consciousness is, in itself, illegitimate. For only this claim could imply that there is no point in talking about consciousness as something that remains unexplained even when all of the possible structuralist analyses of particular states, processes, and phenomena are completed. But this suggestion of comprehensiveness is not earned by any particular explanatory success or set of successes that structuralist analyses can claim. Nothing about the actual successes of analytical methods of analysis and clarification in explaining particular phenomena and pieces of language implies that these methods are comprehensively applicable to *all* meaningful language or to *all* phenomena that we can meaningfully discuss.

In the recent discussion of explaining consciousness, even where the legitimacy and priority of explicitly *linguistic* methods for understanding consciousness have been recognized, this recognition has most often coexisted with a continued maintenance of the structuralist assumption of explanatory totality that continues to falsify the real character and potential of these methods. A prominent recent example of this coexistence is Dennett's (1991) defense of what he calls the method of *heterophenomenology*. Doubting the reliability of purely first-person methods such as introspection, Dennett argues that progress in understanding consciousness requires a method that, even in making sense of the purely phenomenal elements of individual consciousness, respects the objectivity and third-personal character of scientific inquiry.[7] The right way to reconcile these commitments, Dennett suggests, is to adopt a method that is explicitly *interpretive*: in particular, to treat a subject's descriptions of her own conscious states and phenomena as a stable, interpretable, and potentially unifiable text. At this stage, Dennett suggests, the investigator maintains a constitutive *neutrality* with respect to the existence of the phenomena reported in the subject's text.[8] He suggests conceiving of the status of the heterophenomenological text by analogy with the status of a *fictional* text: as defining a "heterophenomenological world" open to questions of consistency and internal coherence, but not necessarily a *real* world in which the entities reported actually exist.[9] Once the heterophenomological text has been completely assembled and understood, however, it becomes possible to inquire into the reality of its objects:

My suggestion, then, is that if we were to find real goings-on in people's brains that had *enough* of the "defining" properties of the items that populate their heterophenomenological worlds, we could reasonably propose that we had discovered what they were *really* talking about – even if they initially resisted the identifications. And if we discovered that the real goings-on bore only a minor resemblance to the heterophenomenological items, we could reasonably declare that people were just mistaken in the beliefs they expressed, in spite of their sincerity.[10]

Dennett's argument for an explicitly interpretive method of understanding consciousness manifests his recognition of the limitations of purely first-personal methods and his appreciation of the linguistic character of the methods that have defined the analytic inquiry into consciousness. The investigation of consciousness is, as Dennett recognizes, always also an investigation into the meaning of the language by which we make claims about consciousness. But like his physicalist predecessors in the analytic tradition, Dennett situates this methodological insight within the ambit of the assumption that our talk about consciousness, if it is to be valid, must be supported or supportable by a general structuralist account of its significance. This assumption is evident, in particular, in Dennett's construal of the interpreted remarks of a subject about his own consciousness as "data" for a physicalistic *theory* of consciousness, and in his suggestion that the *reality* of the entities in a subject's heterophenomenological world can ultimately be settled only by discovering their similarity to physical brain events. The suggestion amounts to the methodological assumption of an unargued physicalism, and it threatens to falsify the results of the very interpretive method that Dennett defends.

The assumption provides the basis for most of the rest of Dennett's explanatory project in *Consciousness Explained*, a project that conceives of itself as providing a physicalistically respectable and scientifically grounded alternative to a Cartesian conception of mind that is still, according to Dennett, prominent in both ordinary and philosophical discussions. In his defense of a method that refutes the Cartesian theory by interpreting the ordinary utterances of untutored subjects about their own conscious experience, Dennett presupposes (without rehearsing) the "ordinary language" methodology of his teacher Ryle. But to subject the language of consciousness to the assumption that its legitimacy and truth depend on its reference to physical events, causally described, is to break essentially with the method defended by Ryle, limiting and modifying the practice of interpretation just where it might prove most revealing. The assumption is licensed only by the general structuralist claim that every describable event or phenomenon is analyzable in structuralist terms, a claim that the dualist shares insofar as he purports to give a positive theoretical description of the nature of the events referred to in our ordinary language of consciousness. The third alternative, ungrasped by Dennett and his dualist opponent alike but actually diagnostic of the debate in which they both participate, is to practice the interpretation of the language of consciousness outside the ambit of any such general assumption, looking for the distinctive kind of intelligibility that it can produce without subjecting this intelligibility to an antecedently held structuralist theory of language.

IV

The present historical analysis locates the origin of the problem of explaining consciousness in the structuralist theory of meaning and in the characteristic structuralist assumption of explanatory totality. This does not suffice, admittedly, to provide any direct *solution* to the problem as it is currently discussed. But it does show how historical and methodological critique can substantially resolve the problem nevertheless. It does this by exposing the methodological assumptions that have organized the problem in a way that is directly *diagnostic* of it; and it can subsequently provide the basis for a reconsideration and replacement of these assumptions that moves beyond diagnosis to substantial *cure*.

The structuralist claim to explanatory totality has seemed plausible, in large part, because of its connection to the characteristic interpretive methods of analytic philosophy, methods that aim to produce philosophical insight by clarifying the meaning of ordinary locutions and sentences. A general structuralist theory of meaning has seemed to offer the only possible way of understanding the possibility and force of these methods, and has accordingly seemed to offer the only plausible account of the nature of meaning itself. At a later stage in the dialectic, what was initially the structuralist theory of meaning became the unified physicalist account of the world, obscuring the original connection of structuralist theory with linguistic reflection, even as this connection remained determinative of the distinctive methods of analytic philosophy. Exposing the structuralist assumption that has underlain the analytic discussion of consciousness throughout its history, however, has the effect of reexposing this assumption to criticism on the level of the methodological grounds that provide its ultimate basis.

In this way, philosophical history provides the basis on which the structuralist claim to explanatory totality can be extracted from obscurity and explicitly reconsidered. The historical analysis cannot demonstrate, by itself, the falseness or incoherence of this claim; to purport to do so would be to offer a kind of theory, even if only a negative one, that historical reflection itself cannot support. But even the exposure of the structuralist claim to explanatory totality has the effect of transforming the debate, opening the logical and rhetorical space for resistance, on the basis of a reconsideration of the method of linguistic analysis itself, to the assumptions that have led to the contemporary discussion of the problem and locked it in the pattern of theoretical oscillation that continues to characterize it today.

Without the structuralist claim to explanatory totality, the problem of explaining consciousness, as it is currently discussed, cannot even arise. For without the structuralist claim to explanatory totality, the comprehensive explanatory claims of structuralism – physicalism's claim to explain every real phenomenon in physical terms, and functionalism's claim to explain every mental phenomenon in functional terms – are themselves unformulable. These claims to explanatory totality have appeared, in recent stages of the dialectic, to be supported by general metaphysical theses about the nature of events and phenomena in the world, but I have argued that they remain decisively grounded in a particular conception of the nature of meaning. It is only because they have seemed to be metaphysical theses, rather than semantic ones, that they have seemed to demand that any consistent resistance to them take the form of the introduction of new processes, states, or events inexplicable in physicalist or functionalist terms. Shifting the rhetorical ground of the discussion back to its real basis in the methods of linguistic insight allows the objection to structuralism to be reformulated, in more self-conscious and revealing terms, as an objection to the totality of the structuralist view of language itself.

Does there not remain, all linguistic and methodological questions aside, a deep and basic mystery about the place of consciousness in nature? The abiding sense of such a mystery has provided the usual backdrop of discussions of consciousness, not just in the analytic tradition but throughout discussions of the metaphysics of mind since Descartes, and it is impossible to deny that the feeling of a mystery here has driven some of the most significant developments in the history of modern philosophical thinking about subjectivity and its relation to the objective world. The response of the historical analysis is not to deny the sense of mystery, but to relocate it by critically questioning the semantic grounds of the terms of its contemporary formulation. For as the historical analysis points out, the place of consciousness in nature can, at any moment of the philosophical dialogue, seem to be the *particular* problem that it is only against the backdrop of a *particular* conception of nature. Just as Descartes' conception of matter as *res extensa* set the terms in which he was able to portray the mind as nonphysical, the structuralist conception of the unity of nature as the unity of physical law has set the terms in virtue of which consciousness has seemed to be an explanatory problem. But this structuralist conception itself, as I have argued, rests ultimately on semantic reasoning about the overall nature of meaning, and it is eminently questionable on this ground. To expose it to this questioning on the level of philosophical method is not only to recover, for the debate, the most decisive innovation of the analytic tradition – its turn toward a specifically linguistic method of investigation – but also to gesture toward the real depth of the mystery of the *meaning* of consciousness, a mystery that subsumes all of the projects and developments of the analytic discussion of consciousness but has not even generally been recognized as such in the most recent stages of this discussion.

Contrary to appearances, consciousness is not the "last frontier," the only important phenomenon still left out of a comprehensive and ever-expanding web of scientific explanation, awaiting only a new discovery or breakthrough to make it tractable. It is, however, the core of some of the deepest concerns and most enduring problems of our human self-understanding. Recognizing the ultimately linguistic origins of the problem of explaining consciousness allows us to see these concerns and mysteries as they exist and have figured, through the twentieth century, in the philosophical practices that have themselves made the structuralist conception of nature possible. That the mystery of consciousness reveals itself, in the twentieth century, as the mystery of the language of consciousness shows that the question about the place of consciousness in the world is decisively linked to the question of meaning, of the precipitous and elusive configuration of the self-consciousness with which we pose the question of the significance of our own kind of existence, reflected in the meaning of our language of it.

V

In the history discussed here, beginning with the Vienna Circle, the structuralist view of language has consistently and repeatedly seemed to analytic philosophers to be both a necessary precondition for the possibility of their various practices of logical, conceptual, and grammatical analysis and insight, and the most significant result of these practices. Structuralism has been, as we have seen in the preceding chapters, the determinative faith of the analytic inquiry into consciousness, held throughout the history we've considered with a tenacity that must be considered remarkable. The remarkable endurance of structuralism within the analytic inquiry into consciousness traces not to any particular result of analysis about language or the mind, but rather to the methodological unity of the tradition of specifically linguistic inquiry itself, across the decades of the twentieth century and the diversity of practices of linguistic analysis. But in fact the historical reconsideration of these practices and their real implications shows that nothing about the specific forms of insight that they allow demands structuralism as an interpretation of or precondition for them. Examined in the new light of historical and methodological reconsideration, structuralism emerges as both the most characteristic temptation of linguistic analysis and the source of its greatest failures with respect to our self-understanding. Understanding the characteristic kinds of insight that linguistic reflection yields about consciousness, then, requires that we reconsider the methodological warrant of structuralism by reflecting on its basis, or lack thereof, in the practice of analysis.

At first, we have seen, the practice of linguistic analysis seems to require a structuralist view of language in that it operates by exposing, describing, or capturing the *genuine* logical form of an utterance, over against the tendency of ordinary language to conceal or obscure it. Beginning with Frege's innovation in *Begriffschrift*, the analysis of meaning seemed to be the identification of the underlying logical laws that determine the inferential and semantic relations of sentences. The work of analysis is, then, the determination of logical form as the structure of abstract rules that govern the significant interrelations of senses and contents in the language; and the analysis of the logical content (as opposed to the psychological content) of sentences in the language seems to be wholly exhausted by the elaboration of these rules. Prominent misinterpretations of the early Wittgenstein's conception of "logical form" gave further support to this understanding of analysis. The practice of analysis seemed, in the *Tractatus* as well, to result in the demonstration of the ineffable, crystalline logical structure of the rules of language, accordance with which was always a precondition for the possibility of meaningfulness.[11] And we have seen, in Chapter 2, how the logical positivists' conception of structure as the essential precondition for the possibility of objective meaningfulness supported their understanding of epistemologically reconstructive analysis as accounting, via structuralization, for the meaning of scientific claims. For each of these projects, the practice of logical analysis seemed to be the revelation of the transcendent, objective structure that makes meaningful language itself possible. The elucidation of this structure was to abstract from the ambiguities and infelicities of ordinary language, revealing the hard core of rule-governed meaning behind the obscuring vestments of ordinary speech.

For these early projects, then, the analysis of meaning, aided by the formal tools of symbolic logic, is the exposure of the real logical form of a proposition, comprehensible as its place in the total, formally defined network of logically possible contents. The demonstration of the logical significance of the proposition is at the same time the description of its place in the total logical structure of language; and it is in virtue of its place in this structure that the proposition has the logically relevant meaning that it does. That language overall has a determinate, describable logical structure seems, then, to be both a necessary precondition for the possibility of elucidatory analysis and a necessary upshot of its practice. Both in general and in specific areas of traditional philosophical puzzlements, analysis moves from the particular sentence toward the increasing revelation of the supra-particular and unified structure that bestows upon it its specific, logically defined and objective, meaning.

The temptation of structuralism arises, then, in the first instance as part of strongly revisionary projects that see the logical structure of language as something entirely distinct from, and comprehensible only by way of abstraction from, the ordinary intersubjective use of language. But it survives, almost as robustly, even in later conceptions of analysis that aim to do nothing more than to expose the logical structure of ordinary linguistic practice. Here, as in Schlick's conventionalism (Chapter 3) and – at least sometimes – in Ryle's conception of his own method (Chapter 4), the logical structure of language, to be revealed by analysis, is no longer located in a super-empirical Platonic realm or as the transcendent structure of the world itself. But the temptation to construe analysis as revealing the logical structure of language remains. Logical structure now figures as "implicit" in practice, as a matter of the stipulative or conventional rules that language users, *qua* language users, follow and agree upon, as a matter of sociological or pragmatic fact, in order to make communication possible. Even if they do not explicitly grasp what they implicitly follow, the real meanings of language users within a concrete, specific practice are to be shown by reflecting on the underlying structure of rules that in fact govern usage in that practice. Here, the methodological warrant for analysis is no longer the thought that meaning must be guaranteed by a set of abstract logical rules, sublimely independent of the actual practice of language. But the now-guiding conception of meaning as use or usage produces a structuralism about the underlying rules of use that is just as robust, and just as potentially misleading in relation to the language of consciousness.[12]

The methodological temptation to structuralism survives, and continues to have the determinative theoretical consequences that we've seen, even within theoretical projects that see themselves as the partially or wholly *empirical* analysis of patterns of intersubjective use, meaning, or reference. As we saw in Chapter 5, at the moment at which the identity theory cedes to functionalism, the authority of functionalist claims about the real meaning or reference of the claims of our ordinary mentalistic discourse comes to depend on the philosopher's insight into the dynamics of semantic changes in the meaning and reference of theoretical terms. And the possibility of this insight itself depends on a structuralist conception of meaning. The ultimate theory of causal-role functionalism depends on the structuralist construal of the logic of ordinary terms of mentalistic description as, at least implicitly or essentially, a *causal* logic. And it hangs its ultimate description of the meaning of ordinary mentalistic terms of description on its preconception that they must, in order to mean what they do, ultimately say something about the causal structure of the world. Their analysis is then the discovery of occupants of the causal roles that define them, a practice that is empirical in the form of its discoveries but thoroughly structuralist in its theory of meaning.

At each of these stages of the analytic tradition, then, structuralism about meaning, in various forms, has seemed to be both the precondition and the result of each of the various concrete practices of logical and conceptual analysis, insight, and reflection that we've considered. But at the same time, the analysis of consciousness has repeatedly manifested a deep resistance to the structuralist theory of meaning and its associated claim to explanatory totality. Understanding, in historical detail, the reasons for this resistance allows us to begin to see an alternative to the structuralist interpretation of the method of analysis itself, an alternative that begins to reveal the language of consciousness as subject to a specific kind of nonstructuralist and self-reflexive intelligibility that is distinctively appropriate to it. This kind of intelligibility emerges, repeatedly and at definitive but isolated moments in the history of the analytic tradition, as the result of linguistic analysis of the language of consciousness, but it is always in imminent danger of being lost again when this analysis is subjected to a structuralist interpretation.

VI

From the beginning of its discussion in the analytic tradition, conscious experience has figured as that field of interiority, subjectivity, or privacy that must be set off against the structural totality of objectively descriptive language, reduced by the progress of scientific structuralization or unspeakable in its vocabulary, its positive implications of resistance to the structuralist order assimilated or dissimulated by the progress of explanation itself. But as we have seen, the successive theoretical projects of structuralism also drew decisive and positive theoretical support, at each moment of their development, from the insights of linguistic reflection about the language of consciousness, even when this support was only the paradoxical one of defining the margin or boundary of explanation that must, at each stage of progress, be successively reduced. It is the suggestion of this work that analytic philosophy's encounter with consciousness has been the locus of its consideration of the human self-image, an encounter that has been as decisive for the development of analytic philosophy as its object is significant in itself, even when (as has typically been the case) this inquiry has operated in the obscuring explanatory modes of assimilation and self-denial. The interpretive investigations of the preceding four chapters read the history of analytic philosophy of mind in terms of its paradoxical, sometimes self-obscuring concern with the image of the human, producing the story of this concern as the story of the unself-aware struggle of distinctively linguistic insight into consciousness with the ever-present theoretical temptation to make the language that relates it the unified description of an objectively present natural phenomenon.

The most significant interpretive result of the historical investigation is its exposure of the historical dynamic of opposition that links and opposes the language of consciousness to structuralism in each of its versions in the history of analytic philosophy of mind. The analytic tradition's concern with the human self-image has, according to the historical analysis conducted here, unfolded in the terms of this opposition and still remains, in the form of the contemporary problem of explaining consciousness, locked within it.

Structuralism subsumes practices of analysis that are as general as the view of language that it formulates. The language of consciousness resists the structuralist picture, not by demonstrating the falseness or incoherence of this picture, but by demanding for its own intelligibility an alternative construal and practice of the work of analysis. This alternative resists the generality of structuralist explanations and the analytic practice that delivers them, on the ground of the language of consciousness itself. The language of consciousness, as we have seen, is the language with which we express (among other things) what is in each case our own: that core of sensations, impressions, memories, and beliefs that we typically think of as most interior to us, even in the publicity of their linguistic expression. And even without proposing or implying a tendentious view of the implications of this interiority, the ordinary language of consciousness, in its very dialectical movement, recognizes and confirms it. The claim that the language of consciousness expresses, and that seeks the recognition of another, in the report of a pain or the articulation of a mental image is immediately misconstrued, in each case, by the structuralism that sees the locutions of these expressions only as descriptions meaningful in that they occupy a position in the total logical structure of language. Reflection on the language of consciousness in its intersubjective, dialectical situation, by contrast, offers to remind us of the inadequacy of structuralism for its comprehension, furthering the expression of consciousness itself as the linguistic articulation, in doctrine and practice, of the self-image that it defines.

As the philosophical tradition since Descartes amply testifies, what is in each case one's own, the privilege of the self, has multiple dimensions and significances, as manifold and far-ranging as the being of the human subject itself. And it is no historical accident that the philosophical self-reflection on subjective experience that once organized a whole metaphysics of Absolute Idealism could be, by the beginning of the twentieth century in the analytic tradition, narrowed down to the merely sensory and phenomenal conception of "experience" that the first analytic philosophers already presupposed. For as we have seen since the first chapter, this narrowing supplements and responds to the widening of a reflection on language that expands to include within the universality and objectivity of concepts everything that is linguistically expressible, seemingly leaving the meaning of bare phenomenal consciousness inexpressible or mute, the last remnant of subjectivity that cannot be reduced by the universality of successive definition. Interrogated as an objectively present phenomenon of nature, phenomenal experience becomes the unarticulated, indefinable presupposition for all articulated awareness or the core of a conceptual illusion that must be explained or explained away by means of an expanding science. Reading the dialectic of consciousness in the analytic tradition as that tradition's way of figuring, and responding to, the human self-conception, however, opens a passage to an alternative conception of the joined significance of the analysis of language and the understanding of consciousness, within a future philosophical practice that would recover the founding and constitutive insights of the analytic inquiry into the mind as revealing, rather than obscuring, the self-consciousness of the language they invoke.

VII

Since Kant, a *critical* philosophical discussion is one that explicitly and centrally considers and evaluates its own method of producing intelligibility, the form and credentials of its own distinctive kind of philosophical insight. The turn to criticism endows philosophical understanding with the self-conscious movement of the articulation of its own limits, expanding and enriching the dialectic of its relation to that which is beyond it. Throughout the twentieth century, structuralism has figured the limits of language as the limits of an objectively present and describable logical structure, reducing conscious experience as mutely exterior to it. In all of its theoretical assumptions and movements, structuralism has presupposed a conception of the limits of philosophical insight and linguistic intelligibility without in general making this conception explicit as an object of investigation. But attention to the language of consciousness already suffices to contest, as it has implicitly at several moments of the analytic inquiry, the conception of all that can be said as the display of a unified, objective logical structure of language. Understanding this contestation at the level of its real generality and methodological implication, historical inquiry recovers the problem of consciousness as the motivation for an explicitly critical discussion of the relation of language to experience. Inflecting the debate critically yields the suggestion that the distinctively linguistic forms of interpretation characteristic of the analytic tradition, read outside the structuralist assumptions to which they have constantly submitted, can bring the joint intelligibility of language and consciousness to view, in a dialectic that does not rest in any stable, theoretical solution but may nevertheless find satisfaction.[13]

The kind of critical limit-fixing work I am suggesting for a descendent of the contemporary debate has, of course, distinguished philosophical ancestors. The idea of a critical fixing of the limits of *knowledge* traces to Kant and results from his concern to limit reason's pretensions to knowledge beyond the bounds of experience. An even more complete parallel is Wittgenstein's limit-fixing project in the *Tractatus*, a project of defining the boundaries of meaningful language in order to gesture at that which is outside them, what can be shown but not said. For Wittgenstein, there is no possibility of a theoretical description of that which is outside the boundaries of theoretically descriptive language. We can only gesture at the showable by showing that any proposition that attempts to describe it is nonsense. The special work of philosophical criticism is to allow the formulation of what appear to be positive theoretical claims about the showable, and then to embarrass them by exposing their nonsensicality. The consistent historical complaint in favor of consciousness, I have argued, has exemplified just such a gesturing, and a future version of the current debate could give it a critical turn by developing structuralist methods into just this sort of practice. The attempt to give a positive philosophical characterization of the nature of consciousness or subjectivity has consistently yielded what must be, by the lights of structuralist analysis, nonsense. But in the light of historical reflection, it is possible to see the significance of this historically important kind of nonsense in terms of its ability to define the limits of a kind of explanation that is otherwise quite general.

The work of criticism, in its self-consciousness about philosophical practice, is immediately the fixation of the limits and boundaries of the specific methods of philosophical insight. But beyond simply fixing their limits, criticism can also sharpen and expand these methods by making them aware of themselves. In the case of the analytic investigation of the mind, we have already seen how attention to the language of consciousness contests the structuralist interpretation of the method of linguistic analysis, suggesting that the question of this method be raised again. An improved, more critical form of the discussion of language and consciousness, dedicated to confronting rather than obscuring the questions of method that the history of analytic inquiry into the mind displays, could bring the practice of linguistic analysis to a new understanding of its own implications, revealing the fateful configuration of self-understanding in which language and consciousness are linked.

VIII

The analysis of language, in each of its moments and methodological versions throughout the twentieth century, aims to produce intelligibility by clarifying meaning, by showing us more clearly what we mean in the various forms of description, explanation, interpretation, and expression that comprise our ordinary discursive practices. Under the sway of the structuralist picture, the clarification of meaning consistently seems to be the description of a unified and total logical structure, underlying the practice of language in each of its instances, accounting from behind the scenes for the possibility of meaningfulness everywhere it occurs. But the language of consciousness, in each of the moments we've considered here, problematizes this picture on the ground of the specific inappropriateness of structuralist forms of explanation to the kind of intelligibility that the language of consciousness, in its ordinary uses, is felt to have. The historical investigation of the problem of explaining consciousness, by taking seriously the intuition that consciousness resists structuralist explanation, provides the basis for an alternative understanding of the method of analysis that construes its capability of clarifying meaning otherwise than as the elucidation of logical structure. The alternative construal reveals analysis, instead, as capable of producing the kind of linguistic understanding appropriate to the intelligibility of consciousness, an understanding that is most elucidatory when it is not the description of a structure of meaning explanatory of the language of consciousness, but rather moves in the self-reflexive element of this language itself.

With an antistructuralist construal of the method of analysis in view, the insights of each of the specific moments of theoretical innovation that we've discussed can be recast in terms that elucidate, in each case, some aspect of the meaning of the language of consciousness. The analyses, recast in the antistructuralist form of a self-reflexive practice of linguistic insight, are in each case partial and specific, responsive to particular philosophical needs rather than instances of a general, self-standing theoretical structure. But collectively, they define the real progress of philosophy of mind, in its joint inquiry into experience and language, over the twentieth century.

The Vienna Circle's protocol sentence debate, as we saw in the first chapter, arose when the structuralist analysis of the meaning of scientific and objective terms of description threatened to render unintelligible the intuition that empirical claims must ultimately be grounded in experience, an intuition upon which structuralism had also in fact relied in the formulation of its central opposition between structure and content. When the question of protocol sentences arose, we saw, the only consistent way to maintain their epistemological primacy given structuralism was to misleadingly assimilate their meaning to an ostensive or demonstrative act of gesturing at contents conceived as in themselves ineffable. Neurath took the alternative route of upholding physicalism while abandoning the kind of epistemological reconstruction that structuralism had originally aimed to facilitate. But despite its misconstrual by all parties to the debate, the underlying insight that objective claims are *responsive* and *responsible* to claims about our own conscious experience summarizes a significant and real aspect of our ordinary discursive practices. The insight that Schlick and Carnap sought to capture in their original project of epistemological reconstruction, and that Neurath subsequently abandoned, was that on each particular occasion on which the credentials of an empirical claim are at issue, a self-reflexive appeal to one's own experience can always play a role in justification, and this role is not simply that of a further empirical description of one's cognitive state. Set outside structuralism, within an alternative conception of analysis, the insight that consciousness is ultimately determinative for empirical claims need not license any general description of the structure of science as an edifice founded on empirical claims, or indeed any *positioning* of these claims within a more general network of meaningful propositions at all. But it nevertheless calls attention to a definitive feature of both our ordinary and our scientific discourse, without which the ordinary practice of giving justifications for empirical claims that terminate in statements about experience would be impossible.

In the third chapter, we saw that Husserl and Schlick shared, despite their substantial methodological differences, an essential insight into the *necessity* of the general statements about experience that Husserl called "phenomenological laws," a necessity rooted in the specific nature of our experience in a way that, as both Husserl and Schlick recognized, is falsified and obscured by any conception of the basis of phenomenological laws as simply factual. Schlick's description of the phenomenological laws included the additional insight that this necessity is perspicuous as a feature of the *meaning* of the terms involved, and accordingly that their nonfactual character additionally excludes any material analysis of their content. But Schlick's further description of meaning generally as grounded in conventional and stipulative rules of use already misconstrued his underlying insight into the language of experience by interpreting its description as the elucidation of a general logical structure of rules responsible for, and explanatory of, meaning. Meanwhile, Husserl's account of phenomenological laws preserved the insight that the only possible epistemic basis for the establishment of these laws is an appeal that adverts in each case to the first-personal form of one's own experience rather than to the objective institution of conventional rules. But missing the *semantic* character of this appeal, Husserl had to resort to a complex and epistemologically problematic account of the necessity of phenomenological laws as arising from abstractive synthesis, an account that Schlick rightly rejected. In this way, both philosophers gestured at, but ultimately failed to capture, the insight that our form of experience has a *necessity* for us that is intelligible in terms of the semantic possibilities of meaning open to us, possibilities that can be shown in each case only by appealing to our ordinary, first-personal insight in practice into the meaningfulness of our own language of experience and that do not rest, in any such appeal, on any further description of their basis or ground.

Ryle's project of conceptual geography represents perhaps the most complete and self-consistent application, within the analytic tradition, of an essentially nonstructuralist project of analysis that methodologically recognizes the essentially linguistic character of our insight into consciousness and locates this insight at its own level of epistemological self-reflexiveness and generality. His insight, for instance, into the dispositional logic of many mentalistic terms expresses a recognition unimpeachable on the level of the kind of pre-theoretical reflection on our own meanings of which we are all capable as users of the English language, but eminently useful in dispelling the falsifications of grammar that philosophical theories such as Descartes' dualism are apt to produce. But the suggestion that analysis *rectifies* the logical grammar of our language by illuminating category mistakes can all too easily, as we have seen, appear to invite a conception of analysis as elucidating the categorical structure of language as a whole. And the specific Rylean analysis of mentalistic terms as having a dispositional grammar can easily seem to support the view that these terms in fact *refer* to substantial dispositions or their microstructural bases. In any case, in the specific case of sensations, Ryle was led by his anxiety to dispel the sense-datum theory to exceed the warrant of his own self-reflexive method and to offer a positive, essentially structuralist theory of the meaning of sensation-language. In this excess, Ryle misunderstood the essential character and limits of his own method, yielding an analysis whose infelicity he himself recognized and that made possible the Identity Theory's criticism of what was subsequently taken to be the Rylean project.

Significantly, the central insight that provided the basis for the early identity theorists' criticism of Ryle was itself a piece of reflection about the meaning of the language of consciousness. Place's and Smart's essential insight against what they took to be Ryle's theory was that ordinary instances of sensation-language, for example the language by means of which we describe our own present perceptual experiences, pains, or after-images, present themselves in intersubjective discourse not as mere expressions, but as genuine *reports*, conceived as describing the objects or events that cause them and accordingly implying the existence of these objects or events. Ryle's failure to grasp this fact about the ordinary grammar of sensation-reports had been, as he himself recognized, the source of the errors and obfuscations of his reductive account of sensation-language, and it was the ultimate source of Place's and Smart's misunderstanding of his project. But to say (what is true) that sensation-reports present themselves in discourse as genuine reports and so imply the existence of their objects, is not yet to imply any particular view of the *nature* of these objects. Place's and Smart's own physicalism led them to slide from the first kind of claim, licensed by ordinary reflection on the language of experience, to the second kind of claim, which is ungrounded in any such reflection and was in fact produced only by the structuralist assumption that any positive reference to the elements of consciousness, in order to be meaningful at all, must be supported by an explanation of this reference in terms of its logical structure. This led, almost inevitably, to new questions about the theoretical grammar of reference to what were now supposed to be physical brain states or events, as this reference figures in ordinary language and in the specialized practice of empirical science.

As we saw in Chapter 4, these questions provided the immediate impetus for the development of functionalism. But the detailed intuitions and considerations about mentalistic language and its relationship to the empirical description of mechanical brain states upon which functionalism relied depended, in each case, on insights into the suggestions and implications of our ordinary language of consciousness. That these suggestions and implications are largely distinct from those of any straightforwardly descriptive or empirical discourse posed, throughout the early history of functionalism, significant problems for the unification of functional-level descriptions with the mechanical-level descriptions that were supposed to underlie them. These problems led to the abandonment of the structuralist model of intertheoretic reduction that Putnam and Oppenheim had originally proposed, and were in the end solved only by Lewis's forceful insistence, at variance with the pre-theoretic result of reflection on the ordinary language of consciousness, that this language is actually primarily descriptive of states and events linked by a *causal* logic of relation. At this moment, as at so many others in the history of analytic philosophy of mind, immanent insights into the meaning of the language of consciousness, significant and decisive in their elucidation of the specific intelligibility of consciousness and in their elaboration of the underlying reasons for the methodological difference between the intelligibility of consciousness and that of any objectively present phenomenon, were lost and obscured almost as soon as they were formulated by their misinterpretation as insights into the special position of consciousness *within* the thematized totality of the structure of language and the objectivity that it describes and delimits.

The insights that have driven the progress of analytic philosophy of mind, then, have arisen in each case from reflection on the meaning of some aspect of our language of consciousness, reflection that clarifies some aspect of the significance or grammar of our multiple and diverse practices of self-description, reporting, and mutual understanding. Each of these insights into the working of the language with which we describe and analyze consciousness *could* be interpreted as contributions to a structuralist picture of language and the mind, elements of a complete or essentially completeable account of the logical structure of the language of experience, an account that would itself define the conceptual form of consciousness without remainder. The preceding chapters portray the theoretical costs and historical effects of doing so. For the positive insights of the analysis of language about consciousness have again and again, as we have seen, been interpreted as results of a structuralist method and components of a structuralist theory. But if it is right that no form of structuralist project offers a suitable account of consciousness, it nevertheless remains possible that these insights can be interpreted otherwise, as illustrative of a distinct method of linguistic insight into consciousness that does not seek, and does not produce, a unified account of the logical structure of language. The results of analytic philosophy's specifically linguistic inquiry into the nature of consciousness are evident in the decisive moments of the historical debate. But the question of the nature of the method that produced them remains an open question for historical inquiry. At each stage in the dialectic, we have seen how a structuralist interpretation of the method of analytic philosophy has assimilated and misconstrued results that can in each case also be read alternatively, as problematizing, in the name of consciousness, structuralism's claim to explanatory totality. Reading their claims otherwise than as structural ones means reopening the question of the character of their specifically linguistic provenance, posing again the question of the nature of the method that produced them in order to challenge the structuralist interpretation of their significance.

This immanent critique of structuralism on methodological grounds should nevertheless not fail to give structuralism its due. For as we have seen, it is impossible to understand the history of the analytic inquiry into the mind without recognizing that structuralism has in fact played a decisive role within it, not only in obscuring the resistance of consciousness but also in facilitating positive insights about it. The positive insights that linguistic analysis and reflection can produce into particular propositions will often seem to have the form of elaborations of their underlying grammar, over against standing temptations to misconstrue it, and there is no reason to suppose that general logical or grammatical principles, demonstrable by analysis, do not indeed govern the grammatical workings of large regions of the intersubjective practice of language. Even if replaced by an alternative interpretation of the method of analysis, structuralization might legitimately remain a normative ideal for this method, an end to which, among others, we expect our partial analyses to aspire. The point of replacing the structuralist interpretation of the practice of analysis with another, more situated one is just to resist the structuralist assumption of totality that holds that every piece of meaningful language *must* be structuralizable if it is meaningful at all. Analysis outside the influence of structuralism might, in many cases, actually coincide in method and result with successful structuralist analysis, especially with those analyses that have comprised the best insights of the analytic tradition. The difference is just that an alternative interpretation of the method of analysis removes the assumption that such analyses must lead to, or converge upon, a single, comprehensive account of the logical structure of language and thereby contests the univocal goal of structuralist theory that that assumption has seemed to sanction.

IX

If the suggestion of the historical analysis is right, analytic philosophy's distinctive turn toward the analysis of language and the clarification of meaning yields a far-reaching and historically decisive source of insight into the nature of consciousness. The identification of the genuine insights of analytic philosophy with respect to consciousness reveals its linguistic turn, if taken consistently and with methodological self-awareness, as definitive of an alternative, nonstructuralist *method of analytic reflection* that recognizably produces a kind of intelligibility that is appropriate to consciousness, and to the kinds of understanding of it that can satisfy our underlying philosophical needs. In the course of the history we've considered, this method of analytic reflection has never been completely and explicitly described, but it is responsible for each of the moments of theoretical insight that we have discussed. The methodological analysis of the history of philosophy of mind provides the basis for a preliminary characterization of this method, in terms that show its distinction from the assumptions of structuralism and its appropriateness for the kind of understanding that we want out of a theory of consciousness.

As we have seen in the preceding chapters, structuralist interpretations of language and of the work of analysis are pervasive and all but exhaustive in the history of analytic philosophy. Nevertheless, we have seen how the language of consciousness repeatedly and decisively provides grounds for resistance to structuralism; and in fact in isolated moments, tentatively and without complete self-clarity, philosophers have begun to understand how the methods of analytic philosophy can produce the intelligibility we seek from an understanding of consciousness, outside the ambit of structuralist assumptions. In this way, certain distinctive moments in the critical history of the tradition intimate an alternative conception of its methods, offering to sensitive interpretation the beginnings of a reading of them against the prevailing grain of structuralism.

One of the most significant such moments is the complicated and critical response of the late Wittgenstein to his own earlier conception of philosophical analysis and method. The response reacts most centrally to a conception of language, one that Wittgenstein says he himself once held, according to which "if anyone utters a sentence and means or understands it he is operating a calculus according to definite rules."[14] This fairly characterizes what I have called "structuralism" in this work; and Wittgenstein's detailed response to it returns to the deepest ground of the consideration of specifically linguistic forms of insight, as these operate in the dialectic of everyday discourse, in order to problematize and complicate the very conceptions of structure, systematicity, and rules that this philosophical conception of language presupposes.[15]

Wittgenstein's partial and situated remarks on the conception of philosophy embodied in the critique do not define anything amounting to a single, general technique of philosophical practice. Nevertheless, they characterize in outline a therapeutic practice of the analysis and interpretation of language that can inflect the traditional methods of analytic philosophy in order to find in them the kind of intelligibility of ourselves that our theories of consciousness desperately and perennially seek. The writing of the *Investigations*, with its multiple and different voices, its various forms of interlocutory exchange (not only the statement of claims but also their immanent problematization, questioning, contestation, and deferral, typically without resolution), its dialectic of the ever-renewed temptations of philosophy and their linguistic deflation, itself practices (I take it) such a method of linguistic analysis, a method in each case ineliminably particular, specific, and situated in the concrete reality of discourse. The method of the *Investigations* produces the intelligibility we seek, not through a general thesis or a single technique, but in particular and situated sketches of journeys that "criss-cross in every direction" through the landscapes of our ordinary language in multiple modes of interpretation, analysis, and critique.[16] Here I enumerate, sketchily and preliminarily, some of the characteristics of this variety of practices that recommend them particularly, against the backdrop of the history here considered, as capable of producing, in a way that is strictly continuous with the methods of analysis and linguistic reflection that have defined the analytic tradition, the intelligibility of ourselves to ourselves that we seek in our attempts to understand conscious experience.

The method of analytic reflection is a method of self-reflection. The clarification of meaning, when conceived and practiced outside the guidance of structuralist assumptions, produces insight by means of an *interrogation of self.* The ordinary question, posed to a speaker, about the meaning of an utterance, asks after something that that speaker, uniquely, can clarify. And the derivation of insight about *what* one oneself means contributes, in the various situations of self-inquiry and self-discovery in which we raise the question, to the authenticity and transparency that the philosophical tradition since antiquity has figured as self-knowledge. Structuralism hides the possibility that linguistic reflection can produce self-knowledge, because it figures language as a structure in itself alien to the particularity of its speakers. The method of analytic reflection, however, recognizes language as an essentially *intersubjective* practice, real and substantial only in the *relationship* between two interlocutors, something not reducible to any kind of objective structure. Failing to situate itself explicitly in this relationship, structuralist analysis cannot be self-reflection. For even when it discusses human experience or selfhood, it treats this selfhood as simply another objective phenomenon or process, thereby missing the decisive significance of the unique dialectical kind of relationality – wherein elucidatory understanding of the self by self is neither simple self-identity nor the relation of one object to another, but rather the essentially *intersubjective* recognition of self in other and other in self – definitive of any practice of inquiry capable of producing self-knowledge.[17] The method of analytic reflection, by contrast, produces the intelligibility it offers within the intersubjectivity of language itself, appealing in each case to the knowledge that speakers already possess, implicitly or explicitly, as this knowledge can be revealed in the intersubjective dialectic of inquiry into meaning.

The conception of philosophical insight as self-discovery, anticipated by philosophical articulations of method since Plato, plays a definitive role in the late Wittgenstein's conception of the nature of philosophical problems and their resolution, and accordingly in the practice of philosophy that he displays. There can be little doubt that Wittgenstein, throughout his life, conceived of philosophical work, including logical and linguistic analysis, as a means of working on *oneself*, and that he conceived of the clarification of philosophical problems as of a piece with the clarification of the problems of life.[18] And the thought that *linguistic* reflection can be *self*-reflection plays a determinative role in his late conception of philosophical insight, as expressed in the *Investigations*. Wittgenstein here says, for instance, that the philosopher's task is not to expose unknown facts or beliefs, but only to clarify what we *already* know, what already lies before us insofar as we speak a language.[19] This is evidently connected, moreover, with Wittgenstein's bold suggestion that there can be no *theses* in philosophy, that the purpose of philosophy is indeed not the advancement of theses or claims but the assembly of reminders of what we already know.[20] This assembly produces the kind of clarity that we lack when we become confused, especially under the influence of philosophical theory, about the grammar that we *already* know: it reveals, not hidden or obscure facts, but those simple and familiar "aspects of things" that are in fact "always before one's eyes" but missed in our philosophical analyses precisely *because* of their familiarity and ordinariness.[21]

Without the support of a structuralist picture of language, it can seem puzzling that this kind of immanent reflection on meaning can produce philosophical insight at all. For how can an inquiry that can reveal only what the inquirers already knew, insofar as they are competent speakers of the language at all, produce any new information or knowledge? Reflection on meaning does not introduce new facts or data. It is no part of its task to contribute to the fund of scientific knowledge or information about any object or phenomenon, even about language itself. But it works by deriving from illustrative examples and particular reminders the kind of insight into our own concepts whose loss threatens us with obscurity before ourselves.[22] We are all, insofar as we are competent speakers of English, more or less competent users of the ordinary repertoire of mentalistic locutions of self-description and reporting; but it is one thing to be able to use the language, and quite another to understand the significance of the concepts that it represents with some degree of perspicuity. Where reflection on the meaning of our self-descriptive language fails, we can be tempted to inaccurate and inappropriate pictures of ourselves.[23] Reflection on the meaning of the language of consciousness remedies this temptation by bringing to our awareness the grammar that underlies our ordinary self-conception in each case. Though it does not thereby produce a single and unified explanatory structure of its own, it delivers the intelligibility that we need, in the particular but also decisive contexts in which the human self-image is in question.

The method of analytic reflection is not a "third-person" method. Structuralism understands the analysis of meaning as the elucidation of the logical structure of language, figuring this structure as a totality, responsible for the possibility of shared, objective meaning in a language, fixed in itself and accessible to theoretical investigation by means and methods that do not essentially involve the subjectivity of the investigator. The elucidation of the logical structure of language is, for structuralism, either the demonstration of the fixed logical rules of inference and derivation sublimely definitive of reason itself, or the empirical description of social patterns and practices of linguistic behavior current in a speech community. But the elucidation of meaning, in the specific, concrete contexts in which we ordinarily require it, never in fact consists solely, or even primarily, in reference to a system or totality of rules of language. The kind of knowledge that is decisive for ordinary inquiries into meaning, outside specialized contexts, is not theoretically derived knowledge of the rules or structure definitive of meaning, but the everyday, lived knowledge of meanings that we gain simply in becoming competent speakers of a language. The "know-how" that we exhibit in using a language, and that is the object of reflective inquiry into meaning, is not reducible to or eliminable, in its actual discursive life, in favor of any item or totality of theoretical "knowledge-that." Instead, the inquiry into the meaning of a particular word or phrase, on a particular occasion, always asks after something that is only accessible from within, and will be displayed as part of, the lived, experienced practice of a language, and never as a component of a total, theoretical description of the preconditions for the possibility of that practice.

The much-discussed but little-understood Wittgensteinian conceptions of "forms of life" and "language games" aim to reveal the kinds of intelligibility possible for, and appropriate to, this lived practice, as it shows itself in the forms of understanding that philosophy is capable of. In employing these heuristic concepts to explain the kind of insight that linguistic investigations can produce, Wittgenstein gestures at the grounding of our linguistic inquiry in the "bedrock" of practices, criteria, and attunements that we share as speakers of a language. The point of this gesture is not to provide, or to provide warrant for, a *theory* of the beliefs or practices that must be shared in order for the intersubjective practice of language to be possible, but rather to gesture at the sort of *inexplicable* agreement that shows itself in our practice of language itself.[24]

The attempt to explain consciousness as a natural phenomenon, comprehensible and explainable by means of the essentially third-person and objective methods of empirical science, naturally produces the complaint that these means and methods are inappropriate for the understanding of consciousness. The complaint grasps that any project of explanation that applies to consciousness the empirical methodology of the experimental sciences risks falsifying or omitting entirely the interpretive kind of access that we have to our own consciousness, a kind of access that is unique and practically definitive of the special problems of explaining it. It can seem difficult, however, to support this complaint with any phenomenologically accurate linguistic account. The linguistic analysis of the first-person utterances and locutions with which we describe our own consciousness can all too easily seem to amount simply to the description of conventionally established and socially enforced speech behavior, leaving the special character of our access to consciousness mysterious. If, on the other hand, the analysis of the language of consciousness is never the *third-person, empirical* description of speech behavior, but rather the essentially intersubjective clarification of meanings between practitioners who mobilize their knowledge of the language in the very practice that explicates it, then the analysis of the language of consciousness can bring out its phenomenology in a way that does not falsify it by subjecting it to essentially third-person means. If the nature of consciousness is misunderstood whenever it is subjected to the methods of third-person description, misconstrued in its essence by means of an inquiry that takes the language of consciousness to exemplify a structure objectively present for all inquirers, the method of analytic reflection offers the alternative thought that the language of consciousness, like consciousness itself, always essentially eludes any such inquiry. For its genuine analysis essentially involves the position and situation of the analyst in a discursive movement that cannot be reduced to the description of, or inquiry into, an objectively present structure. Instead, any possible analysis unfolds in the intersubjective discourse that makes sense of claims about consciousness by staking these claims themselves on the possibility of mutual understanding that defines their meaningfulness.

The method of analytic reflection is not a "first-person" method. Even though the analysis of the language of consciousness, purged of the structuralist picture, never demonstrates an objective logical structure of language, independent from or explanatory of its practice, each specific analysis it offers nevertheless elucidates meanings that are transcendent to the individual in being shared. In intersubjective discourse, the analysis of language remains the analysis of a language that is, to the extent that it is meaningful, normative for a speech community; and even if this analysis in each case depends on an appeal to one's own meaning or intention, still it can clarify the meaning of a locution only insofar as this meaning is shared. The method of analytic reflection thus integrates the realization that one's meaning is, in each case, one's own with the recognition that meaning something by something one says is always a *social* act, an act that presupposes, or stakes, the mutual attunement that makes meaning possible to begin with. Analytic reflection therefore appeals in each case to something that is one's own, but also, at the same time, to something that is what it is only in its essential publicity. The analysis of a particular word or phrase, on a particular occasion, reflects what its user meant by using *that* locution on *that* occasion, but it also essentially presupposes, and helps to reveal, what the locution itself *means*, in the intersubjective practice of the community. The appeal of linguistic reflection is in each case to an individual, but it appeals in a decisive and singular way to the individual's sociality in asking after her meanings.[25]

In the recent discussion of the problem of explaining consciousness, discomfort with third-person methods often produces a recoil to first-person methods such as phenomenology and introspection. As we saw in the third chapter, phenomenology aims to describe consciousness by means of a self-reflection that is always individual. But introspectionism, even in its sophisticated phenomenological version, fails in that it dissimulates and obscures the essentially intersubjective character of the language that necessarily frames any statement of its own process or results. The method of linguistic reflection, by contrast, figures this sociality *inherently*, as part of what is involved in the individuality that is displayed by the language of consciousness. Rather than rest its appeal to the individual on items or contents that are inherently private, essentially hidden from the view of any inquisitive other, and therefore in themselves unsayable, the method of linguistic reflection necessarily depends upon the very relational situation of communication that is the medium of the individual language of consciousness in each case. Again, though, this "social order" never figures in the method of analytic reflection as the thematizable totality of a set of beliefs, practices, or empirical behaviors. Reference to it gestures, instead, to the *ungrounded* ground of inexplicable agreement or attunement that makes possible the practice of language itself. Rather than reducing objectivity or trying to account for it subsequently as a construction of subjectivities, the method of linguistic reflection already moves within the linguistic consensus among subjectivities, deeper than any thematizable agreement on facts, behaviors, or practices, that in fact defines objectivity in each case of successful intersubjective recognition.

The method of analytic reflection produces clarifications, not accounts. Outside the structuralist picture of language, there is no reason to suppose that the clarification of the meaning of ordinary locutions and propositions will illuminate a fixed and self-consistent structure of meaning. Indeed, the method of analytic reflection provides no reason to believe that our ordinary conceptual scheme, insofar as it is thematizable at all, is not fragmentary, ill-defined, and internally contradictory. The method of analytic reflection operates, in each case, to clarify the meaning of an expression or a proposition, answering to a doubt or obscurity that itself is, in each case, specific and situated. As far as it goes – and reflection on meaning can go no further without falsifying itself – it provides no reason, moreover, to believe that it ought to be possible to provide *the* unique or final analysis of any term or expression. The analyses it offers are, by contrast, situated and partial, applicable within the contexts in which the need for them arises, but not necessarily generalizable. It follows that the method of analytic reflection, in application to the language of consciousness, cannot produce anything like a unified and general *account* of the nature of consciousness. Its conclusions are not proofs of a theory, but clarificatory reminders, partial and situated, of what we ourselves mean.

One of the most central methodological insights of Wittgenstein's late critique of his own earlier conception of philosophy is that the relationship of linguistic investigation to philosophical theory is not one of direct support, but rather one of diagnosis, therapy, and unavoidable dialectical self-contestation. In these modes of interpretation, the method of analytic reflection produces the intelligibility of ourselves to ourselves by assembling, in the particular cases where such intelligibility is needed, specific reminders of the forms of our language, what is already before us in the everyday life of our linguistic practice.[26]

The aim of the assemblage of particular reminders is to produce a "perspicuous representation" of the grammar of our language, a kind of clarity that we sometimes lack about which way to go on among the many branching paths of our language.[27] But the perspicuity it produces is not that of a unified, general, or total representation of the language as a whole. It is, rather, simply the *complete* clarity that means the complete dissolution of the philosophical problem.[28]

The method of analytic reflection answers to specific philosophical needs. The project of structuralism presents itself as the necessary precondition for any possible clarification of meaning, and in so doing obscures the alternative kind of clarification that operates nontheoretically in the practice of a language itself, responsive to the specific demands and needs in pursuit of the satisfaction of which we inquire into meaning. Refusing to recognize their own origin as anything other than the neutrality of a pure inquiry, structuralist theories of consciousness hide and dissimulate the specific theoretical needs that they in fact aim to satisfy. The method of analytic reflection, by contrast, responds in each case of its application to a specific *need* for clarification, a desire to make the significance and import of some piece of ordinary language clearer or more obvious. Its yield is not a general theory; instead, its "reminders for a particular purpose" answer in each particular case to a specific ambiguity or obscurity that threatens the intelligibility of consciousness. Responding in each case to the specific needs for which we inquire into meanings, the method of analytic reflection allows these needs themselves to be described and examined rather than obscured. In this way, it raises anew the question of our own involvement in our theoretical activities with respect to consciousness. In response to the "preconceived idea of crystalline purity" – the idea that organized the structuralist picture of language – the specific therapies of linguistic reflection remind us of our real reasons for wanting to understand ourselves. In this way, it turns our investigation around the "fixed point of our real need," our need for the kind of mutual intelligibility that the language of consciousness incessantly seeks, and only sometimes finds, in the ordinary practice of its speech.[29]

In the course of the ordinary discourse with which we express claims about our own experience, willingness to clarify what we mean by our particular, contextual utterances is often the essential prerequisite for our being understood, for our own experience to be made intelligible to the other. In the theoretical context where our goal is not the intelligibility of an individual's experience but the intelligibility of consciousness itself, philosophical analysis of the meaning of the language of consciousness produces this intelligibility in the medium of linguistic self-reflection. But even if the latter kind of reflection yields results that are more general and require a greater development of specialized practice for their derivation, it would be wrong to suppose that the clarification of meaning can ever lend insight except as a response to a specific kind of obfuscation or unclarity. As we saw in Chapter 4, *one* significant source of a kind of obfuscation that philosophical reflection on language can aptly remedy is philosophical theory itself. Here, philosophical analysis derives its purpose and import from that of the particular conceptions of the human being that it confronts. Ryle's practice of ordinary-language analysis operated by detecting, by means of reflection on the meaning of our ordinary concepts of consciousness, the infelicities and absurdities of the Cartesian theory, a theory that falsified the concepts of mind by obscuring their ordinary grammar. But philosophical theory is not the only general source of the kind of confusion that reflection on the meaning of the language of consciousness can address. These confusions are possible, and often tempting, wherever a general image of the nature of the human self is offered or contested. They provide ample ground for the work of analytic clarification in domains ranging from the scientific to the cultural and political. In these wide-ranging domains, the stakes of the interpretation of the language of consciousness are as manifold and significant as its ordinary and specialized uses. Responsive to our particular needs in understanding ourselves in each case, analysis practices this interpretation as a linguistic self-consciousness that reveals our needs by illuminating their source.

These heuristic specifications, partial and impressionistic, gesture toward a practice of linguistic interpretation that contests some of the most pervasive theoretical assumptions definitive of the tradition of analytic philosophy. But the practice toward which they point is, at the same time, not distinct, in general or in detail, from the one that has produced some of analytic philosophy's best results. Methodologically, rereading these results as instances of the practice of analytic reflection rather than within the matrix of structuralism allows them to be read as distinctively linguistic contributions to self-knowledge, to the ongoing development of our ways of understanding and defining ourselves as human. So read, the real method of analytic interpretation allows the exploration of language to clarify the meaning of consciousness as it is shown in our concrete, everyday speaking. The movement of linguistic interpretation then occurs as a mode of, rather than in opposition to, the intelligibility of what the language of consciousness in each case aims to say. Its very practice, thought and applied outside the interpretation of saying as the description of contents indifferently present to the sayers, reveals and furthers the situated, irreducibly relational linguistic intelligibility of other to self or of self to self that the language of consciousness always, from its simplest cries to its most complicated and articulated self-examinations, aims to produce.

What I have called the method of analytic reflection is not the definition of the logical structure of language or the adumbration of the implicit rules of our language games. But its immanent reflection on meaning recovers the tradition's methods of logical and grammatical analysis as specialized modes of a practice of interpretation whose significance is as comprehensive as our needs for self-understanding. The analytic tradition has often, in recent years and decades, been declared dead or moribund, consigned to an irrelevance and sterility resulting from the exhaustion of its method. If the argument of the present analysis is right, however, to abandon the analytic tradition would be to lose its best linguistic insights by failing to understand the genuine depth and relevance of its true practice. That this practice has constantly been obscured by even the best analytic philosophers should not prevent the historical overview from revealing it, and the insights that it allows, in the concrete interpretation of the dialectic of experience and explanation in the analytic tradition over the course of the twentieth century.

Read historically and methodologically, the best insights of the analytic tradition reveal the understanding of consciousness and the understanding of language as fatefully linked, mutually dependent in the ever-emerging dialectic of our self-knowledge. Structuralism would make this linkage an opposition, figuring consciousness outside the boundary of a comprehensive totality of structure without considering the incessant dynamic of the joined movement of language and consciousness toward this boundary, yielding characteristic fantasies of the privacy, unintelligibility, or insignificance of what is most significant to us, the muteness of what is most telling. But the recovery of the true method of analytic philosophy, against its structuralist misinterpretation, *is* the recovery of the mutual implication of consciousness and language by means of the movement of interpretation that reveals and furthers it. The result is the most enduring and still unexplored legacy of the analytic tradition, for our many futures, not only the philosophical one but the cultural one, and the linguistic one that still gives the specific being of the human to be heard.

Notes

Chapter 1

1. Older discussions of consciousness often used Nagel's memorable phrase "what it's like" to gesture at the problematic properties of consciousness; in particular, Nagel (1974) argued that knowing all of the objective facts about a bat would not help to establish "what it's like" to be a bat. Except in the specialized context of Jackson's "Knowledge Argument" – where what is at issue is the cognitive or epistemological status of learning "what it's like" to see red (Jackson 1982) – this language has largely ceded to talk of the "qualitative" character of conscious states. Still, explanation of the meaning of "qualitative" usually just repeats Nagel's phrase (e.g., Chalmers 1996, pp. 4–5). The claim that consciousness is "subjective" captures a different thought; perhaps the clearest formulation in the contemporary literature – Searle's (1992, p. 95) – defines the subjectivity of a conscious state as its property of existing *only* for a single person or from a single point of view. (This language, though clearer than most contemporary descriptions of "subjectivity," of course demands additional clarification of the phrase "point of view.") The notions of states of consciousness as "ineffable" and "private" are, perhaps, more popular with those who affirm the explainability of conscious states than with those who deny it; for instance, Dennett (1988, p. 639) characterizes the concept of qualia as the concept of the "ineffable, intrinsic, private, directly apprehensible properties of experience" in order to show that there are no such properties. A third set of associations clusters around descriptions of conscious states in terms of their alleged *epistemic* properties – for instance, their epistemic immediacy. For these descriptions, conscious states (or, more often, the qualitative component or aspect of them) are immediately recognizable or capable of being grasped in advance of other, more highly structured items of knowledge. For illuminating discussion of some of these alleged

properties of qualia and the arguments that they issue in, see Lormand (1994) and Lycan (1990). Finally, some discussions of conscious states as epistemically immediate emphasize their being accessible to awareness preconceptually or nonconceptually; see, e.g., Peacocke (1983) and Crane (1992).

2. See, e.g., Price (1996).

3. In this study, I use the terms "experience" and "consciousness" more or less synonymously. The former term is generally more prevalent in older discussions, while the latter term has largely displaced it in the discussions of recent decades.

4. In this study, I always use "structure" and "structural" in this sense, to refer to a network of relations or to the explanation, definition, or designation of items in terms of their place in such a network. "Structural properties" are properties defined by an item's position in such a network of relations, as opposed to "intrinsic properties," which can be attributed to an item in itself, apart from any consideration of its relations to other items. There is another sense of "structure" in which it means something like "composition"; in this latter sense, understanding the "structure" of an item means understanding what it itself is made of or composed of. When talking about "structure" in this latter sense, I will refer to it as "microstructure" or "compositional structure" in order to avoid ambiguity.

5. What I am calling "structuralism" here has certain suggestive parallels to the school of thought about language, founded by the semiotics of Saussure and prominent in European thought throughout the twentieth century, that also goes by that name; but the two kinds of structuralism ought in general to be kept separate to the extent that the traditions they represent are themselves distinct.

6. Of course, as we shall see in detail in Chapter 5, there are various ways of conceiving of these relations and their *relata*, corresponding to the various versions of functionalism that are still hotly debated today. One prominent and historically decisive version, the "causal-role" functionalism that traces to David Lewis, defines these relations, as does physicalism, as causal relations between physical events. But there are other ways of characterizing the essential functional relations, and not all versions of functionalism are (as we shall see) necessarily congenial to physicalism.

7. For the failure-of-supervenience point, see Chalmers (1996); for the explanatory gap, see Levine (1983).

8. Commentators who have drawn (at least cautiously) the conclusion that qualia are incapable of functionalist or physicalist explanation include Kim (1998), Chalmers (1996), Levine (1993), and McGinn (1991); commentators who hold that qualia are real but reducible include Shoemaker (1982), Churchland and Churchland (1982), and Tye (1995). Deniers of the theoretical utility of the concept of qualia include Dennett (1988) and, at least implicitly, Rorty (1979).

9. Peirce sometimes also suggests that, because the experiential given is complex, qualia are nonrelational *abstractions* from a sensory manifold

(e.g., Peirce 1867, p. 4) or even that they are mere logical possibilities. This appears to sit in some tension with the claim that qualia are the basis of sensory experience; for more on this tension, see Goudge (1935).

10. James (1879), pp. 333–7.
11. Lewis (1929), pp. 124–5.
12. Ibid., p. 119.
13. Lewis's theoretically motivated description of qualia as ineffable should be compared to Ned Block's more recent "definition" of qualia: "You ask: What is it that philosophers have called qualitative states? I answer, only half in jest: As Louis Armstrong said when asked what jazz is, 'If you got to ask, you ain't never gonna get to know'" (Block 1978, p. 278).
14. Lewis (1929), pp. 127–8.
15. Chalmers (1996), p. 107.
16. For other formulations in the contemporary literature of the thought that qualia resist structural explanation because they are in some way nonrelational, see, e.g., Loar (1990), Harman (1990), and Levine (1995).
17. Chalmers (1996), Chapter 1.
18. Kim describes the widespread influence of the layered model:

> "For much of this century, a layered picture of the world like this has formed a constant – tacitly assumed if not explicitly stated – backdrop for debates on a variety of issues in metaphysics and philosophy of science – for example, reduction and reductionism, the mind-body problem, emergence, the status of the special sciences, and the possibility of a unified science. In fact this picture has had a strong and pervasive influence on the way we formulate problems and their possible solutions in many areas. Sometimes the layered model is couched in terms of concepts and languages rather than entities and their properties. Talks of levels of organization, descriptions or languages, of analysis, of explanation, and the like is encountered everywhere – it has thoroughly permeated primary scientific literature in many fields, in particular, various areas of psychology and cognitive science, systems theory, and computer science – as well as philosophical writings about science." (Kim 1998, p. 16)

Moreover, it is the same picture to which J. J. C. Smart already appealed in defending his early articulation of the Identity Theory (see Chapter 3 for more on this).

19. In this way, the *micro*structural decomposition of an item that is not basic in the explanatory order itself ultimately requires a structuralist explanation. Any possible description or explanation of a nonsimple item ultimately identifies the simple items that make it up by referring to their relational structure.
20. Carnap (1928), section 16.
21. Carnap (1932a).
22. See, for instance, Hardin (1987, 1988) and van Gulick (1993). These authors differ from Lewis in that they do not explicitly develop a conception of the intrinsic properties of qualia in order to oppose such a conception to their relational description; instead, they hold that qualia can be *fully* explained structurally and relationally. However, the motivation for this is

the same as the motivation for Lewis's argument for the solely structural identifiability of qualia.

23. The view traces to Russell (1927). For recent expressions of it, see, e.g., Chalmers (1996, pp. 153–5), Lockwood (1989), and Maxwell (1978). Something like this view is also discussed in Feigl's influential "The 'Mental' and the 'Physical'" (Feigl 1958).

24. See, e.g., Frege (1879), Russell (1918), and Wittgenstein (1921).

25. See, e.g., the highly polemical debate conducted between John Searle and Daniel Dennett in the *New York Review of Books* and reprinted in Searle (1997).

26. See, e.g., Goldman (1993), Harman (1990), and Levine (1995).

27. Of course, it remains possible to adopt a stable position, even while recognizing the resistance of consciousness to structuralist explanation, by refusing to give any positive characterization whatsoever of the content of consciousness, even any characterization of it *as* ineffable or indescribable. This position is a stable one and cannot be ruled out by any structuralist argument, but it puts its adherent in the difficult position of having nothing to say about his most central object of theoretical concern. Moreover, consistent maintenance of the position that the contents of consciousness are literally unspeakable threatens to require the theorist to deny the intelligibility of much of our ordinary language of self-description and explanation.

28. Shoemaker (1982) made the inverted spectrum case newly relevant to the question of qualia by suggesting that a modified form of functionalism can provide for the possibility of inverted spectra after all. Ned Block's (1978) fairly early article "Troubles with Functionalism" developed the famous case of the "Chinese Nation," the hypothetical scenario in which the citizens of China are wired into a functional web mirroring the functional organization of a brain. Other variations on this are Searle's "Chinese Room" argument (under some interpretations), Bogen's (1979), and Searle's (1992) thought experiment involving the replacement of brain parts with functional duplicates. The *absent qualia* or *zombie* thought experiment, central to Chalmers's argumentation, seems to have appeared as early as Kirk and Squires (1974); see also Kirk's (1994) recent discussion. Finally, Jackson's so-called knowledge argument first appears in Jackson (1982), with responses by Lewis (1990), Nemirow (1990), Churchland (1989), and Loar (1990), among others. Other recently influential thought experiments have focused on the relationship between qualitative content and intentional content; for two representative examples, see Block (1990) and Tye (1995).

Chapter 2

1. The roots of the interpretation of the protocol sentence debate as a debate between the correspondence theory and the coherence theory extend to the late suggestions of the debaters themselves and especially to

the contemporary reconstruction of Hempel (1935a). Subsequently, this interpretation was influentially formulated by Ayer (1936a) and has been followed up by Davidson (1982).

2. See, e.g., Quine (1951, 1960).

3. See, e.g., Uebel (1992b), Oberdan (1996), Coffa (1991), and Friedman (1999). Interpreters who connect structuralism with the debate include Turner (1996), Coffa (1991), Richardson (1996), and Uebel (1992a).

4. Uebel (1992a), p. 288; Oberdan (1996), p. 270.

5. Carnap (1928) (henceforth *Aufbau*), section 1.

6. *Aufbau*, section 2, section 120.

7. *Aufbau* section 67, section 78.

8. See, e.g., Friedman (1999), Chapters 5 and 6.

9. *Aufbau*, section 59, section 62.

10. *Aufbau*, sections 71–3.

11. For instance (section 71), the musical chord produced by striking c, e, and g on the piano might be quasi-analyzed by determining its acoustic similarity and difference relations with other chords. This would provide the basis for our grouping this chord in "similarity circles" along with other chords "containing" c, e, and g. But we can still treat each of the chords as basic and undecomposable: the grouping into similarity circles does not analyze the chord into constituent parts but rather quasi-analyzes it by adumbrating the structure of resemblance relations into which it fits. Quasi-analysis, rather than proper analysis, is appropriate, Carnap argues, when, as in the case of basic experiences, the elements to be analyzed are in fact basic and undecomposable.

12. For more on the importance to the *Aufbau* of structural definite descriptions, and on the way that appreciation of their role undermines a traditional "empiricist" interpretation of Carnap's project, see Friedman (1999), Chapters 5 and 6.

13. *Aufbau*, section 2.

14. *Aufbau*, section 16.

15. Ibid.

16. *Aufbau*, section 14.

17. *Aufbau*, section 15.

18. The idea of the purely structural nature of logic already had a rich history when Carnap picked it up. As Friedman (2000) illuminatingly discusses, in 1910 Cassirer had already described formal logic in terms of Russell's theory of relations in *The Principles of Mathematics*; this conception became the key to Cassirer's sophisticated use of modern logic in developing the Marburg school's neo-Kantianism, which was itself a decisive influence on the young Carnap. For more detail, see Friedman (2000), Chapters 3 and 5. See also Richardson (1998) for an illuminating account of the development of Carnap's philosophical concerns prior to, and leading up to, the *Aufbau*.

19. Russell (1927). According to Russell, all physical descriptions are structural descriptions; the ultimate elements of the structures described are

elementary experiences or basic units of experience. And like Carnap, Russell held the doctrine of the structural nature of physical description for broadly *logical* reasons; it was the possibility of an *analysis* of the entities of physical description as logical constructions from more basic entities that licensed treating propositions of physical description as structural (Russell 1927, pp. 2–4). For more on Russell's own development toward structuralism and its relation to the developing method of "construction theory," see Hylton (1990).

20. *Aufbau*, section 14.
21. *Aufbau*, section 16.
22. *Aufbau*, section 59.
23. *Aufbau*, section 64.
24. *Aufbau*, section 54.
25. *Aufbau*, sections 15–16.
26. Schlick (1925) (henceforth *AE*), section 6.
27. Hilbert (1899).
28. *AE*, section 11.
29. *AE*, section 5, section 11.
30. *AE*, section 7.
31. *AE*, section 12.
32. Here I partially follow the instructive reconstruction given by Turner (1996).
33. Following Wittgenstein, Schlick held that a proposition could not *express* or *designate* the logical or relational form of an object; rather, the logical form of the object shows up in the language in the possibilities established by the language's grammar for the formation of meaningful propositions about it.
34. Schlick (1932) (henceforth "Form and Content"), p. 295.
35. "Form and Content" p. 296.
36. "Form and Content," pp. 296–7.
37. "Form and Content," p. 310.
38. Quoted in Uebel (1992a), p. 71.
39. Ibid., p. 87.
40. Neurath (1932a), p. 62.
41. Interestingly, then, Neurath's official argument for the claim that all expressible states of affairs are physicalistic derives from his claim that linguistic signs are themselves physical.
42. Uebel (1992a), p. 123.
43. Neurath (1931a), pp. 54–5.
44. Neurath (1932a), p. 63.
45. Schlick (1934), p. 215.
46. Ibid.
47. Ibid., pp. 212–13.
48. Ibid., pp. 220–1.
49. Ibid., pp. 221–2.
50. Ibid., p. 225.

51. Neurath (1934).
52. Neurath (1932b).
53. This interpretation is suggested, anyway, by Neurath (1933, p. 2) and developed by Thomas Uebel (1992a, pp. 272–3).
54. Neurath (1934), p. 111.
55. Schlick suggests this interpretation especially when he says that the demonstratives he uses in describing the content of affirmations have "rules of usage [that] provide that in making the statements in which they occur some experience is had" (Schlick 1934, p. 225).
56. Oberdan (1996) has also recently argued that the location of Schlick's theory of affirmations as demonstrative within his general theory of meaning based on application rules gives him a defensible account of their content.
57. It must be admitted that Schlick often talked as if he meant his affirmations to be linguistically formulable propositions employing demonstrative terms like "here" and "now," and that the attempt to make sense of such formulations leads to notorious difficulties. Some of these difficulties are instructively developed by Chisholm (1982); for instance, because of the problems involved in explaining just what is described as yellow in the affirmation "yellow here now," Chisholm suggests an "adverbial" construal employing a first-personal pronoun and a specially constructed predicate: "I sense-yellowly." As becomes evident under consideration of the meaning of such adverbial predicates, this suggestion tends in the direction of replacing the propositional form of an affirmation with the description of an otherwise indescribable action. But since this may have been Schlick's intent anyway, it is not clear that we need any description of the propositional form of an affirmation at all. Coffa (1991, p. 362) has similarly argued that Schlick's account of affirmations must be considered incoherent because it holds that an affirmation can be understood only in the course of verifying it.
58. But the philosophical distance between the two positions was by no means very great; for instance, as Haller (1985, p. 290) has noted, Schlick's account of the connection between verification and sense is already present, at least in outline, in the *General Theory of Knowledge.*
59. Thomas Uebel (1996, 1999) and Thomas Oberdan (1998, 1999) have recently debated whether Schlick's conception of affirmations and protocols made him a foundationalist. According to Uebel (1996, p. 423), affirmations are primarily semantic media for the connection of the abstract symbols of language with the world. As such, Uebel argues, their epistemic function is secondary and dependent upon their general semantic function of connecting language and the world, even in particular cases of verification and falsification. Against this, Oberdan (1998, pp. 305–6) objects that the construal of affirmations as semantic media void of empirical content fails to account for the role of affirmations in connecting observation to scientific claims. Oberdan concludes that the psychological function of affirmations was to provide empirical content

for a special set of intersubjective claims – the protocol sentences – which could then, in turn, provide the foundation of knowledge.

But whether or not Schlick should be considered a "foundationalist," it is clear that he intended affirmations to do more than provide psychological support for protocol sentences. Because the empirical content of protocol sentences itself derives from affirmations, affirmations must have empirical content even if they do not stand in straightforward derivational relationships with protocol sentences. Owing to its essential subjectivity, the empirical content of an affirmation remains inexpressible (as on the "Form and Content" model); but it can be the occasion for the formulation of a protocol that bears empirical content that is at least *structurally* similar to the content of the affirmation (i.e., content that occupies the same place in the abstract, intersubjectively communicable relational structure of experience).

60. Hempel (1935).
61. Schlick (1935a), p. 403.
62. Schlick (1935b), pp. 407–8.
63. Carnap (1932a), p. 52.
64. Ibid., p. 49.
65. Ibid., p. 50.
66. Ibid., p. 61.
67. Ibid., p. 64.
68. Ibid., p. 88.
69. Ibid., pp. 89–91.
70. Ibid., p. 92.
71. Ibid., p. 93.
72. Ibid., p. 86.
73. Ibid., p. 459.
74. Ibid., pp. 460–1.
75. Carnap (1932b), p. 465; Popper made the suggestion in conversation with Carnap.
76. Ibid., p. 467.
77. Ibid., pp. 459–60.
78. Philosophical interpretation and description of the Vienna Circle has, of course, often collapsed these distinctions by construing logical empiricism as committed to a "verification theory of meaning." But the verification theory was Wittgenstein's suggestion, and when used by members of the Circle it most often simply expressed the demand that all meaningful sentences be verifiable, rather than any theory of meaning articulated in its own right.
79. Perhaps the first expression in the analytic tradition of something like the doctrine of the incommunicability of content can be found in a somewhat similar argument given by Frege (1918) in "The Thought":

My companion and I are convinced that we both see the same field; but each of us has a particular sense impression of green. I glimpse a strawberry among the green strawberry leaves. My companion cannot find it, he is colour-blind. The colour impression he gets from the strawberry is not noticeably different from the one he gets from the leaf. Now does my companion see the green leaf as red, or does he see the red berry as green, or does he see both with one colour which I am not acquainted with at all? These are unanswerable, indeed really nonsensical, questions. For when the word 'red' is meant not to state a property of things but to characterize sense impressions belonging to my consciousness, it is only applicable within the realm of my consciousness. For it is impossible to compare my sense impression with someone else's. For that, it would be necessary to bring together in one consciousness a sense impression belonging to one consciousness and a sense impression belonging to another consciousness. Now even if it were possible to make an idea disappear from one consciousness and at the same time make an idea appear in another consciousness, the question whether it is the same idea would still remain unanswerable. It is so much of the essence of any one of my ideas to be a content of my consciousness, that any idea someone else has is, just as such, different from mine. (pp. 334–5)

Although Frege seems to suggest that it is the *essential* difference between my ideas and another's that makes questions about the qualitative character of ideas unanswerable, he also seems to agree with Schlick in holding that, because of the impossibility of comparison between qualitative contents in distinct minds, talk of their similarity is itself unintelligible. But if similarity is unintelligible, then presumably difference is, too; so Frege's argument, like Carnap's, seems to undermine itself by taking as a premise a distinction that, by its own conclusion, is nonsensical.

80. It was this feature of Carnap's argument that Neurath, for instance, reacted most favorably to in his endorsement of the *Aufbau* project; the elimination of *individual* and *idiosyncratic* differences of perspective seemed to Neurath an essential prerequisite for the furtherance of communal scientific inquiry.

81. Schlick (1932), pp. 296–7.

82. Following Kaplan (1977), I use "indexical" to designate any term (such as "here," "I," "now," "this," and "that") whose referent, in each case of its use, depends on the context of that use; within the category of indexicals, "demonstratives" are those terms (such as "that" but not "I") whose referent, in each case, depends not only on the context of use but also on an act of demonstration or pointing. In the context of the present discussion, where what is at issue is the indication of experiences or states of affairs, all of the relevant indexicals are also demonstratives.

83. For instance, in "Physical Language" he describes even ostensive definitions as translational:

A translation is a rule for transforming a word from one language to another, (e.g. 'cheval' = 'horse'); a definition is a rule for mutual transformation of words in the same language. This is true both of so-called nominal definitions (e.g. 'Elephant' = animal with such and such distinguishing characteristics) and also, a fact usually forgotten, for so-called ostensive definitions (e.g. 'Elephant' = animal of the same kind as the animal in this or that position in space-time); both definitions are translations of words. (Carnap 1932a, p. 39)

84. This notion of private ostension, understood as something like the demonstrative tokening of an experience before oneself, would become one of the targets of Wittgenstein's private language argument.

85. In the sense that Schlick suggests, a proposition is self-verifying if understanding its meaning suffices to establish its truth. Demonstrative propositions are not ordinarily self-verifying in this sense, although certain propositions *combining* two or more demonstratives ("I am here now"; "This thing is here before me") might be thought to be self-verifying though nontautological. Because of the possibility of error or falsehood in what one says about an object even when it is indicated demonstratively, demonstrative propositions can be construed as self-verifying only if they are construed as *including* the objects that they indicate. Keith Lehrer (1982, pp. 54–5) objects to Schlick's account of self-verifying ostensive affirmations along these lines. To say that an affirmation has *partly* demonstrative content, Lehrer points out, is not to say that its content is *exhausted by* its ostensive or demonstrative character. It follows that, even if affirmations are necessarily partly demonstrative, they may be understood but still be incorrect, owing to inaccuracies in the part of their content that is not demonstrative; therefore, Lehrer maintains, affirmations cannot be self-verifying, as Schlick claims. Schlick might have answered the objection by holding that the content of an affirmation is *purely* demonstrative – amounting, for instance, to something like "this here now"; and it might seem impossible to understand *this* content without having the experience that it indicates. Correctly put, then, an affirmation would not have the form of a demonstrative term attached to an empirical *description*, but would rather essentially *involve* the tokening of a particular experience. (Schlick suggests this interpretation especially when he says that the demonstratives he uses in describing the content of affirmations have "rules of usage [that] provide that in making the statements in which they occur some experience is had" [Schlick 1934, p. 225].) But since a purely demonstrative utterance is not a proposition, it is impossible to construe this involvement as a matter of self-verification. Indeed, if affirmations essentially involve the experiences that they indicate, then they are not expressible in demonstrative or any other terms; the loose propositional expression of an affirmation employs a demonstrative term only to *allude to* (without really capturing) its essential dependence on experience.

86. Consider, for instance, Quine's description of the role of consciousness in the program that he recommends in "Epistemology Naturalized":

> This attitude is . . . one that Neurath was already urging in Vienna Circle days. . . . In the old epistemological context the conscious form had priority, for we were out to justify our knowledge of the external world by rational reconstruction. Awareness ceased to be demanded when we gave up trying to justify our knowledge of the external world by rational reconstruction. What to count as observation now can be settled in terms of the stimulation of sensory receptors, let consciousness fall where it may. (Quine 1969, p. 231)

87. For the classic exposition of the "deductive-nomological" model of expla-
    nation, according to which a theory explains particular events causally
    by subsuming them deductively under general causal laws, see Hempel
    (1948); see also Hempel (1942). For Nagel's conception of theories at
    different levels as linked by relations of biconditional, definitional reduc-
    tion, see Nagel (1960). Nagel (1974) distinguishes between *homogeneous*
    intertheoretic reductions licensed by definitions and *inhomogeneous* reduc-
    tions between theories with terms that are not mutually definable, hold-
    ing that inhomogeneous reductions require additional empirical "bridge
    laws" to mediate between the reducing theory and the reduced one; see
    also Nagel (1960).
88. Feigl (1958).
89. Of course, it remains possible to affirm ontological physicalism – the
    doctrine that all processes and events are ultimately physical or material in
    nature – while nevertheless denying the semantic reducibility of all claims
    to claims in the physical language. Exposing the origin of physicalism
    in the analytic method of structuralism does not render this position
    untenable in principle, but it does expose its theoretical sterility. Given the
    methods of analytic philosophy, any theoretical application of ontological
    physicalism in order to produce the intelligibility or explanation of some
    hitherto mysterious phenomenon will in fact amount to the semantic
    reduction of claims about that phenomenon to claims in the physical
    language.

Chapter 3

1. Husserl (1929), sections 1 and 2.
2. Ibid., section 11.
3. Ibid.
4. Ibid., section 12.
5. See, e.g., Depraz (1999), Varela and Shear (1999), and many of the essays
   collected in Petitot et al. (1999). Chalmers (1997, p. 36) holds that "[a]
   phenomenological] approach must be absolutely central to an adequate
   science of consciousness."
6. Schlick (1910), pp. 51–61, where Schlick somewhat misleadingly
   understands Husserl's antipsychologism as committing him to an
   "independence" theory of truth whereby the truth of a proposition is
   conceived in complete independence of any concrete act of judgment or
   comprehension.
7. Schlick (1910), pp. 59–61.
8. Schlick (1913), pp. 146–7.
9. Ibid., p. 149.
10. Schlick (1925) (henceforth *AE*), section 5.
11. *AE*, section 18, p. 139.
12. *AE*, section 18, pp. 138–41.
13. Husserl (1900) (henceforth *LI*), pp. 663–4.

14. *AE*, section 18, p. 139.
15. Schlick (1930).
16. Ibid., p. 166.
17. Ibid., p. 167.
18. Ibid., p. 169.
19. Schlick (1930), p. 168. Wittgenstein himself had rejected Husserl's account of phenomenological propositions as synthetic a priori in response to a query from Schlick. For a description of the reason for Wittgenstein's rejection in the context of the "phenomenological" focus of Wittgenstein's own project, see Hintikka and Hintikka (1986), pp. 151–4.
20. Ibid., p. 165, p. 169.
21. Ibid., p. 169.
22. Schlick's article was entitled "Gibt es ein materiales apriori?"; Wilfred Sellars' translation of this title as "Is there a factual a priori?" somewhat obscures the relevance of the formal/material distinction to the basis of Schlick's critique.
23. Van de Pitte (1984), p. 202.
24. Husserl (1913) (henceforth *Ideas*), section 22, p. 41.
25. Van de Pitte (1984), p. 211.
26. Shelton (1988), p. 559.
27. *LI*, section 67.
28. This interpretation is outlined in Smith (2000).
29. *LI*, pp. 237–8.
30. *LI*, p. 238.
31. *LI*, Investigation II, section 38, pp. 394–5; section 31, pp. 399–401.
32. *LI*, Investigation II, Chapter 1, section 1, pp. 338–9; section 4, p. 345.
33. *LI*, section 63, p. 825.
34. In *LI*, Investigation IV, sections 12–14, Husserl gives this example in connection with the "grammatical" distinction between nonsense and absurdity. This distinction, too, depends on the formal/material distinction: nonsensical propositions violate the formal, categorial laws of the possibility of meaning, whereas absurd propositions violate synthetic a priori laws grounded in nonformal concepts. Thus, "There is a round square" violates none of the formal laws governing the combination of parts of speech to form a meaningful proposition, but runs afoul of specific, phenomenological laws governing the particular material region involved.
35. *Ideas*, vol. 1, section 5.
36. *Ideas*, vol. 1, section 11.
37. Husserl (1948) (henceforth *E&J*), Part II, Chapter 1, section 47, pp. 198–9, 238–9.
38. *E&J*, Part III, Chapter 1, pp. 317–18.
39. *E&J*, Part III, Chapter 3, pp. 374–5.
40. *E&J*, Part III, Chapter 1, pp. 332–3.
41. Ibid., p. 342.
42. J. N. Mohanty (1989, pp. 25–35) illuminatingly explains Husserl's method of imaginative free variation in detail, and considers the relationship

of arbitrariness to the universality of the results. Mohanty suggests that Husserl conceives of the arbitrariness of examples in free variation on analogy with the arbitrariness of the concrete example used for a mathematical (for instance, a geometrical) proof, and that this analogy is misleading. For there is little reason to suppose that the realm of phenomenologically discoverable essences is *constituted* or defined by underlying laws, principles, and regularities such as those that allow us to be assured of the genuine arbitrariness of an example in mathematics. Mohanty also considers possible objections to Husserl's method on the ground of its similarity to induction, its apparent assimilation of possibility to conceivability, and its circular presumption of already existing knowledge of categorial types.

43. *E&J*, III.1, pp. 321–3.

44. *E&J*, III.1, pp. 321–3.

45. In Wittgenstein (1929), p. 31, he claims only that *magnitudes* are part of logical form, so that the logical form of the simplest propositions describing colors or spatial relations in the visual field ineleminably refers to numerical quantities. In *Philosophical Remarks*, he seems to go further, considering that the logical form of, e.g., a proposition attributing color already contains the whole system of color relations.

46. Wittgenstein (1921), 3.327–3.328.

47. Hintikka and Hintikka (1986, pp. 116–36) consider at length the relationship between the exclusionary structure of color terms and the *Tractatus* picture of meaning. They conclude that, *contra* such interpretations as Anscombe's (1959, pp. 25–8), the incompatibility of color terms does not vitiate the *Tractatus* thesis of the independence and truth functionality of simple propositions. For, Hintikka and Hintikka (p. 122) point out, there is no reason to suppose that a color ascription such as "This is red" has the subject-predicate form that it superficially appears to have. This leaves open the possibility – which Wittgenstein himself appears to have considered – of a more complex analysis of the relations among such propositions that would reveal them as reducible to genuinely logical relations; for instance, the mutual exclusivity of color terms might simply reflect that color discourse represents each color with a different *name* because the function ascribing colors to visual field points is essentially one-valued. Hintikka and Hintikka in fact recommend such a possibility as a legitimate extension of the *Tractatus* picture. Whatever the extent of the consistency of the *Tractatus* with such a picture, however, it was (as Hintikka and Hintikka themselves explain [p. 131]) the question of color attributions that, at least in part, led Wittgenstein to abandon the Tractarian doctrine that propositions can be compared to reality individually in favor of the alternative picture that Schlick now recommended.

48. See, e.g., *Philosophical Remarks* (henceforth *PR*), pp. 1–4, where Wittgenstein speaks of phenomenology as establishing grammatical possibilities, and considers the possibility of establishing the "grammatical" structure of color space. See also the comprehensive and enlightening treatment of

Wittgenstein's move from considering a "phenomenological" language to favoring a "physical" one in Hintikka and Hintikka (1986), pp. 145–60.

49. One sort of problem that Wittgenstein thematizes in the *Philosophical Remarks* (Wittgenstein 1930) traces to the Tractarian doctrine of the unrepresentability of logical form. If the structure of experience is part of logical form, then it, too, must be unrepresentable:

> If I could describe the point of grammatical conventions by saying they are made necessary by certain properties of the colours (say), then that would make the conventions superfluous, since in that case I would be able to say precisely that which the conventions exclude my saying. Conversely, if the conventions were necessary, i.e. if certain combinations of words had to be excluded as nonsensical, then for that very reason I cannot cite a property of colours that makes the conventions necessary, since it would then be conceivable that the colours should not have this property, and I could only express that by violating the conventions." (*PR*, section 4, p. 53)

50. See, e.g., *PR*, section 82: "It isn't a proposition which I put against reality as a yardstick, it's a *system* of propositions." Waissman's notes of Wittgenstein's discussion with the Circle on December 25, 1929, give a fuller explanation of this:

> I once wrote: "a proposition is laid like a yardstick against reality. Only the outermost tips of the graduation marks touch the object to be measured." I should now prefer to say: a *system of propositions* is laid like a yardstick against reality. It's not the individual graduation marks that are applied, it's the whole scale. . . . If, for instance, I say that such and such a point in the visual field is blue, I not only know that, I also know that the point isn't green, isn't red, isn't yellow etc. I have simultaneously applied the whole colour scale. This is also the reason why a point can't have different colours simultaneously; why there is a syntactical rule against fx being true for more than one value of x. For if I apply a system of propositions to reality, that of itself already implies – as in the spatial case – that in every case only one state of affairs can obtain, never several. (*PR*, p. 317)

51. I have argued elsewhere that structuralism originates, in each case, from totalizing theoretical reflection on the nature of linguistic meaning. Though Husserl does not make the specific consideration of language the basis of his phenomenological method – and indeed misses much of the specific insight of the linguistic turn in failing to do so – the structuralism of his method should not be seen as an exception to this claim. We have seen how Husserl's method of abstractive reflection essentially parallels Schlick's favored, linguistically informed method of conceptual analysis. And the metaphysical picture underlying Husserl's conception of the logical structure of meaning and logical insight is not different, in any way essential to the current analysis, from Frege's roughly contemporaneous Platonist conception, even if it does not as explicitly develop tools of specifically *linguistic* analysis.

52. Wittgenstein already had this idea – a descendent of the Tractarian doctrine of the unrepresentability of logical form – in the *Philosophical Remarks* (see note 44).

Chapter 4

1. Some of the philosophers who emigrated were Carnap, Neurath (to Holland and then to England), Hempel, Gödel, Feigl, and Reichenbach. For a detailed personal recollection of the reception of these philosophers in the United States, see Feigl (1969). For a supplementary account, see also Hacker (1996), Chapter 7.

2. American philosophers sympathetic to the Vienna Circle, even before the emigration of many of its members, included C. I. Lewis, Charles Morris, and Ernest Nagel. In 1929, Schlick made the first substantial contact with American philosophers, by visiting at Stanford. Following this, in 1931, Herbert Feigl and Albert Blumberg published "Logical Positivism: A New Movement in European Philosophy" in the *Journal of Philosophy*, making the principles and methods of logical positivism accessible to a wide audience. The spread of logical positivism at this time was further aided by the visits of young foreign scholars to the meetings of the Vienna Circle, including the visits of A. J. Ayer and W. V. O. Quine in 1932 and 1933. For more, see Hacker (1996).

3. The most decisive link between these two strands of philosophical analysis was, of course, Wittgenstein. Since the mid-1920s, Wittgenstein had been intermittently present in the discussions of the Vienna Circle, and in 1929 he returned to Cambridge. Beginning at this time, he sought to extend and reconceive the ideas expressed in the *Tractatus*, communicating his new ideas at first only to a close circle of disciples and students. Nevertheless, the influence of Wittgenstein's ideas through the 1930s and into the 1940s quickly and decisively altered the philosophical landscape, informing the methods and procedures of a host of Cambridge and Oxford philosophers, including Austin, Ryle, von Wright, Hampshire, Wisdom, and Strawson.

4. Instructive examples are Norman Jacobs's "Physicalism and Sensation Sentences" (1937), which theorized the Vienna Circle's problems with protocols as arising from the "linguo-centric predicament" of "using language to try to communicate the non-linguistic" (p. 603), and "Quality, Physicalism, and the Material Mode," by Bertram Morris (1941). The latter article includes a lengthy discussion of Schlick's original "Form and Content" picture of the relationship between the elements of experience and their logical structure, and argues that sensory qualities must ultimately be defined as lying beyond any communicable logical structure.

5. Ryle (1970), p. 12.

6. Ryle (1962), p. 188.

7. Ryle (1949), p. 16.

8. Ibid., pp. 16–17.

9. Ibid., pp. 18–19.

10. Ryle (1932).

11. Ryle (1949), p. 19. In the analytic tradition, the idea that ordinary language has a superficial grammatical form that is misleading with respect to the real logical form of the underlying states of affairs traces,

of course, to Frege's analytic project and connects closely with his idea of an improved language that more perspicuously exhibits the logic of the facts. In Ryle's work, by contrast, there is no suggestion that an analysis that exhibits the real logical form of the facts should yield a new notation or language to replace the ordinary-language expression. Still, the consistent dependence of Ryle's analytic program on the idea of the possible *misleadingness* of the grammar of ordinary language should be borne in mind when considering the meaning of his "ordinary language philosophy."

12. Ibid., p. 23.
13. Ryle (1949), p. 37.
14. Ryle (1938).
15. Ibid., p. 281.
16. Ibid., p. 291.
17. Ryle (1949), pp. 294–5.
18. For a methodologically sensitive treatment of this point, see also Urmson (1956), p. 167.
19. Ryle (1949), p. 29.
20. Ibid., pp. 31–32.
21. Ibid., p. 117.
22. Ryle's notion of the background of the use of a dispositionalist mental concept invites comparison to Husserl's notion of the phenomenological "horizon," an idea of which Ryle was well aware, having written and lectured on Husserl early in his career (Ryle 1970, pp. 8–9). This similarity and others show that there is no particular tension between Ryle's program and phenomenological explanations of mental terms. Ryle wrote in 1962 that *The Concept of Mind* "could be described as a sustained essay in phenomenology, if you are at home with that label" (Ryle 1962, p. 188). Cf. Thomasson (forthcoming), which points out many of the detailed and instructive connections between Ryle's program and phenomenology.
23. Ryle (1949), p. 117.
24. Ibid., p. 118.
25. "Dispositional statements are neither reports of observed or observable states of affairs, nor yet reports of unobserved or unobservable states of affairs. They narrate no incidents" (ibid., p. 125).
26. Ibid., p. 124.
27. Ibid., p. 123.
28. Ibid., p. 124.
29. Ibid., pp. 124–5.
30. Ibid., pp. 327–30.
31. In this, Ryle's position differs sharply from a behaviorist doctrine such as that of Carnap (1931) and Hempel (1935b), who advanced a version of dispositionalist behaviorism on epistemological grounds. For Carnap, psychological terms must really describe behavioral dispositions, since all we know of another's inner mental states is shown in behavior. Ryle's analytic project, by contrast, aimed to clarify logical grammar and had

no special relationship to epistemology. The term "logical behaviorism" itself appears to originate in Hempel (1935b).

32. The only book-length study of Ryle gets this point only partly right. Lyons (1980, pp. 43–9) sketches Ryle's nonfactual, semantic account of dispositional language as licensing inferences, but concludes that Ryle's doctrine also requires, or implies, a "genetic" account of the origin and nature of dispositions, and that it is inadequate on this count. For, Lyons takes it, Ryle is, at least in part, using his account of disposition to argue for "ontological conclusions." For instance, Lyons says, Ryle "was accusing the Cartesian dualists of thinking mind was one sort of ontological category, substance, when in fact it was another, a disposition" (p. 50). Lyons further concludes that, despite Ryle's official refusal of a structural or causal explanation of dispositions, his account might usefully be augmented by such an explanation. But this gets Ryle wrong in two ways. First, if Ryle's account of disposition-language is genuinely nonfactual in the way I have sketched, it cannot be any part of Ryle's analysis to show that the objects of mental concepts are *in fact* dispositions. To say of knowledge, for instance, that it is a disposition is just to say that it is an ability or habit. These terms get their meanings from their logical relationship to, not their standing for, particular things and events, and it would be wrong to suppose that this construal involves one in commitment to any such ontological items as "abilities" or "habits." For dispositional terms do not *refer* to *any* facts, events, states, or processes (even, as Lyons [p. 55] supposes, hypothetical ones); instead, they have the logical job of *licensing* certain inferential movements among facts. Ryle's "ontological conclusions" with respect to the Cartesian theory are strictly negative, tending to show that we need not believe in the sorts of things the Cartesian theorist says there are, not that we should believe in other sorts of things. Second, it is misleading to construe Ryle as offering an account congenial to, or even on the same level as, an "explanation" of the referents of mentalistic terms as shown in ordinary use. For given Ryle's sense of category mistakes as absurdities displayed in ordinary language, the remedy to a category mistake can, at best, be a descriptive reminder of its tendency to lead to such absurdities. Such reminders rest on our recognition that we speak as we do, and do not rely on, presuppose, or even invite an "explanation" for our doing so.

33. Ryle (1949), pp. 210–11. Though Ryle does not refer by name to any actual adherent of the sense-datum theory, his considerable care in sketching the theory reveals his sensitivity to the variety of versions of it that had been suggested. For instance, he distinguishes between those sense-datum theorists who hold that sense-data are ultimately physiological and those who hold them to be irreducibly mental, and also between those who use ordinary-language verbs such as "see" or "taste" to characterize our relationship to sense-data and those who, perhaps particularly concerned with the special epistemological characteristics of sensation, replace these ordinary verbs with specialized ones such as "intuit" or with verb phrases

such as "have direct acquaintance with" that suggest an objectual (rather than factual) relationship to sensed sense-data.

34. Ibid., p. 214.

35. Ibid., pp. 229–30.

36. Examples include Sellars (1956) and Austin (1962).

37. Ryle (1949), pp. 202–3. This observation about the origin of sensory language has sometimes been discussed as the "topic-neutrality" of some mental terms.

38. The idea of attacking sense-datum theory on the ground that sense-data are defined in terms drawn from public language traces at least to Paul (1936), who argued on various grounds that sentences describing sense-data are logically equivalent to public sentences about how things seem, and who disputed, on that ground, the claim that sense-data exist as further entities, over and above physical objects. On Paul's article, see also Urmson (1956), pp. 183–7.

39. Ryle (1949), pp. 219–20.

40. Ryle's story about the origin of sensation-language should be compared to Wilfred Sellars' (1956) influential and similar (but somewhat more developed) account in "Empiricism and the Philosophy of Mind." Like Ryle, Sellars points out the constitutive dependence of sensation-language on public language. And like Ryle, Sellars concludes from this (and on other grounds) that sensation-language originates in the recognition of the possible nonveridicality of some instances of observing and experiencing, as this recognition is internalized and deployed in reports of one's own experience.

41. Place (1956), pp. 29–30.

42. Whatever warrant there is for ascribing this view to Wittgenstein is based on *Philosophical Investigations*, section 244, where Wittgenstein considers the suggestion that, in the process of a child's adoption of language, "words are connected with the primitive, the natural, expressions of the sensation and used in their place." But even here, the suggestion is explicitly offered only as a "possibility," and the context shows that Wittgenstein does not mean to definitively adopt or defend this suggestion.

43. Smart (1959), p. 141.

44. Ibid., p. 144.

45. Already, then, the beginnings of an important consideration of the historical dynamics of theoretical identification in science visibly influences Smart's thinking. See Chapter 5 for more discussion of this.

46. It would be another decade before Kripke and others would begin to suggest that a posteriori theoretical identifications might after all be necessary.

47. The attempt to preserve some elements of the "conceptual analysis" approach alongside the physicalist's claim to exorcize irreducibly mentalistic entities soon issued, however, in the doctrine and program of *eliminative materialism* (see, e.g., Rorty 1965; Churchland 1979), which promised that mentalistic terms, whatever unreal entities they refer to today, would one

day, under the influence of advancing science, come to refer to physiological states and processes or simply be dropped from ordinary language.
But from the perspective of the history here sketched, this attempted
reconciliation of the Rylean's conceptual and the physicalist's empirical
analysis combines the worst features of both. As a bet on the influence
of future science, the doctrine puts the semantic horse before the empirical cart, demanding – what has seldom in the history of science been
possible – an account of how ordinary concepts will change under the
weight of new scientific results; and as a description of present meaning,
the doctrine can only construe contemporary speakers as grossly in error
about the reference of their language.

48. The best Smart can do is to suggest defining the reference of sensation-
reports on terms of public description, so that a sensation-report like "I
see a yellowish-orange after-image" means "There is something going on
which is like what is going on when I have my eyes open, am awake, and
there is an orange illuminated in good light in front of me, that is when
I really see an orange" (p. 149).

49. Smart (1970), p. 304.

50. The point would be made again, much later (if more perspicuously),
by "externalist" philosophers of mind who pointed out the many and
complex ways in which the identities of the referents of mentalistic terms
depend on relations between the subject and the world.

51. Ryle makes this clear at several points in *The Concept of Mind*. Discussing
skills, he says that a skill "is not a happening at all. It is a disposition, or
complex of dispositions, and a disposition is a factor of the wrong logical
type to be seen or unseen, recorded or unrecorded" (p. 33). Of dispositional statements, he says that they are "neither reports of observed or
observable states of affairs, nor yet reports of unobserved or unobservable
states of affairs. They narrate no incidents" (p. 125).

52. Ryle (1949), p. 240.

53. Ibid., pp. 241–2.

54. Ibid., p. 243.

55. Ibid.

56. Ryle (1956), pp. 195–6.

57. Hampshire (1950), pp. 20–1.

58. Wisdom (1950), pp. 53–4.

Chapter 5

1. Smart (1959), pp. 144–5.

2. Ibid.

3. Ibid., p. 146. To show this, Smart uses both Frege's classic example of the
terms "Morning Star" and "Evening Star," which are conceptually different but refer to the same object, and the lightning/electrical discharge
example.

4. Ibid., p. 151.

5. Ibid., p. 152.
6. Black's objection, made in discussion at a conference, is reported in Putnam (1960), pp. 376–7.
7. Brandt and Kim, p. 531.
8. Ibid., p. 537.
9. Putnam (1957), p. 100.
10. Ibid., pp. 98–9.
11. Putnam (1957), p. 95. As we have seen (Chapter 4), it is unlikely that many of the figures usually identified with "logical behaviorism" actually held this view. Ryle certainly did not, and Wittgenstein would have disavowed both this behaviorist outlook and the reductive program it implies. Only Carnap believed – for a time – that psychological states are in any sense "logical constructions" from behaviors, and even then he treated their grammar as akin to the grammar of dispositional terms, which ultimately, he thought, refer to nondispositional internal structures that underlie and explain them. The term "logical behaviorism" itself originates with Hempel's (1935b) defense of this view.
12. Putnam (1960), p. 375.
13. Ibid.
14. Ibid., p. 376.
15. "[W]ith the development of new scientific theories it is constantly occurring that sentences that did not previously 'have a use', that were previously 'deviant', acquire a use – not because the words acquire new meanings, but because the old meanings as fixed by the core of stock uses, determine a new use given the new context" (Putnam 1960, p. 377).
16. Ibid., p. 380.
17. Oppenheim and Putnam (1958).
18. Putnam (1960), p. 379.
19. Turing (1936).
20. Turing (1950).
21. Putnam (1960), p. 363.
22. Ibid., p. 372.
23. Ibid., pp. 372–3.
24. Ibid., p. 362.
25. Putnam (1963), p. 337.
26. Fodor's doctrine thus has motivations that parallel, and somewhat overlap, those of Davidson's "anomalous monism" about the mental: the view that although each (token) mental state is in fact identical with a token physical state, there are no strict psychophysical laws connecting the two types of states. The classic expression of this view is Davidson (1970), and the "type-token" distinction suggested there would soon give philosophers a natural language in which to express and investigate the insights of functionalism. It is not clear to what extent Davidson's thinking about the anomalous character of the mental, growing from his investigations of the ontology of events and the logical form of actions, influenced the thinking of Fodor and Putnam in the 1960s. But it should be noted

that Davidson's 1963 article "Actions, Reasons, and Causes," in which he defends the traditional view that rationalizations are a kind of causal explanation, already contains a statement of the anomaly of the mental:

> The laws whose existence is required if reasons are causes of actions do not, we may be sure, deal in the concepts in which rationalizations must deal. If the causes of a class of events (actions) fall in a certain class (reasons) and there is a law to back each singular causal statement, it does not follow that there is any law connecting events classified as reasons with events classified as actions – the classifications may even be neurological, chemical, or physical. (p. 699)

The position thereby defined agrees with Fodor's in holding that psychological explanation is both genuinely causal explanation and irreducible to purely physical terms of explanation. Fodor draws many of the consequences of this antireductionist picture of psychology in Fodor (1974). Unlike Davidson, however, Fodor continues to construe psychological explanation as dependent on genuine causal laws (though these laws will be irreducible to physical laws and, owing to the absence of strict psychophysical bridge laws, will not have the strictness and exceptionlessness of physical laws).

27. Fodor (1964), p. 168.
28. A visible influence on Fodor's thinking here is Chomsky's (1959) review of Skinner's *Verbal Behavior*. In it, Chomsky argues that the Skinnerian notions of stimulus, response, and reinforcement, however well defined they may be in the context of particular experiments, resist extension to real-life behavior:

> The notions stimulus, response, reinforcement are relatively well defined with respect to the bar-pressing experiments and others similarly restricted. Before we can extend them to real-life behavior, however, certain difficulties must be faced. We must decide, first of all, whether any physical event to which the organism is capable of reacting is to be called a stimulus on a given occasion, or only one to which the organism in fact reacts; and correspondingly, we must decide whether any part of behavior is to be called a response, or only one connected with stimuli in lawful ways. Questions of this sort pose something of a dilemma for the experimental psychologist. If he accepts the broad definitions, characterizing any physical event impinging on the organism as a stimulus and any part of the organism's behavior as a response, he must conclude that behavior has not been demonstrated to be lawful. . . . If we accept the narrower definitions, then behavior is lawful by definition (if it consists of responses); but this fact is of limited significance, since most of what the animal does will simply not be considered behavior. (p. 51)

Like Fodor, Chomsky argues that there is no helpful reduction of the Skinnerian notions to physicalistic terms. Fodor supplements this realization, however, with the suggestion that the Skinnerian notions *do* characterize the organism under consideration on an autonomous level of functional description.

29. Fodor (1964), pp. 171–4.
30. Ibid., pp. 173–4.
31. Ibid., p. 174.

32. Ibid., p. 176.
33. See, e.g., Putnam (1964), p. 391.
34. Putnam (1967a), pp. 421–2; a similar argument is suggested in Putnam (1967b), pp. 438–9.
35. Putnam (1967b), p. 437.
36. Its most usually cited version is ibid., pp. 436–7; compare Putnam (1964), pp. 392–3 (quoted later), and Putnam (1969), p. 451.
37. Putnam (1967a), pp. 414–15.
38. Ibid., p. 418.
39. Lewis (1966), p. 21.
40. Ibid., p. 22.
41. Lewis (1969).
42. Armstrong (1968), p. 83.
43. Lewis (1969), p. 116.
44. It is worth noting, though, one slight difference of emphasis between Armstrong's and Lewis's ways of putting the point. Lewis draws more clearly than Armstrong does the distinction between causal roles and their contingent occupiers. This allows him to envision a program comprising two clearly distinct levels of analysis: first, the logical description of causal roles, and second, the empirical identification of their occupiers. Armstrong, by contrast, does not draw the role/occupier distinction and therefore often seems to consider the causal relationship between a physicalistically described brain state and a mental state to be logically on a par with the causal relationships among mental states. Although this leads to a less well-defined distinction between the two components of the suggested analysis, it also allows Armstrong's analysis more room to exploit the suggestion that the logic of many of our concepts of mental phenomena – for instance, the concepts of sensation – already implies that they are caused by internal brain states, even before empirical results are available to verify this implication.
45. For more on the logic of Lewis's suggestion for the nature of theoretical identifications and comments on its relation to Putnam's developing account, see Lewis (1972).
46. Fodor (1968), pp. 108–9.
47. Over the last three decades, various versions and inflections of functionalism have taken different perspectives with respect to the central issue of the conceptual nature of a "functional" description. Subsequent literature often distinguishes between Putnam's original "machine functionalism," which takes functional descriptions to be computational ones, and Lewis's "causal-role" functionalism. "Teleological" functionalism (Sober 1985) explicitly affirms the irreducibly teleological character of the functional description of a system. "Biological" functionalism (e.g., Millikan 1984) further specifies the teleological functions involved as, in the case of humans at least, biological functions that have developed adaptively through natural selection. Finally, Dennett's "homuncular" functionalism (Dennett 1978; Lycan 1987) begins with intentionally characterized,

fully teleological functions but seeks to "discharge" the teleology involved in functional description by reducing these functions to the mechanisms that realize them. These approaches have led to a rich and interesting discussion of teleology and function in biological explanation (see also Dennett 1995); but it is interesting to see the way in which the conceptual space for all of these positions is opened by Lewis's original invocation of the "normal" causal role of an experience.

48. See Block and Fodor (1972).
49. Ramsey (1929).
50. Lewis (1970), p. 207.
51. Lewis writes: "Yet the principle that experiences are defined by their causal roles is itself behaviorist in origin, in that it inherits the behaviorist discovery that the (ostensibly) causal connections between an experience and its typical occasions and manifestations somehow contain a component of analytic necessity" (pp. 20–1).

Chapter 6

1. For an illuminating defense of the idea that reflection on the history of analytic philosophy can inform contemporary philosophy by exposing its methodological determinants, see Hylton (1990), Chapter 1.
2. See Chapter 1 of this volume.
3. The form of protest can be supported by the natural-enough thought, clearly operative in Carnap's and Schlick's original description of the analytic project, that explanations of linguistic structure must after all advert to the structure of *something*, in itself unstructured; analysis cannot yield structure "all the way down," so it seems compelling to suppose that the unstructured elements revealed by a completed analysis are themselves primitive or immediate experiences. Nevertheless, I do not think that the underlying protest, at least once the explanation of objectivity in terms of structure is standardized, necessarily requires this further thought.
4. A typical attack on the concept of "qualia" is found in Dennett (1988). For its setting within Dennett's own theory of consciousness, see Dennett (1991).
5. Chalmers (1996), Chapter 4.
6. Much the same objection applies to other traditional theories, such as epiphenomenalism and some versions of panpsychism, that also attempt to solve the problem by adding consciousness to the physical world as an additional constituent of objective reality.
7. Dennett (1991), pp. 70–2.
8. Ibid., pp. 74–8.
9. Ibid., pp. 78–81.
10. Ibid., p. 85.
11. Recent literature on the *Tractatus*, however, challenges this traditional interpretation by questioning, on the ground of Wittgenstein's own description of his method, the assumption that the book presents a *theory*

of language at all. See the essays collected in Crary and Read (2000), especially Conant (2000).

12. As we saw in Chapter 3, the kind of structuralism that adumbrates an implicit structure of conventional rules of use is at times even more misleading than the kind that looks to Platonic rules; for insofar as it accounts for the logical structure of language as conventional or stipulative, it fails almost inevitably to capture the *necessity* of forms of language that are grounded in our specific character.

13. In a series of publications, Colin McGinn has recently argued that the problem of consciousness is insoluble for us because of our own *cognitive limitations*: our minds are simply not constituted in the right sort of way to understand consciousness. McGinn suggests that the special difficulty of the problem results from the inadequacy of our current concepts for solving it. He goes on to argue that this inadequacy is a matter of our being *cognitively closed* to the explanation of consciousness, of our simply lacking the cognitive capacities which would be needed to explain it (McGinn 1991, 1999). For instance, McGinn argues, we are able to understand many elements of the objective world because they are spatial in nature. But consciousness does not present itself to us as having a determinate spatial character. The conditions for the possibility of our understanding empirical phenomena are not fulfilled in the case of consciousness; barring a radical change in our cognitive capacities, McGinn concludes, consciousness is destined to remain a mystery. The limit-fixing suggestion offered by the historical analysis resembles McGinn's conclusion in certain respects. But it attributes the intractability of the problem of consciousness not to our fixed cognitive constitution, but rather to the history of the concepts and methods in terms of which it has been discussed.

14. *Philosophical Investigations* (henceforth *PI*) 81.

15. I do not offer, here, anything like an interpretation of the *Investigations'* most important arguments or results overall; nor do I even claim a comprehensive understanding of its method. I aim only to relate certain methodological suggestions present in it to parallel ones that emerge from the reading of philosophical history undertaken here. What is important for the current discussion, accordingly, is not so much the substance of Wittgenstein's critiques of rule following and "private language" as the method of philosophical understanding that these critiques embody and practice. Of course, in taking Wittgenstein's partial articulations of method to coincide with the best prospects for a practice of analysis that could resist structuralism by producing the kind of intelligibility at which our ordinary language of consciousness aims, I do not construe the so-called private language argument as criticizing anything that this language should like to say. (Rather, it contests a particular, and ultimately incoherent, conception of this language as *private*, a conception to which philosophers are prone, and which is in fact evident, as we have seen, in the projects of philosophers such as Russell, Carnap, and Schlick.)

16. *PI*, Preface.

17. Cf. Moran (2001), who argues that self-knowledge is unintelligible outside the specific possibilities of self-alienation that specify its meaning for us, particularly as these emerge from the commitments we can make before one another; and also Cavell (1969, Chapter 9), who argues that the language of consciousness – for instance an avowal of pain – does not so much formulate a claim inviting endorsement or dispute as an item of knowledge as seek the *acknowledgment* of another, the recognition of one's suffering.

18. See, e.g., Monk (1991).

19. "[Logical investigation] takes its rise, not from an interest in the facts of nature, nor from a need to grasp causal connexions: but from an urge to understand the basis, or essence, of everything empirical. Not, however, as if to this end we had to hunt out new facts; it is, rather, of the essence of our investigation that we do not seek to learn anything *new* by it. We want to *understand* something that is already in plain view. For *this* is what we seem in some sense not to understand." (*PI* 89).

20. *PI* 127, 128. Compare the penetrating discussion of Wittgenstein's remark about theses in Cavell (1979), pp. 33–4.

21. *PI* 129.

22. The essays collected in Cavell (1969), especially the title essay "Must We Mean What We Say?" and "Knowing and Acknowledging," develop, at length and in detail, the thought that the forms of analysis and investigation definitive of Oxford "ordinary language" philosophy embody a distinctive form of linguistic insight as self-knowledge, grounded on the authority of what is in each case one's own knowledge as a speaker of language. I am deeply indebted to Cavell's groundbreaking work on ordinary-language philosophy in what I say about the method of analytic reflection here.

23. "For we can avoid ineptness or emptiness only by presenting the model as what it is, as an object of comparison – as, so to speak, a measuring-rod; not as a preconceived idea to which reality must correspond. (The dogmatism into which we fall so easily in doing philosophy.)" (*PI* 131)

24. "241. 'So you are saying that human agreement decides what is true and what is false?' – It is what human beings *say* that is true and false; and they agree in the *language* they use. That is not agreement in opinions but in form of life.

    242. If language is to be a means of communication there must be agreement not only in definitions but also (queer as this may sound) in judgments. This seems to abolish logic, but does not do so." (*PI* 241–2)

25. Cf. Cavell's remarkable description of the appeal of ordinary language philosophy in *The Claim of Reason*:

    In philosophizing, I have to bring my own language and life into imagination. What I require is a convening of my culture's criteria, in order to confront them with my words and life as I pursue them and as I may imagine them; and at the same time to confront my words and life as I pursue them with the life my culture's words may imagine for me: to confront the culture with itself, along the lines in which it meets in me. (Cavell 1979, p. 125)

26. "Philosophy simply puts everything before us, and neither explains nor deduces anything. – Since everything lies open to view there is nothing to explain. For what is hidden, for example, is of no interest to us. . . . The work of the philosopher consists in assembling reminders for a particular purpose." (*PI* 126, 127)

27. *PI* 122, 123.

28. "For the clarity that we are aiming at is indeed complete clarity. But this simply means that the philosophical problems should completely disappear. The real discovery is the one that makes me capable of stopping doing philosophy when I want to. – The one that gives philosophy peace, so that it is no longer tormented by questions which bring *itself* into question. – Instead, we now demonstrate a method, by examples; and the series of examples can be broken off. – Problems are solved (difficulties eliminated), not a *single* problem.

   There is not *a* philosophical method, though there are indeed methods, like different therapies." (*PI* 133)

29. *PI* 108.

Works Cited

Anscombe, G. E. M. 1959. *An Introduction to Wittgenstein's* Tractatus. New York: Harper and Row.

Armstrong, D. M. 1968. *A Materialist Theory of the Mind*. London: Routledge.

Austin, J. L. [1947] 1962. *Sense and Sensibilia*. New York: Oxford University Press.

Ayer, A. J. 1936a. Verification and experience. Reprinted in Ayer (1959).

Ayer, A. J. [1936b] 1952. *Language, Truth and Logic*. New York: Dover.

Ayer, A. J. [1940] 1958. *Foundations of Empirical Knowledge*. London: Macmillan.

Ayer, A. J. (ed.) 1959. *Logical Positivism*. New York: The Free Press.

Block, N. 1978. Troubles with functionalism. In *Readings in the Philosophy of Psychology*, vol. 1, ed. N. Block. Cambridge, MA: Harvard University Press.

Block, N. 1990. Inverted Earth. *Philosophical Perspectives* 4, pp. 53–79.

Block, N., and J. A. Fodor. [1972] 1980. What psychological states are not. In *Readings in the Philosophy of Psychology*, vol. 1, ed. N. Block. Cambridge, MA: Harvard University Press.

Bogen, J. 1979. Agony in the schools. *Canadian Journal of Philosophy* 11:1, pp. 1–21.

Brandt, R., and J. Kim. 1967. The logic of the identity theory. *Journal of Philosophy* 64:17, pp. 515–37.

Carnap, R. [1928] 1967. *The Logical Structure of the World*. Translated by Rolf A. George. Berkeley: University of California Press.

Carnap, R. [1931] 1959. Psychology in physical language. In *Logical Positivism*, ed. A. J. Ayer. New York: The Free Press.

Carnap, R. [1932a] 1934. The physicalist language as the universal language of science. *Erkenntnis* 2, pp. 432–65. Translated by Max Black as *The Unity of Science*. London: Kegan Paul, 1995.

Carnap, R. 1932b. On protocol sentences. *Nous* 21 (1987), pp. 457–70.

Carnap, R. 1934. *The Logical Syntax of Language*. London: Kegan Paul.

Cavell, S. [1969] 1976. *Must We Mean What We Say?* Updated edition. Cambridge: Cambridge University Press.

Cavell, S. [1979] 1999. *The Claim of Reason.* New edition. New York: Oxford University Press.

Chalmers, D. 1996. *The Conscious Mind.* New York: Oxford University Press.

Chalmers, D. 1997. Moving forward on the problem of consciousness. *Journal of Consciousness Studies* 4:1, pp. 3–46.

Chisholm, R. M. 1982. Schlick on the foundations of knowing. *Grazer Philosophische Studien* 16/17, pp. 149–57.

Chomsky, N. [1959] 1980. A review of B. F. Skinner's *Verbal Behavior.* In *Readings in the Philosophy of Psychology,* vol. 1, ed. N. Block. Cambridge, MA: Harvard University Press.

Churchland, P. M. 1979. *Scientific Realism and the Plasticity of Mind.* Cambridge: Cambridge University Press.

Churchland, P. M., and P. S. Churchland. 1982. Functionalism, qualia, and intentionality. In *Mind, Brain, and Function,* ed. J. Biro and R. Shahan. Norman: University of Oklahoma Press.

Churchland, P. M. 1984. *Matter and Consciousness: A Contemporary Introduction to the Philosophy of Mind.* Cambridge, MA: MIT Press.

Churchland, P. M. [1989]1997. Knowing qualia: A reply to Jackson. In *The Nature of Consciousness: Philosophical Debates,* ed. N. Block, O. Flanagan, and G. Guzeldere. Cambridge, MA: MIT Press.

Coffa, J. A. 1991. *The Semantic Tradition from Kant to Carnap.* Cambridge: Cambridge University Press.

Conant, J. 2000. Elucidation and nonsense in Frege and the early Wittgenstein. In Crary and Read (2000).

Crane, T. 1992. The nonconceptual content of experience. In *The Contents of Experience,* ed. T. Crane. Cambridge: Cambridge University Press.

Crary, A., and R. Read (eds.) 2000. *The New Wittgenstein.* New York: Routledge.

Davidson, D. 1963. Actions, reasons, and causes. *Journal of Philosophy* 60:23, pp. 685–700.

Davidson, D. [1970] 1980. Mental events. In *Readings in the Philosophy of Psychology,* vol. 1, ed. N. Block. Cambridge, MA: Harvard University Press.

Davidson, D. 1982. Empirical content. *Grazer Philosophische Studien* 16/17, pp. 471–89.

Dennett, D. C. [1975] 1990. Why the law of effect will not go away. In *Mind and Cognition: A Reader,* ed. W. G. Lycan. Oxford: Blackwell.

Dennett, D. C. 1988. Quining qualia. In *The Nature of Consciousness: Philosophical Debates,* ed. N. Block, O. Flanagan, and G. Guzeldere. Cambridge, MA: MIT Press, pp. 619–42.

Dennett, D. C. 1991. *Consciousness Explained.* Boston: Little, Brown.

Dennett, D. C. 1995. *Darwin's Dangerous Idea.* New York: Simon and Schuster.

Depraz, N. 1999. The phenomenological reduction as praxis. In *The View from Within: First-Person Approaches to the Study of Consciousness,* ed. F. Varela and J. Shear. Imprint Academic, Thorverton, pp. 95–110.

Feigl, H. 1958. The 'mental' and the 'physical'. *Minnesota Studies in the Philosophy of Science* 2, pp. 370–497.

Feigl, H. 1969. The Wiener Kreis in America. In *Herbert Feigl: Inquiries and Provocations, Collected Writings 1929–1974*, ed. R. S. Cohen. Dordrecht: Reidel.

Feigl, H., and A. Blumberg 1931. Logical positivism: A new movement in European philosophy. *Journal of Philosophy* 28, pp. 281–96.

Fodor, J. A. 1964. Explanations in psychology. In *Philosophy in America*, ed. M. Black. Ithaca, NY: Cornell University Press.

Fodor, J. A. 1968. *Psychological Explanation: An Introduction to the Philosophy of Psychology*. New York: Random House.

Fodor, J. A. [1974] 1980. Special sciences, or the disunity of science as a working hypothesis. In *Readings in the Philosophy of Psychology*, vol. 1, ed. N. Block. Cambridge, MA: Harvard University Press.

Frege, G. [1879] 1997a. *Begriffschrift*. Excerpts translated in *The Frege Reader*, ed. M. Beany. Oxford: Blackwell.

Frege, G. [1918] 1997b. Thought. Reprinted in *The Frege Reader*, ed. M. Beany. Oxford: Blackwell.

Friedman, M. 1987. Carnap's *Aufbau* reconsidered. *Nous* 21:4, pp. 521–45.

Friedman, M. 1999. *Reconsidering Logical Positivism*. Cambridge: Cambridge University Press.

Friedman, M. 2000. *A Parting of the Ways: Carnap, Cassirer, and Heidegger*. Chicago: Open Court.

Goldman, A. I. [1993] 1997. Consciousness, folk psychology, and cognitive science. In *The Nature of Consciousness: Philosophical Debates*, ed. N. Block, O. Flanagan, and G. Guzeldere. Cambridge, MA: MIT Press.

Goudge, T. A. 1935. The views of Charles Peirce on the given in experience. *Journal of Philosophy* 32, pp. 533–44.

Hacker, P. M. S. 1996. *Wittgenstein's Place in Twentieth-Century Analytic Philosophy*. Oxford: Blackwell.

Haller, R. 1985. Problems of knowledge in Moritz Schlick. *Synthese* 64, pp. 283–96.

Hampshire, S. [1950] 1970. Critical review of *The Concept of Mind*. In *Ryle: A Collection of Critical Essays*, ed. O. P. Wood and G. Pitcher. New York: Doubleday.

Hardin, C. L. 1987. Qualia and materialism: Closing the explanatory gap. *Philosophy and Phenomenological Research* 48, pp. 281–98.

Hardin, C. L. 1988. *Color for Philosophers*. Indianapolis: Hackett.

Harman, G. [1990] 1997. The intrinsic quality of experience. In *The Nature of Consciousness: Philosophical Debates*, ed. N. Block, O. Flanagan, and G. Guzeldere. Cambridge, MA: MIT Press.

Hempel, C. G. 1935a. On the logical positivists' theory of truth. *Analysis* 2:4, pp. 49–59.

Hempel, C. G. [1935b] 1980. The logical analysis of psychology. Reprinted, with revisions, in *Readings in the Philosophy of Psychology*, vol. 1, ed. N. Block. Cambridge, MA: Harvard University Press.

Hempel, C. G. 1942. The function of general laws in history. *Journal of Philosophy* 39, pp. 35–48.

Hempel, C. G. 1948. Studies in the logic of explanation. *Philosophy of Science* 15, pp. 135–75.

Hilbert, D. [1899] 1962. *The Foundations of Geometry.* Translated by E. J. Townshend. Chicago: Open Court.

Hintikka, J., and M. B. Hintikka. 1986. *Investigating Wittgenstein.* Oxford: Blackwell.

Hung, T. 1985. Remarks on affirmations. *Synthese* 64, pp. 297–306.

Husserl, E. [1900] 1977. *Logical Investigations.* Translated J. N. Findlay. London: Routledge and Kegan Paul.

Husserl, E. [1913] 1983. *Ideas Pertaining to a Pure Phenomenology and to a Phenomenological Philosophy, First Book.* Translated by F. Kersten. The Hague: Martinus Nijhoff.

Husserl, E. [1929] 1988. *Cartesian Meditations: An Introduction to Phenomenology.* Translated by D. Cairns. Dordrecht: Kluwer.

Husserl, E. [1937] 1970. *The Crisis of European Sciences and Transcendental Phenomenology.* Translated by D. Carr. Evanston, IL: Northwestern University Press.

Husserl, E. [1948] 1973. *Experience and Judgment.* Translated by J. S. Churchill and K. Ameriks. Evanston, IL: Northwestern University Press.

Hylton, P. 1990. *Russell, Idealism, and the Emergence of Analytic Philosophy.* Oxford: Clarendon.

Jackson, F. [1982] 1990. Epiphenomenal qualia. In *Mind and Cognition: A Reader,* ed. W. Lycan. Oxford: Blackwell.

Jacobs, N. 1937. Physicalism and sensation sentences. *Journal of Philosophy* 34:22, pp. 602–11.

James, W. 1879. The sentiment of rationality. *Mind* 4, pp. 317–46.

Kaplan, D. [1977] 1989. Demonstratives. In *Themes From Kaplan,* ed. J. Almog et. al. Oxford: Oxford University Press.

Kim, J. [1972] 1980. Physicalism and the multiple realizability of mental states. In *Readings in the Philosophy of Psychology,* vol. 1, ed. N. Block. Cambridge, MA: Harvard University Press.

Kim, J. 1998. *Mind in a Physical World.* Cambridge, MA: MIT Press.

Kirk, R. and J. E. R. Squires. 1974. Zombies vs. materialists. *Proceedings of the Aristotelian Society* 48 (suppl), pp. 143–7.

Kirk, R. 1994. *Raw Feeling.* New York: Oxford University Press.

Lehrer, K. 1982. Schlick and Neurath: Meaning and truth. *Grazer Philosophische Studien* 16/17, pp. 49–61.

Levine, J. 1983. Materialism and qualia: The explanatory gap. *Pacific Philosophical Quarterly* 64, pp. 354–61.

Levine, J. 1993. On leaving out what it's like. In *Consciousness: Psychological and Philosophical Essays,* ed. M. D. and G. W. Humphries. Oxford: Blackwell.

Levine, J. 1995. Qualia: Intrinsic, relational, or what? In *Conscious Experience,* ed. T. Metzinger. Place of Publication: Publisher.

Lewis, C. I. 1929. *Mind and the World Order.* New York: Dover.

Lewis, D. K. 1966. An argument for the identity theory. *Journal of Philosophy* 63:1, pp. 17–25.

Lewis, D. K. [1969] 1980. Review of Putnam. In *Readings in the Philosophy of Psychology*, vol. 1, ed. N. Block. Cambridge, MA: Harvard University Press.

Lewis, D. K. 1970. How to define theoretical terms. *Journal of Philosophy* 67:13, pp. 427–46.

Lewis, D. K. 1972. Psychophysical and theoretical identifications. *Australian Journal of Philosophy* 50, pp. 249–58.

Lewis, D. K. 1990. What experience teaches. In *Mind and Cognition: A Reader*, ed. W. Lycan. Cambridge: Blackwell.

Loar, B. [1990] 1997. Phenomenal states. In *The Nature of Consciousness: Philosophical Debates*, ed. N. Block, O. Flanagan, and G. Guzeldere. Cambridge, MA: MIT Press.

Lockwood, M. 1989. *Mind, Brain, and the Quantum.* Oxford: Blackwell.

Lormand, E. 1994. Qualia: Now showing at a theater near you. *Philosophical Topics* 22, pp. 127–56.

Lycan, W. G. [1987] 1990. The continuity of levels of nature. In *Mind and Cognition: A Reader*, ed. W. G. Lycan. Oxford: Blackwell.

Lycan, W. G. 1990. What is the subjectivity of the mental? *Philosophical Perspectives* 4, pp. 109–30.

Lycan, W. G. 1995. A limited defense of phenomenal information. In *Conscious Experience*, ed. T. Metzinger. Paderborn: Schoningh.

Lyons, W. 1980. *Gilbert Ryle: An Introduction to His Philosophy.* Sussex: Harvester.

Maxwell, G. 1978. Rigid designators and mind-brain identity. In *Perception and Cognition: Issues in the Foundations of Psychology*, ed. C. W. Savage. Minneapolis: University of Minnesota Press.

McGinn, C. 1989. Can we solve the mind-body problem? In *The Nature of Consciousness: Philosophical Debates*, ed. N. Block, O. Flanagan, and G. Guzeldere. Cambridge, MA: MIT Press.

McGinn, C. 1991. *The Problem of Consciousness.* Oxford: Blackwell.

McGinn, C. 1999. *The Mysterious Flame: Conscious Minds in a Material World.* New York: Basic Books.

Millikan, R. G. 1984. *Language, Thought, and Other Biological Categories.* Cambridge, MA: MIT Press.

Mohanty, J. N. 1989. *Transcendental Phenomenology.* Oxford: Blackwell.

Monk, R. 1991. *Ludwig Wittgenstein: The Duty of Genius.* New York: Penguin.

Moran, R. 2001. *Authority and Estrangement: An Essay on Self-Knowledge.* Princeton, NJ: Princeton University Press.

Morris, B. 1941. Quality, physicalism, and the material mode. *Philosophical Review* 50:1, pp. 64–74.

Nagel, E. 1960. The meaning of reduction in the natural sciences. In *Philosophy of Science*, ed. A. C. Danto and S. Morgenbesser. New York: Melidian Books.

Nagel, E. 1974. Issues in the logic of reductive explanations. In his *Teleology Revisited.* New York: Columbia University Press.

Nagel, T. [1974] 1997. What is it like to be a bat? In *The Nature of Consciousness: Philosophical Debates*, ed. N. Block, O. Flanagan, and G. Guzeldere. Cambridge, MA: MIT Press.

Nemirow, L. 1990. Physicalism and the cognitive role of acquaintance. In *Mind and Cognition: A Reader*, ed. W. Lycan. Cambridge: Blackwell.

Neurath, O. 1931a. Physicalism. Reprinted in Neurath (1983), pp. 52–7.

Neurath, O. 1932a. Sociology in the framework of physicalism. *Erkenntnis* 2, pp. 393–431. Reprinted in Neurath (1983), pp. 58–90

Neurath, O. 1932b. Protocol sentences. Reprinted in Ayer (1959), pp. 199–208.

Neurath, O. [1933] 1987. Unified science and psychology. Reprinted in *Unified Science*, ed. B. McGuinness. Dordrecht: D. Reidel.

Neurath, O. 1934. Radical physicalism and the 'real world.' Reprinted in Neurath (1983).

Neurath, O. 1983. *Philosophical Papers, 1913–1946*. Edited and translated by R. S. Cohen and M. Neurath. (Vienna Circle Collection, vol. 16). Dordrecht: Reidel.

Nisbett, R. E., and T. Wilson. 1977. Telling more than we know: Verbal reports on mental processes. *Psychological Review* 84, pp. 231–59.

Oberdan, T. 1996. Postscript to protocols: Reflections on empiricism. In *Origins of Logical Empiricism*, ed. R. Giere and A. Richardson. Minneapolis: University of Minnesota Press.

Oberdan, T. 1998. The Vienna Circle's 'anti-foundationalism.' *British Journal for the Philosophy of Science* 49, pp. 297–308.

Oberdan, T. 1999. Deconstructing protocols: reply to Uebel. *British Journal for the Philosophy of Science* 50, pp. 301–4.

Oppenheim, P., and H. Putnam. 1958. Unity of science as a working hypothesis. In *Minnesota Studies in the Philosophy of Science, Vol. 2*, ed. H. Feigl, M. Scriven, and G. Maxwell. Minneapolis: University of Minnesota Press.

Paul, G. A. 1936. Is there a problem about sense-data? *Proceedings of the Aristotelian Society* (suppl.) 15, pp. 61–77.

Peacocke, C. 1983. *Sense and Content: Experience, Thought, and Their Relations*. Oxford: Clarendon.

Peirce, C. I., [1867] 1992. On a new list of categories. In *The Essential Peirce*, vol. 1, ed. N. Houser and C. Kloesel. Bloomington: Indiana University Press.

Petitot, J., et al. (eds.) 1999. *Naturalizing Phenomenology: Issues in Contemporary Phenomenology and Cognitive Science*. Stanford, CA: Stanford University Press.

Place, U. T. [1956] 1990. Is consciousness a brain process? In *Mind and Cognition: A Reader*, ed. W. Lycan. Oxford: Blackwell.

Price, H. H. [1932] 1961. *Perception*. London: Metheun.

Price, M. C. 1996. Should we expect to feel as if we understand consciousness? *Journal of Consciousness Studies* 3:4, pp. 303–12.

Putnam, H. 1957. Psychological concepts, explication, and ordinary language. *Journal of Philosophy* 54, pp. 94–9.

Putnam, H. [1960] 1975. Minds and machines. In Putnam (1975).

Putnam, H. [1963] 1975. Brains and behavior. In Putnam (1975).

Putnam, H. [1964] 1975. Robots: machines or artificially created life? In Putnam (1975).

Putnam, H. [1967a] 1975. The mental life of some machines. In Putnam (1975).

Putnam, H. [1967b] 1975. The nature of mental states. In Putnam (1975).

Putnam, H. [1969] 1975. Logical positivism and the philosophy of mind. In Putnam (1975).

Putnam, H. 1975. *Mind, Language, and Reality: Philosophical Papers, Vol. 2.* Cambridge: Cambridge University Press.

Quine, W. V. 1951. Two dogmas of empiricism. *Philosophical Review* 60, pp. 20–43.

Quine, W. V. 1960. *Word and Object.* Cambridge, MA: MIT Press.

Ramsey, F. P. [1929] 1960. Theories. In his *The Foundations of Mathematics.* Patterson, NJ: Littlefield.

Richardson, A. 1996. From epistemology to the logic of science: Carnap's philosophy of empirical knowledge in the 1930s. In *Origins of Logical Empiricism*, ed. R. Giere and A. Richardson. Minneapolis: University of Minnesota Press.

Richardson, A. 1998. *Carnap's Construction of the World.* Cambridge: Cambridge University Press.

Rorty, R. 1965. Mind-body identity, privacy, and categories. *Review of Metaphysics* 19(1), pp. 24–54.

Rorty, R. 1979. *Philosophy and the Mirror of Nature.* Princeton, NJ: Princeton University Press.

Rosenthal, D. 1996. A theory of consciousness. In *The Nature of Consciousness: Philosophical Debates*, ed. N. Block, O. Flanagan, and G. Guzeldere. Cambridge, MA: MIT Press.

Russell, B. [1918] 1985. *The Philosophy of Logical Atomism.* Chicago: Open Court.

Russell, B. 1927. *The Analysis of Matter.* London: Allen and Unwin, 1954.

Ryle, G. [1932] 1971. Systematically misleading expressions. In his *Collected Papers, Volume 2: Collected Essays 1929–1968.* Bristol: Thoemmes.

Ryle, G. [1938] 1971. Categories. In his *Collected Papers, Volume 2: Collected Essays 1929–1968.* Bristol: Thoemmes.

Ryle, G. 1949. *The Concept of Mind.* Chicago: University of Chicago Press.

Ryle, G. [1956] 1971. Sensation. In his *Collected Papers, Volume 2: Collected Essays 1929–1968.* Bristol: Thoemmes.

Ryle, G. [1962] 1971. Phenomenology versus *The Concept of Mind*. In his *Collected Papers, Volume 1: Critical Essays.* Bristol: Thoemmes.

Ryle, G. 1970. Autobiographical. In *Ryle: A Collection of Critical Essays*, ed. O. P. Wood and G. Pitcher. New York: Doubleday.

Schlick, M. [1910] 1979. The nature of truth in modern logic. In *Moritz Schlick: Philosophical Papers*, vol. 1, ed. H. L. Mulder and B. F. B. Van de Velde-Schlick. Dordrecht: Riedel.

Schlick, M. [1913] 1979. Is there intuitive knowledge? In *Moritz Schlick: Philosophical Papers*, vol. 1, ed. H. L. Mulder and B. F. B. Van de Velde-Schlick. Dordrecht: Riedel.

Schlick, M. [1925] 1974. *General Theory of Knowledge.* Translated by Albert E. Blumberg. Vienna: Springer-Verlag.

Schlick, M. [1930] 1979. Is there a factual *a priori?* In *Moritz Schlick: Philosophical Papers,* vol. 2, ed. H. L. Mulder and B. F. B. Van de Velde-Schlick. Dordrecht: Riedel.

Schlick, M. 1932. Form and content. Reprinted in Schlick (1979), pp. 285–369.

Schlick, M. 1934. The foundation of knowledge. Reprinted in Ayer (1959), pp. 209–27.

Schlick, M. 1935a. Facts and propositions. *Analysis* 2, pp. 65–70. Reprinted in Schlick (1979), pp. 400–4.

Schlick, M. 1935b. On 'affirmations'. Reprinted in Schlick (1979), pp. 407–13.

Schlick, M. 1979. *Philosophical Papers,* vol. 2. Edited by Henk L. Mulder and B. F. B. Van de Velde-Schlick. (Vienna Circle Collection, vol. 11). Dordrecht: Riedel.

Searle, J. 1992. *The Rediscovery of the Mind.* Cambridge, MA: MIT Press.

Searle, J. 1997. *The Mystery of Consciousness.* Including exchanges with Daniel C. Dennett and David J. Chalmers. New York: New York Review.

Sellars, W. 1956. Empiricism and the philosophy of mind. *Minnesota Studies in the Philosophy of Science* 1, pp. 253–329. Reprinted as *Empiricism and the Philosophy of Mind.* Cambridge, MA: Harvard University Press, 1997.

Shelton, J. 1988. Schlick and Husserl on the foundations of phenomenology. *Philosophy and Phenomenological Research* 48, pp. 557–61.

Shoemaker, S. [1982] 1997. The inverted spectrum. In *The Nature of Consciousness: Philosophical Debates,* ed. N. Block, O. Flanagan, and G. Guzeldere. Cambridge, MA: MIT Press.

Shoemaker, S. 1997. The first-person perspective. In *The Nature of Consciousness: Philosophical Debates,* ed. N. Block, O. Flanagan, and G. Guzeldere. Cambridge, MA: MIT Press.

Smart, J. J. C. 1959. Sensations and brain processes. *Philosophical Review* 68, pp. 141–56.

Smart, J. J. C. 1970. Ryle in relation to modern science. In *Ryle: A Collection of Critical Essays,* ed. O. P. Wood and G. Pitcher. New York: Doubleday.

Smith, D. W. 2000. What is 'logical' in Husserl's *Logical Investigations?* Paper delivered at the Conference on *Logische Untersuchungen,* May 26–28, 2000, Copenhagen.

Sober, E. [1985] 1990. Putting the function back in functionalism. In *Mind and Cognition: A Reader,* ed. W. G. Lycan. Oxford: Blackwell.

Thomasson, A. Forthcoming. Analyzing concepts, language, experience: phenomenology and the development of analytic philosophy.

Turing, A. M. 1936. On computable numbers, with an application to the Entsheidungsproblem. *Proceedings of the London Mathematical Society* 2:42, pp. 230–65.

Turing, A. M. 1950. Computing machinery and intelligence. *Mind* 59, pp. 433–60.

Turner, J. L. 1996. Conceptual knowledge and intuitive experience: Schlick's dilemma. In *Origins of Logical Empiricism,* ed. R. Giere and A. Richardson. Minneapolis: University of Minnesota Press.

Tye, M. 1995. *Ten Problems of Consciousness.* Cambridge, MA: MIT Press.

Uebel, T. 1996. Anti-foundationalism and the Vienna Circle's revolution in philosophy. *British Journal for the Philosophy of Science* 47, pp. 415–50.

Uebel, T. 1999. Protocols, affirmations, and foundations: Reply to Oberdan. *British Journal for the Philosophy of Science* 50, pp. 297–300.

Uebel, T. E. 1992a. *Overcoming Logical Positivism from Within: The Emergence of Neurath's Naturalism in the Vienna Circle's Protocol Sentence Debate.* Amsterdam: Rodopi.

Uebel, T. E. 1992b. Neurath vs. Carnap: naturalism vs. rational reconstructionism before Quine. *History of Philosophy Quarterly* 9:4, pp. 445–70.

Urmson, J. O. 1956. *Philosophical Analysis: Its Development between the Two World Wars.* Oxford: Oxford University Press.

Van de Pitte, M. 1984. Schlick's critique of phenomenological propositions. *Philosophy and Phenomenological Research* 45, pp. 195–226.

Van Gulick, R. 1993. Understanding the phenomenal mind: Are we all just armadillos? In *Consciousness: Psychological and Philosophical Essays,* ed. M. Davies and G. Humphreys. Oxford: Blackwell.

Varela, F. J. and J. Shear. 1999. First-person accounts: Why, what and how. In *The View from Within: First-Person Approaches to the Study of Consciousness,* ed. F. Varela and J. Shear. Thorverton, UK: Imprint Academic.

Warnock, G. J. 1969. *English-speaking Philosophy since 1900.* Second edition. Oxford: Oxford University Press.

Wisdom, J. [1950] 1962. The concept of mind. In *The Philosophy of Mind,* ed. V. C. Chappell. Englewood Cliffs, NJ: Prentice-Hall.

Wittgenstein, L. [1921] 1961. *Tractatus Logico-Philosophicus.* Translated by D. F. Pears and B. F. McGuinness. London: Routledge.

Wittgenstein, L. [1929] 1993. Some remarks on logical form. In *Philosophical Occasions, 1912–1951,* ed. J. C. Klagge and A. Nordmann. Indianapolis: Hackett.

Wittgenstein, L. [1930] 1975. *Philosophical Remarks.* Chicago: University of Chicago Press.

Wittgenstein, L. 1958. *Philosophical Investigations.* Third edition, translated by G. E. M. Anscombe. New York: Prentice Hall.

Index